# The Theological Aesthetics of Hans Urs von Balthasar

---

Louis Roberts

The Catholic University of America Press
Washington, D.C.

For my mother and father



Printed in the United States of America

LIBRARY OF CONGRESS CATALOGING-IN-PUBLICATION DATA
Roberts, Louis.
The theological aesthetics of Hans Urs von Balthasar.
Bibliography: p.
Includes index.
1. Christianity and the arts—History of doctrines—20th century. 2. Aesthetics, Modern—20th century. 3. Balthasar, Hans Urs von, 1905– . 4. Catholic Church—Doctrines—History—20th century. I. Title.
BR115.A8R63 1987 230'.2'0924 86-28321
ISBN 0-8132-0634-0

# Contents

# Introduction

HANS URS von Balthasar celebrated his eightieth birthday on August 12, 1985. That year also marked the close of two decades of post–Vatican II Catholicism, a period characterized by major changes in theological method. An examination of Balthasar's achievement provides an opportunity to review the great intellectual tradition in theology and ask whether it might not still have validity in a world that has been knocked about by both structuralists and deconstructionists.

My claim in this book is that the theological aesthetics of Hans Urs von Balthasar constitute a promising combination of the old and new for the future direction of theology. In particular, Balthasar's revival of the patristic doctrine of Christian universalism comes at a most opportune moment. As Edward Schillebeeckx has noted, "For the first time in human history, mankind as such finds itself faced with the task of accepting world-wide responsibility for the consequences of its activities. This need for a joint assumption of accountability calls for an *ethic* of world-wide responsibility."[1]

Theological aesthetics begins with the term "beauty." Bal-

1. Edward Schillebeeckx, "Questions on Christian Salvation of and for Man," in David Tracy, Hans Küng, and J. B. Metz, eds., *Toward Vatican III* (New York: Seabury, 1978), p. 28.

thasar argues that the loss of this dimension in theology has been disastrous. His conviction is built on his insight into the nature of beauty, an insight which he would argue was the foundation of the myths, philosophy, art, and literature of the classical world and was carried over by the Fathers into a theology of the church. The concept of beauty illuminated and found fulfillment in the biblical concepts of *khabod* and *doxa*. This insight grew dim in the waning Middle Ages and was rejected by the Reformers. Protestant theologians from Friedrich Wilhelm Ritschl to Rudolf Bultmann and Catholic theologians such as Karl Rahner and Bernhard Welte have been so heavily influenced by Immanuel Kant that the role of aesthetics has been greatly diminished in modern theology. Balthasar intended that his work counter both tendencies.

This book examines Balthasar's elucidation of "beauty" within the tradition of Western culture. It is not a complete appraisal of Balthasar's theology. Many facets of his work had to be skimmed or ignored altogether. For example, it was not possible to review Balthasar's reading of modern dramatic literature and his interpretation of writers such as Dante, Pascal, Buber, Romano Guardini, Paul Claudel, Rainer Maria Rilke, and Georges Bernanos.

Balthasar has taken a new and different approach to theological aesthetics. Although theology has always contained a latent aesthetic dimension, the degree of explanation, development, and reflection exercised by Balthasar is unique. Aesthetic theories as developed by Gyorgy Lukacs, Theodore Adorno, Hans Georg Gadamer, and Abraham Moles are for Balthasar only partial compared to the all-embracing transcendental aesthetics in which he believes.

The technological revolution with its capacity for instant communication brings home to everyone how much our confessions and theologies are indebted to their respective cultures. The classical tradition with its Hellenic and Judaic roots provided the linguistic framework for developing Christian doctrine. In this book I try to bring forward Balthasar's insight into this development. I also attempt to situate his work in the context of a contemporary literary and critical theory.

Important movements, whether in history or theology, start from particular occasions and moments of time in which perceptive individuals recognize, even if obscurely, larger changes than those to which the occasions themselves bear witness.

The Christian interpretation of human life has been created within a particular culture. Hans Urs von Balthasar has built a system based on an examination of this culture. I wish to demonstrate some significant features of this examination by Balthasar, whom Henri de Lubac called "the most cultured man in Europe."

Although not as well known in the English-speaking world as Yves Congar, Henri de Lubac, or Hans Küng, Balthasar is one of the European theologians who has helped shape contemporary theology.

His reception has been complicated by his criticism of certain movements and theologians such as Rahner and Küng and his consequent adoption by an intellectually conservative minority. According to Leo O'Donovan, "One hears he is a Barthian, a mystic, a papalist. The true Balthasar, however, is not an integrist but a cultural theologian whose work ranges from the ecclesiological to the mystical and whose works are collages of culture and Christianity."[2]

This book attempts to explain Balthasar's theological aesthetics, which is an interpretation of faith through the leitmotif of art. Balthasar compares the light of faith to aesthetic

2. Leo O'Donovan, "Evolution under the Sign of the Cross," *Theological Studies* 32 (1971):602.

contemplation. Only when the truth is beautiful, when its form is intrinsically luminous, is its objectivity evident. Each section of the trilogy, in the manner of Hegel, flows from a different power: from aesthetic contemplation, from moral action, and from reason. Balthasar's aesthetics is the first section of an integrated tripartite system. In the first part, the focus is on the first transcendental, the "beautiful." The other two sections cover the "good" and the "true." In the second, the *Theodramatik*, the "dramatic ethic" is played out on the world stage of freedom and sin. Creator and creatures act out a play of ethical action and moral reflection. We see the dialectic of revelation and tragedy hidden and disclosed in the epic of a single life and the life of the human race.

Theology is primarily a work of the imagination. On one hand the theologian must continually question what the image/concept of God has meant, how it has been understood, how it has functioned in human life from ancient Israel to the present. On the other hand, the theologian examines what the imagination does for human existence, how it creates a worldview within which existence is understood. Theologians in an attempt to appear to be conversant with current "scientific method" have overlooked the long-range dangers associated with a positivistic attitude. The thoroughly admirable concern for process philosophy (David Tracy) or strict methodology (Bernard Lonergan) has contributed immensely toward reestablishing theology as a legitimate discipline. The neglect of tradition and especially the humanities needs to be addressed. Scientists who have begun to realize the implications of quantum mechanics and the implied necessity for metaphorical description are beginning to turn to a study of the problem of chaos.

Consequently, scientists have begun to use chaos as a technique or a framework on which to hang some of their most treasured notions about the role of causation. The realization that the simplest, most deterministic equations can look like random noise suggests that the deterministic view of the world can be reconciled with the appearance of free will.

Art can be viewed as a theory about the way the world appears. There are beautiful things in the world and there is what can be called splendor. Interest in the relationship of theology and art has become a central issue. It would be truly ironic if Balthasar's work, which has been ignored because of its focus on art and literature, turns out to be among the most significant contributions to the future of theology. Despite their differences (and I shall have more to say on this in the body of the book), Karl Rahner could say of Balthasar's work, "Perhaps the effectiveness of such a theology inevitably takes longer than our impatience is ready to tolerate."[3]

This book is not a substitute for reading the original. It is not an abstract of Balthasar's thousands of pages. It is critical while it respects the text of Balthasar. Gerard Reedy may well have been correct when he wrote ten years ago: "His full contribution will perhaps only be recognized in a more irenic age, when believers, freed from polemics, will have the leisure better to savor his rich oeuvre."[4] If this book provokes a wider reading of this oeuvre, it will have served its purpose.

3. Karl Rahner, "Hans Urs von Balthasar," *Civitas* 20 (1965): 604.

4. Gerard Reedy, "The Christology of Hans Urs von Balthasar," *Thought* 45 (1970): 419.

## Chapter 1

# The Man and His Work

WHEN I first visited Hans Urs von Balthasar in his rooms at number 42 Arnold Böcklin Street in Basel a dozen years ago, I thought of Kant working alone in his cold room in Königsberg—not because Balthasar's room was cold and not because both men lived in relative physical and social isolation. Rather, Balthasar's incredible productivity and encyclopedic mind reminded me of Immanuel Kant. In addition, Balthasar's chief work, his theological synthesis, seems destined to suffer a fate similar to that of the great *Critiques*, which received the attention they deserved long after Kant wrote them. A final reason for this comparison was the structural similarity in Balthasar's system to that of Kant and the basic similar approach to aesthetics.

I concur entirely with an observation made by J. K. Riches: "It is hard to avoid a note of crusading zeal when writing about the work of Hans Urs von Balthasar. His contribution to theology in a number of fields is remarkable and remarkably little known."[1]

Many theologians today apparently concur with a judgment

1. J. K. Riches, "The Theology of Hans Urs von Balthasar," *Theology* 75 (1972): 562.

of Balthasar made some years ago by Rosemary Ruether. She narrated somewhat nostalgically: "Daniélou, Urs von Balthasar and others were sustained by this vision of the 'Mystical Body,' and it was this generation that gave birth to the wake of the Second Vatican Council. The pathos of this generation is that when they succeeded, they succeeded so suddenly and so totally that they themselves became almost entirely superseded and left behind, so that now they sound musty and old-fashioned."[2] Ruether admitted that Balthasar helped dissolve the bonds of legal institutional thought, but she charged that he and his colleagues fled to the realm of "angelic contemplation," failing to bring their vision into relation with the reality of the institution. They preferred, she said, to dissolve its categories into a "shimmering light of celestial glory." Consequently, she claimed, Balthasar has become irrelevant to a generation that demands theological realism. I have selected Ruether as an initial critic because she herself was educated in the classical tradition and did her doctoral dissertation on Gregory Nazianzen.

I will argue in this book that any judgment that pronounces Balthasar "old-fashioned" betrays a lack of understanding not only of his work but of the true meaning of the classical tradition and its role in the development of philosophical and theological method. I will attempt to show the contemporary relevance of Balthasar's work by focusing on his fresh presentation of classical and patristic thought. Rosemary Ruether, para-

2. Rosemary Ruether, "New Thinking on the Church," *Cross Currents* 13 (Winter 1968): 111. Balthasar is himself aware of such criticism. He notes that the theologian, whether engaged in dogma, moral theology, or exegesis, is asked today to produce definite results "black on white," which men can take home with them, but he must resist this temptation because, as a theologian, his task involves preserving the incomprehensible marvel of divine revelation, which cannot be exhausted definitively or expressed in portable formulas. See his explanation in *Das Ganze im Fragment*, pp. 12ff.

doxically, could be a paradigm. She wrote: "But if I have had, or can continue to have, anything really significant to say, I cannot afford to take my cues from what is *au courant*. I have to work primarily out of a sense of my personal integrity. The content of cultural critique cannot be the current mood of the year or the decade, but must be a systematic exploration of the pathologies and redeeming graces of the Christian tradition over its whole history, in its many branches, and in its implications for worldwide culture today and in the future."[3] Whenever one confronts this tradition, the hermeneutical problem must be faced. Every great thinker will make a contribution toward the solution. Balthasar's contribution may be among the most significant in this century. Although such a claim sounds inflated, I will argue that it is not. Dennis J. Keefe has called Balthasar's work "the most sustained and comprehensive theological enterprise by a Catholic scholar in this century, and one which must rank with the classic theological achievements of the Catholic past."[4]

Although common theological enterprises on the European Continent often contain contributions from Balthasar—for example, *Mysterium Salutis* or *Absolutheit des Christentums*[5]—Balthasar does not have frequent contacts with other scholars. Events in his own life partially explain the neglect of his work. His physical and social isolation increased when he

3. Rosemary Ruether, *Disputed Questions: On Being a Christian* (Nashville: Abingdon Press, 1982), p. 32.

4. D. J. Keefe, Review of *The Glory of the Lord*, vol. 1, *Thomist* 48 (1984):663.

5. These works contained contributions from many theologians and were intended to present the latest theology in a readable form in the post–Vatican II context. The latter was published in 1977. *Mysterium Salutis*, vol. 3, pt. 2 (Einsiedeln: Benziger, 1969), contains a long article, "Mysterium Paschale," by Balthasar, pp. 133–326.

began work on the manuscripts of Adrienne von Speyr. The lack of translation of much of Balthasar's major work is another reason for his relative obscurity outside German- or French-speaking countries. This lack is twice to be lamented, for his style is beautiful. He has won the coveted Grand Prize for Literature of the Swiss Foundation for Culture, a distinction enjoyed by few other philosophical or theological writers. The few articles by Balthasar that have been translated as well as the translated volumes have for the most part been concerned with particular questions. Nevertheless, the swelling tide of his thought has not approached English or American shores. In addition, Balthasar's continuing emphasis on mysticism and the spiritual associations of theology have not always evoked a sympathetic response. Yet his viewpoint is not extreme or shocking, as, for example, in Teilhard de Chardin; nor is it confined to a single genre such as biblical theology or archaeology. Some have been misled by his criticism of aspects of the work of Rahner and Schillebeeckx to consider him a reactionary and "antiprogressive" thinker. What other theologians apparently find most disconcerting, however, is his insistence on the role and place of the humanities, including the fine arts, in his theological system—a position espoused by patristic and classical authors but seemingly anathema to contemporary theology.

Rather than "dehellenize" Western thought, Balthasar demands a basic return to this classical tradition. He insists upon a thoroughly grounded metaphysics, study of patristics, and solid exegesis of the literary text. Such a view is the antithesis of some modern approaches. Thomas J. J. Altizer may stand as a typical representative of this modern view. Altizer wrote: "What is requisite in our situation is an application of the analogical method to the dynamic or process categories of contemporary scientific and historical thinking. No longer can we think in terms of analogical relation between two eternally given or unchanging forms of being but rather of a moving or evolving series of analogical relationships between the integrally related poles of a forward moving process."[6] Where thinkers such as Altizer call for a transformation in consciousness in accordance with the movements of history, Balthasar insists upon insight into the traditional *analogia entis* and sees no necessity for positing a strictly linear evolution or process. Balthasar continues the tradition of "universalism," the teaching of the Alexandrians and Scholastics (whose last representative was Nicholas of Cusa in the fifteenth century). Balthasar is a master of this traditionalist viewpoint. He unites various "forms" of life, thought, and perception with the "form" of language in the manner of Ludwig Wittgenstein, who, curiously, shared Balthasar's master view that ethics and aesthetics are one.[7]

Paradoxically, the ethics of belief that founds Balthasar's aesthetics has become a central theme in the current debates on the philosophy of religion. If "aesthetics of belief," were substituted, one could fix Balthasar as a star in this debate. Yet one will search and search English publications on the philosophy of religion in vain to find a serious acquaintance with the thought of Balthasar.

Balthasar holds no appeal to thinkers convinced that a simple or even a complex reinterpretation of tradition is adequate. He attempts not just a reinterpretation and reevaluation

6. Thomas J. J. Altizer, "Catholic Philosophy and the Death of God," *Cross Currents* 12 (Summer 1967): 273.

7. See, for example, Erich Heller, "Ludwig Wittgenstein: Unphilosophical Considerations," *Cross Currents* 12 (Summer 1967): 317–32. For development of the whimsical as well as the serious sides of this question see G. E. Moore, *Philosophical Papers* (New York: Collier, 1962), pp. 247–318.

but a total integration. Such an attempt revolves around the nucleus of traditional epistemology and metaphysics.[8] The current cry is for abandoning the Western tradition that has dominated culture from the time of the Greeks.

Among the most important reasons why individuals such as Balthasar tend to be neglected is that they are accused of being dilettantes. Balthasar wears several hats—literary critic, translator, editor, classical and patristic scholar; it is casually assumed that not one really could fit.

I will not claim that all of Balthasar's work is solid, nor that in some respects he is innocent of the charge of dilettantism. Some of his readings of ancient authors are questionable. Some of his logic is faulty. Redundancies occur in his thousands of pages. Yet he would be the first to admit to these and other weaknesses. Nevertheless, competent critics will grant the general correctness of Balthasar's conclusions, whether of interpretations of ancient authors or contemporary writers.[9] Balthasar's reading of some texts in Plotinus and Iamblichus may well be wrong, but the noted Iamblichus scholar and Regius Professor of Greek at Trinity College, Dublin, John Dil-

8. Balthasar's maintenance of tradition is opposed by many American thinkers. For example, Eugene Fontinell holds that "nothing will do which suggests that some truths—or even some 'substantial' or 'essential' part of these truths—escape process and development" (Religious Truth in a Relational and Processual World," *Cross Currents* 12 [Summer 1967]:285). Others have appreciated selected aspects of Balthasar's work; Grover E. Foley, for example, wrote, "It may even be that the criticism here offered of von Balthasar's interpretations instead of weakening his and his followers' material agreement with the theologial *and* anthropological (because christological) fulness of the *Church Dogmatics*, may only strengthen their careful avoidance of any theoretical consequences which could only undermine Barth's Christocentrism" ("The Catholic Critics of Karl Barth in Outline and Analysis," *Scottish Journal of Theology* 14 [June 1961]:718).

9. In addition to the comments in this chapter, specific instances of Balthasar's possible misreadings will be indicated in subsequent chapters, especially those dealing with patristics.

lon, concedes the essential correctness of Balthasar's interpretation of the *De Mysteriis*. Balthasar himself readily confesses his weaknesses, but he asks that his general purpose be kept in mind—to put these studies to the service of theology. Major patristic scholars such as Henri Charles Puech, Alois Lieske, Henri Crouzel, Marguerite Harl, and Heinrich Karpp have reviewed his work on the Fathers, and from them we can obtain a sense of their reception of his work.[10]

It is important from the beginning to recognize that Balthasar's theological work is set in the context of his studies of German Idealism, classical literature, patristics, especially Origen, Gregory of Nyssa, and Maximus the Confessor, and the field of European literature and drama.

## Biographical Sketch

Hans Urs von Balthasar was born in Lucerne, Switzerland, on August 12, 1905, the son of architect Oskar von Balthasar and Gabrielle Pretzker. His ancestry includes some of the most illustrious names in Swiss and Hungarian history. His grand-

10. Reviewers spoke favorably of his work on Origen. Puech wrote: "I do not know any better introduction to the thought of Origen than this anthology of extracts from his works, translated into German and presented in an elegant and spacious format. Everything moves toward situating the reader in a direct, profound, and living contact with the thought of the great Alexandrian, not only to open the sum of his ideas in their very intent and context but also to sensitize the reader to the unique attraction of his spirit and the exaltation of his heart" (*Revue de l'histoire des religions* 62 [1941]: 214–15). Crouzel called the work an "important introduction which constitutes a certain guide for penetrating the thought of the man of steel" (*Revue d'ascétique et de mystique* 37 [1961]: 235). Karpp said, "The book with its plenitude of good, legible texts, valuable introductions to the individual sections, and the thoughtful introduction, which was written with enthusiasm, is, though it contains almost no scholarly references and will not find universal scholarly agreement with its conclusions . . . useful for scholarly work" (*Theologische Rundschau* 14 [1942]: 207).

mother was Hungarian. One of his great uncles, a bishop, was murdered by the Nazis on their invasion of Hungary. Another uncle was a member of the Maltese Order in Rome and as a Swiss Guard wielded considerable influence at the papal court. A sister joined the community of Franciscan nuns of Angers and worked for years as Sister Mary of the Angels in a nursing home near Southhampton in England.

The family influence in a typical turn-of-the-century bourgeois setting provided a thorough introduction to the best in Western high culture. One example was the early development in the young child of a love of music, which made him an accomplished pianist. It might have been possible for him to become a concert pianist, had he chosen to pursue music instead of literature and philosophy.

From 1917 to 1921 he was a student in the grammar school and Gymnasium (Stiftschule) conducted by the Benedictine Order in Engelberg, Switzerland, and from 1921 to 1924 at the Stella Matutina Gymnasium of the Jesuits in Feldkirch, Austria. He matriculated at the University of Zurich in 1923–24 as a student of German language and literature and of philosophy. He pursued the typical German university student life and spent semesters enrolled in the Universities of Vienna and Berlin. During the course of his studies in Vienna, Balthasar came to know the physician-psychiatrist and philosopher Rudolf Allers. The multitalented doctor, philosopher, and theologian shared with Balthasar his theory of "love of one's fellow human being as the objective medium of human existence . . . in this turning away from the ego to a reality filled with the other lay philosophical truth and the psychotherapeutic method for him."[11] Allers remained a lifelong friend and

11. See Werner Löser, "Das Sein—ausgelegt als Liebe," *Internationale katholische Zeitschrift* 4 (1975):416.

inspiration. It was also during this period in Vienna that Balthasar attended the lectures of Hans Eibl on Plotinus's *Enneads* and was greatly influenced by Eibl's interpretation of the transcendentals. Similarly, in Berlin, Romano Guardini, whose lectures he followed closely, became an important inspiration, turning the thoughts of the young "Germanist" more and more in the direction of philosophy and theology. It was Guardini who suggested the contrast between Kierkegaard and Nietzsche, which became the springboard for examining Gotthold Ephraim Lessing in Balthasar's doctoral dissertation.

On October 27, 1928, he completed his doctoral examinations and was awarded a doctorate for his dissertation, "The History of the Eschatological Problem in Modern German Literature." In the summer of 1927 he had made a thirty-day Ignatian retreat for laymen conducted by Father Friedrich Kronseder, S.J., at Whylen near Basel. Some thirty years later he reflected that he could still find the tree on a path in the Black Forest under which he felt the call to become a priest. On October 31 of the following year he entered the novitiate of the Society of Jesus at Feldkirch. During this period he was immersed in Ignatian spirituality. The thirty-day retreat early in the course of the first year profoundly affected the young novice and apparently gave him an insight into the discernment of spirits which was to remain with him.

After the normal two-year period of trial and probation in the novitiate in Feldkirch, he was sent to study Scholastic philosophy at Berchamanskolleg at Pullach near Munich. He later termed these three years as a period in which he wandered about in the desert of Neoscholasticism. There were a few oases. One was Father Peter Lippert, whose deep spirituality was a spring from which the young philosopher could drink. The other was the teaching of Erich Przywara. In Przywara Balthasar discovered the "greatest mind I was ever privileged to encounter."[12] Przywara gave Balthasar his first in-depth understanding of the relation between faith and reason. The philosophical categories developed by Przywara made him one of the few Catholic philosophers of the time to escape the false boundaries of Scholasticism. Along with Joseph Maréchal, Przywara fought against "extrinsicism" in the teaching on nature and grace and in all doctrinal questions.

"Extrinsicism" involved a theory of a complete human nature (*natura pura*) to which grace was added as a new and separate supernatural end. The issue of saving grace for the person as human tended to be overlooked in favor of an emphasis on the gratuity of salvation. Przywara helped Balthasar to escape this manner of thinking. In addition, Przywara suggested a line of thought that Balthasar was later to develop thoroughly: the relation of the individual to the Redeemer. These issues will be discussed in more detail in a later chapter, but Balthasar never tired of crediting his original inspiration for this line of development to Erich Przywara.

Upon completion of the three-year course at Pullach, Balthasar was sent to study theology at Lyons (Fourvière) in France. This four-year period (1933–37) was also meaningful for the personal contacts he made. The encounter with Henri de Lubac infused his younger colleague with his own love for the intellectual riches of tradition, especially the patristic treasury, which became the determining influence on the future course of Balthasar's work. De Lubac helped Balthasar see in the Church Fathers, especially the Greek Fathers, a neglected source for innovative theological development. Others joined him in this work in addition to de Lubac. The group included Henri Bouillard, Gaston Fessard, and Jean Danièlou. None of

12. *Rechenschaft* 1965, p. 34; see also his portrait of Przywara in *Tendenzen der Theologie*, pp. 354–59. For the citations of works by Balthasar used in this book see the Bibliography.

these theologians, however, dedicated themselves to the Fathers to the extent that Balthasar did. Balthasar later wrote that de Lubac opened the world of the Greek Fathers, the philosophical mysticism of the East, and modern atheism to the group of young theologians and also that Balthasar himself owed to de Lubac gratitude for sparking an interest in patristic studies: "For Patristics meant for us: Christianity, which still stretches into the limitless space of the non-Christian world and holds the hope of redeeming the world."[13]

Michael Cardinal Faulhaber ordained Balthasar a priest on July 26, 1936, in the Church of St. Michael in Munich. Upon completing his theological studies at Lyons, Balthasar served on the editorial staff of the Jesuit periodical *Stimmen der Zeit* in Munich from the autumn of 1937 until the summer of 1939. Again he made important contacts: "Meeting with Erich Przywara . . . working together with Karl Rahner[14] and patristic 'syntheologein' [common study of the Fathers] with Hugo Rahner"[15] strengthened his resolve to live for God alone. He then underwent the final stage of Jesuit preparation, the "tertianship," in 1939 back at the Berchmanskolleg. This final year is like a repetition of the novitiate and includes another thirty-day retreat based on the "Spiritual Exercises" of Ignatius of Loyola.

The exercises gave Balthasar a sense of his ultimate mission as a theological writer. He eventually translated them into a lucid German that recaptured the spirit of Ignatius's original: "I translated the exercises and must have given them a hundred times; if anywhere, this is where it is made evident what

13. *Rechenschaft* 1965, pp. 5–6.

14. Together with Karl Rahner Balthasar developed an outline of a new dogmatic theology which Rahner later published in the first volume of his *Schriften zur Theologie* on his own initiative.

15. *Rechenschaft* 1965, pp. 6ff.

being a Christian in one's 'origins' means: the attentive listening for the Word that summons and becoming free for the anticipated answer. This is where, more than any place else, there is also intimate contact with the sense and genius of the reformation from Luther to Karl Barth."[16]

In 1940 Balthasar left Munich to take up a position as student chaplain in Basel. In that same year Adrienne von Speyr, a Swiss physician, became a convert to the Catholic faith under Balthasar's direction. This mystic was from that time on the most important personal influence on Balthasar's work and life. He himself wrote: "It was Adrienne von Speyr who pointed out the fulfilling way from Ignatius to John, and so laid the foundation for most of what has been published by me since 1940. Her work and mine is neither psychologically nor philosophically separable, two halves of a whole which, as center, has but one foundation."[17]

Balthasar and Adrienne von Speyr developed what they saw as the most appropriate form for living the Christian life in the contemporary world. They determined to found a "secular institute." They believed this a God-given commission. At first they attempted to achieve such a body within the context of the Society of Jesus. The provincial superior, the Father General at Rome, and even Balthasar's close Jesuit friends, all thought this inappropriate. Because this duty appeared so clear to him, even though it did not appear feasible to his superiors, Balthasar felt he had no choice but to leave the Jesuit order, which he did in 1950 with great sorrow. The new Johannesgemeinschaft (Community of St. John) was then founded in Basel, and Balthasar has continued ever since to direct and in-

16. Ibid., p. 8; cf. *Spiritus Creator,* pp. 76ff. Balthasar contrasts Luther and Ignatius as "types" of different modes of existential belief.

17. *Rechenschaft* 1965, p. 35.

spire it. His goal was to live the "true, unabridged church program for today." He believed this form of life the best available for holding together the "concrete universality" of Christian belief with all its stresses and strains.

Balthasar remained in his student chaplaincy until 1948. During this time he met the French writer and thinker Albert Béguin, whom Balthasar eventually baptized. Béguin opened the door for Balthasar's acquaintance with Charles Péguy and Georges Bernanos. In addition, the constant work with young students who questioned their faith and yet wanted to be Christian led Balthasar to seek a better way to give witness to this life. The way he found was the above-mentioned "secular institute." In the meantime he sought to organize groups of students and alumni. He kept these groups together after they had graduated from the university primarily by means of the journal *Civitas*.

In 1947 Balthasar founded his own publishing house, the Johannesverlag, at Einsiedeln. A primary motive was to provide the students with the necessary literature. The series of publications subsequently brought out for students carried names such as *Christ Heute, Sigillum, Adoratio, Horizonte, Lectio Spiritualis, Der Neue Weg*, and *Kriterien*.

The lengthy period in Basel provided Balthasar opportunity for frequent contact with Karl Barth. Barth called Balthasar's study of his work (*The Theology of Karl Barth*) "incomparably more powerful than most of the books which have clustered around me."[18] This contact developed into a friendship that endured until Barth's death.

Almost six years after leaving the Jesuit Order Balthasar was received by the bishop of the Diocese of Chur as a member of that diocese on February 2, 1956. Balthasar has never really

18. Karl Barth, *Church Dogmatics* (Edinburgh: T. & T. Clark, 1936), vol. 4, pt. 1, p. 71.

functioned, however, as a member of the secular clergy. Instead, he devoted himself all the more to his writing. For many years after leaving the Jesuit Order, Balthasar was virtually shunned. He was ignored during the Second Vatican Council. But time and the importance of his work eventually brought recognition by the church officials. At the Synod of Bishops held at Rome in 1971 Balthasar was summoned as a *peritus* (expert) on the question of the priestly office. Gradually the recognition and honors he earned have come to him. He has been awarded honorary doctorates by the Universities of Edinburgh, Munster, Fribourg, and the Catholic University of America. He is a corresponding fellow of the British Academy and a foreign associate of the Institut de France (Académie des Sciences Morales et Politiques).

In his essay on Balthasar, Jakob Laubach mentions a remark of Reinhold Schneider: "Balthasar's publications are variations on one theme, the theme of time."[19] Others have put together bibliographies of the work of Hans Urs von Balthasar.[20] Here I will give only a general view of the breadth of the scholarly and publishing activity of this unusual and often unknown theologian. The Bibliography gives a list of most of the important works of Balthasar, including all those cited in this book.

## Bibliographical Sketch

### Patristic Works

I noted above the significance of patristic study in the development of Balthasar's thought. The Fathers he chose to read,

19. Jakob Laubach, "Über Hans Urs von Balthasar," in *Theologen unserer Zeit, eine Vortragsreihe des Bayrischen Rundfunks*, ed. L. Reinisch (Munich: Kösel 1965), p. 179.

20. For the most recent bibliography see Cornelia Capol, *Hans Urs von Balthasar, Bibliographie*, 1925–1980 (Einsiedeln: Johannesverlag, 1981).

edit, and interpret were those whose themes interested him most. This study influenced both the thought and style of the young writer. Like that of the Greek Fathers, Balthasar's style is elegant and picturesque. His contemporaries tended to write theology in a turgid, scholastic, idealistic, or existentialist frame, which was most marked by being abstruse and abstract. Balthasar, however, writes a beautiful prose, full of images, and the multiple allusions demonstrate his command of the breadth of Western literature without overwhelming the reader with erudition.

The influence of patrology extends throughout the corpus—from earliest up to and including Balthasar's most recent works. An early article on Origen in 1936 led two years later to the collection of texts with introduction, *Geist und Feuer.* This work has been elegantly translated into English by Father Robert J. Daly, S.J.[21] Daly noted in his foreword that Balthasar's introduction still remains the best brief statement of the heart, soul, and spirit of Origen's writings.

In 1937 Balthasar edited and published a shortened version of Gregory of Nyssa's "Song of Songs" with the title, *Der versiegelte Quelle.* Balthasar formulated Gregory's philosophy of religion in 1942 under the title *Présence et pensée.*

Balthasar reintroduced Evagrius Ponticus to modern theology in the series of studies published in 1939. Balthasar dedicated his most extensive and intensive efforts to the study of Maximus the Confessor. In 1941 he published the two volumes *Kosmische Liturgie* and *Die Gnostischen Centurien des Maximus Confessor.* The first volume was redone completely and in 1961 published under the title *Kosmische Liturgie.* The

21. *Origen, Spirit and Fire: A Thematic Anthology of His Writings*, trans. Robert J. Daly, S.J. (Washington, D.C.: Catholic University of America Press, 1984).

reedited version included the Scholia of John of Scythopolis and versions of the "mystagogie" and "Viermal hundert Sprüche über die Liebe." These editions achieved recognition and review by eminent patristic scholars. Henry Chadwick, for example, in reviewing *Kosmische Liturgie*, wrote, "This book is more than a learned contribution to the finer points of the monothelite controversy or the immediate impact of the Areopagite. Balthasar invites us to see in Maximus Confessor an intelligence of the first rank and a bridge-thinker between East and West."[22]

In 1943 Balthasar published a selection from the writings of Irenaeus of Lyons—translations plus introduction—titled *Geduld des Reifens*. Four years later he published an edition of the "rules" of Basil. In the second volume of *Herrlichkeit* Balthasar devoted a chapter to Dionysius the Areopagite as well as to Irenaeus and Augustine. Among the Latin Fathers it was Augustine who had the greatest influence on Balthasar. In 1936 a selection from Augustine's "On the Psalms" was published. In 1942 Balthasar published *Das Antlitz der Kirche* and in 1955, an edition with commentary of the *Confessiones*. In 1961 he published a selection from the "De Civitate Dei" as *Die Gottesbürgerschaft*. Herbert Vorgrimler in his brief portrait of Balthasar includes among the patristic works Balthasar's translation in 1943 of Henri de Lubac's *Catholicism*. De Lubac had published the volume in 1938. It produced a true change in the direction of Catholic theology in France.[23] Balthasar's original translation was published as *Katholizismus als Gemeinschaft*. In 1970 he reedited it under the title *Glauben aus*

22. Henry Chadwick, review of *Kosmische Liturgie*, *Journal of Theological Studies* 13 (1953):431.

23. See Herbert Vorgrimler, "Theologische Porträts: Hans Urs von Balthasar," in Robert Vander Bucht, ed., *Bilanz der Theologie im 20. Jahrhundert* (Freiburg, Basel, and Vienna: Herder, 1970), p. 124.

*der Liebe* as part of the handsome Lubac series Balthasar published beginning in 1968.

## Translations of French Authors

At the same time Balthasar undertook to transmit the inheritance from the Fathers he also seized the opportunity to introduce the German-speaking world to contemporary French Catholic literature. Balthasar became the German voice of Paul Claudel. As a student of theology at Lyons Balthasar together with a group of fellow students read *The Satin Slipper*, of which Balthasar published a literary translation in 1939. Several editions of this work have subsequently appeared, including the pocket book edition of 1965. Also in 1939 he published the German edition of the *Five Great Odes* and in 1943, the *Way of the Cross*. He translated Claudel's play on the Annunciation in 1946 as *Maria Verkündigung*. Balthasar spent more than twenty-five years perfecting the translation of the poems until they were published as the first volume of the complete German edition of Claudel's works.

Balthasar also introduced Charles Péguy to Germany through the 1943 edition, *Tor zum Geheimnis der Hoffnung*. Ten years later a selection of Péguy's prose was translated as *Wir stehen alle an der Front*. This French writer also enjoys a prominent place in volume 2 of *Herrlichkeit*. The third French Catholic writer whose works Balthasar translated was Georges Bernanos. Balthasar published translations of the *Letters* in 1951, 1953, and 1954. The three novellas were translated as *Eine Nacht*, and that same year (1954) Balthasar's critical monograph, *Bernanos*, appeared.

German literary artists also interested Balthasar. He called Reinhold Schneider a "tragic Aeolian harp—who later truly fell apart and in place of the exact tones only produced lost, off-key sounds (*Winter in Wien*), which appeared interesting to the decadents and shadowed the truly prophetic elements of his greatest work."[24]

## Principal Philosophical Works

Balthasar's initial philosophical work grew out of his doctoral dissertation and encompassed the three-volume *Apokalypse der deutschen Seele: Studien zu einer Lehre von letzten Haltungen*. In this work Balthasar attempted an existential interpretation of modern German philosophy and literature from the time of Lessing to 1930 from an eschatological viewpoint. Volume 1, titled *Der deutsche Idealismus* appeared in 1937; Volume 2, *Im Zeichen Nietzsches*, in 1939; and Volume 3, *Die Vergöttlichung des Todes*, also in 1939. The first volume was republished in 1947 under the title *Prometheus*. Also in 1947 Balthasar published volume 1 of his *Wahrheit: Wahrheit der Welt*: and in 1954 his book on Thomas of Aquinas, *Thomas von Aguin Besondere Gnadengaben und die zwei Wege menschlichen Lebens, Kommentar zu Summa Theologica II-II*.

The projected set of studies on truth (*Wahrheit*) was never completed. The ten years from 1955 to 1965 were a time of "genuine decision" during which Balthasar reformulated his writing program and began work on the great theological trilogy. A resolve to present in a comprehensible manner the focus of Christianity throughout history led to the notion of writing a theological aesthetics, dramatics, and logic. The volume on truth (*Wahrheit*, vol. 1) was republished as the first volume in the third part of the trilogy, the *Theologik*. Volume 1 was published in 1985 as *Wahrheit der Welt*. Volume 2, *Wahrheit Gottes*, also appeared in 1985. Balthasar is working on the

24. *Rechenschaft* 1965, p. 25.

final volume of the trilogy. One contemporary philosopher has continued to interest Balthasar, however—Gustav Siewirth—particularly his philosophy of language.

## Major Theological Works

Balthasar published two volumes of *Skizzen zur Theologie* in 1960. The first volume, *Verbum Caro*, translated into English by A. V Littledale and Alexander Dru, was called *Word and Revelation* (1964). The second volume, *Sponsa Verbi* was also translated by Dru and Littledale as *Church and World* (1967). Volume 3 of the *Skizzen* appeared in 1967: *Spiritus Creator*; and volume 4, *Pneuma und Institution*, in 1974.

Balthasar's major theological work is his trilogy: a theological aesthetics, a theological dramatics, and a theological logic. *Herrlichkeit* is in the process of being translated under the title *The Glory of the Lord: A Theological Aesthetics.*[25] John Riches is the general editor. The complete translation of the first part of the trilogy is projected to constitute seven volumes: 1. *Seeing the Form*; 2. *Studies in Theological Style: Clerical Styles*; 3. *Studies in Theological Styles: Lay Styles*; 4. *The Realm of Metaphysics in Antiquity*; 5. *The Realm of Metaphysics in the Modern Age*; 6. *Theology of the Old Covenant*; and 7. *Theology: The New Covenant*. The first two volumes are now in print. The publisher anticipates that most of these volumes of the English translation will be in print by the end of 1986.

Balthasar began work on the trilogy in 1961 and has not yet finished. The work synthesizes his literary, philosophical, theological, exegetical, and systematic knowledge. The divisions come from the medieval doctrine of the "transcendentals"—those apects of being which surpass the categories: the

25. Volume 1 was translated by Erasmo Leiva-Merikakis; volume 2 by Andrew Louth, Francis McDonagh, and Brian McNeil. Volume 2 (San Francisco: Ignatius Press and New York: Crossroad) appeared in 1984.

good, the true, and the beautiful. Theological aesthetics, the theme of the six volumes of *Herrlichkeit*, published between 1961 and 1969, involves the classical and patristic teaching on the perception of the beauty of the selfless, divine love of God in its "appearing glory." This subject dominates the greater part of this book.

In the center of the trilogy stands theodramatic: the doctrine of the human person's openness to God's historical action. This is the point of transition from aesthetics to drama, the expression of the real "drama of life." Balthasar explains:

> Nowhere is the character of existence represented more clearly than in acted drama: we wish to view it ourselves, no matter for the moment whether we are looking for ourselves or fleeing from ourselves, whether they are presenting for us the serious or the ludicrous, the annihilating or the transforming, the meaningless or the hidden depths of insight into our being. Through this drama of relationships inherent to theater, the questionable and ambiguous character not only of the theater but also of existence too which holds it up to the light, becomes clear as perhaps nowhere else.[26]

The first volume provides "categories and forms of expression for the principal undertaking."[27] These categories then have to be transformed into those of history and anthropology. In the concepts of "sending" and "choosing," this anthropology provides a framework for the decisive "Persons in the play," Jesus Christ (so the title of Volume 2, part 2, *Die Personen in Christus*). Volume 3, *Die Handlung*, and Volume 4, *Das Endspiel*, present the dramatic event of God's love in the history of Christ. Balthasar deliberately chose this order for his theological dramatics to avoid the danger of appearing to allow God and the other actors to be absorbed into their historical activity and run the risk of simple identification with history.

26. *Theodramatik*, 1:17.
27. Ibid., p. 24.

History can be comprehended only as the revelation of the possibilities inherent in the persons.

The third part of the trilogy, theological logic, remains as yet unfinished, although the two volumes mentioned above have been published. It involves the truth of divine action in history. Elaboration of the relation between theological aesthetics and dramatics will occupy the remaining chapters of this book.

I commented above on Balthasar's remarkable literary style. His sentences have a rhetorical rhythm that almost demands that they be read aloud. He consciously avoids an "academic" style, and his use of the concept of "sketches" (*Skizzen*) helps explain his manner of writing. In his preface to one of the *Skizzen* Balthasar noted,

> Also it is no surprise if often in a book of sketches a couple of themes circulate like fixed ideas and are approached and tested from every side; a certain fascination for the impalpable middle is responsible for such repetition and overemphasis. Emphases of Rodin or Marais place multiple outlines of an arm or leg alongside or over one another; one does not know—is this a grasping for the only proper curve or rather the only possible way to represent an action, an act of living.[28]

28. *Verbum Caro*, p. 7.

## Chapter 2

# Philosophical Presuppositions

THE HISTORICAL question whether Plato abandoned or sharply modified his theory of ideas in later life serves to situate the problem of considering Balthasar's philosophical perspective. The question is historical, but the answer one gives is likely to be influenced by presuppositions. If one believes that the theory of ideas is in some sense true and that the questions it answers are philosophically important, one will be reluctant to think that Plato ever abandoned or discounted his theory. One will be less reluctant to think this if one supposes that the theory is false, or, more than false, irrelevant—an answer to mistaken questions. For it will then seem reasonable to suppose that a philosopher of Plato's acumen came to see its irrelevance for himself. This latter view has gained approval in recent years, the result of current emphases in philosophy. A similar case can be made for the patristic work of Hans Urs von Balthasar. If one supposes that metaphysics as the science of being as being has importance for the study of theology, one will grant Balthasar's work more relevance. All theology, including patristics, proceeds upon assumptions of this kind, of which some may be apparent, others, more or less hidden.

This chapter focuses on some of the more or less apparent presuppositions necessary for understanding Balthasar's theological aesthetics. I wish to emphasize that Balthasar disclaims either belonging to any system or having one of his own. This Swiss thinker is thoroughly classical, however, and his metaphysics springs from the Greeks. Balthasar takes *metaphysics* in its most comprehensive sense, not separated from sacred (mythical) knowledge. It includes the transcendental aspects of the one, true, good, and beautiful. Balthasar attempts "to develop a Christian theology in the light of the third transcendental, that is to say: to complement the vision of the true and the good with that of the beautiful (*pulchrum*)."[1] The category of the *beautiful* comprehends his particular concern. When philosophy struggles with this part of itself, the real aesthetic problem, it cannot escape its "*mythical*" past. Even before Plato began to philosophize, the high period of Greek art was nearly over. All that came later in Greece and Rome was but an echo of the original impulse of artistic creation which sprang from the earlier mythic drive. I shall examine this process in detail in the next two chapters on the classical tradition. All great art is religious, and Balthasar sees it as an act of adoration of the *doxa* of being. When this religious dimension fades from art, its worship degenerates into a superficial fascination with the sensuous. As Goethe remarked with astonishing humility for his time to his friend Riemer: "Men are productive in poetry and art only so long as they are religious; when they become simply imitative and repetitive as in our age, their works become fantastic imitations."[2]

## Relation of "Theologik" to Aesthetics

Because the third part of his major work, the theological logic, is not finished and probably will not be, the material

1. *The Glory of the Lord*, vol. 1, Preface.
2. Johann Wolfgang Goethe, *Werke*, vol. 12 (Hamburg: Hegner, 1953), p. 79.

covered in this chapter may help in understanding what that section of the trilogy was intended to accomplish. It is important, however, to give some sense of the content of the *Theologik* and its relation to theological aesthetics, even though in Balthasar's system it comes last.

The *Theologik* questions the meaning of "truth" against the background of the Incarnation of the Logos and the Pentecost event. The question about the Logos is the question about the truth of being. Balthasar begins the *Theologik* with an outline of the entire trilogy ordered around the transcendentals and their analogous interrelationships. In the aesthetics worldly beauty and divine glory share an analogous relation; in the "dramatics" limited worldly and unlimited divine freedom are discussed. The "theologic" considers the relation between the structure of divine and created truth and asks whether divine truth can be expressed within the structures and diverse forms of created truth: "Theological knowledge of God's glory, goodness, and truth presupposes a structure of worldly being that is not only formal or gnoseological but also ontological: without philosophy, no theology."[3]

The question of the analogy of being is transposed into the question whether worldly Logos is capable of containing divine Logos. Balthasar says that the "theologic" will call to attention many teachings that have been lost since the time of antiquity and the patristic tradition—for example, that on the "circuminsessio."

Balthasar gave five reasons why he thinks his philosophical viewpoint deserves consideration:[4]

1. He says his position allows the truth contained in myth and in the study of the history of religions to be revealed pre-

3. *Theologik*, Vol. 1, Preface, p. 1.

4. See *Herrlicheit*, vol. 3, pt. 1, Introduction, for elaboration of these five reasons.

cisely as the *wholly other* of biblical revelation. His position thus avoids the problem found in German Idealism and Romanticism (and romantically inclined theologians) of making a unified cosmic history out of divine revelation.

2. He claims his position respects the attitude of those who take seriously the call of Scripture for penance and conversion, for immediate hearing of the Word. Thus he is open to the thought of Luther, Kierkegaard, Bultmann, and the like.

3. It is a position that views the formality of Christ's revelation precisely in the radical destruction of the beauty and form (Is. 53:2) of Him who became sin for all. It emphasizes the scriptural view of the decisive illumination of the glory of being in that event (the cross) wherein every form becomes formless. It is the union of theological aesthetics and dramatics.

4. It is a Christian and Catholic position, which promises gospel freedom without at the same time wholly discarding ecclesiastical and theological tradition. Balthasar fears the growing numbers of conceptual iconoclasts, especially those who would cleanse Catholicism of Hellenic influence. Balthasar says such men argue that Greek philosophical influence tainted Paul, grew chronic in the Alexandrian Fathers, and became toxic in the work of the Council of Constantinople. This viewpoint fails to appreciate the basic unity of early Mediterranean culture—as if Herodotus or Joseph and his brothers had never visited Egypt or Antiochus IV Epiphanes never came to Jerusalem.

5. Finally, Balthasar says his position is not blind to the blindness of the modern world for the beauty and glory of reality (the reflected glory of God).

These five "reasons" we may take as presuppositions influencing Balthasar's thought and his approach to the Fathers. Two issues should be clarified at this point. The first is the question of using supposedly outmoded categories. Balthasar himself answered this charge in his book on Karl Barth:

Anyone who wants to exist in the world has to learn languages. The person who wants to penetrate the intellectual world must learn its languages: the concepts and modes of thought that change with different cultures and with succeeding generations. Thus the Catholic, who feels a responsibility to preserve the deposit of faith intact, should make every effort to learn modern modes of thought. If he does not do this, if he knows only the terminology and outlook of the Middle Ages, he will not be able to give directions to his contemporaries.[5]

The second issue is the question of "God-talk." The indirectness of speaking-of-God means that humans can use such language only analogically. This analogous character is independent of the way divine reality is conceived or where it is encountered. Balthasar works out of the classical theory of analogy, which holds that the divine reality stands in an analogical relation to the world in the sense of the "analogy of being." Traditionally this means a combination of the "analogy of attribution" and the "analogy of proportionality." Although the analogates that make up the analogy of attribution are unequal, that is, only one of the two really deserving to have predicated of it the common abstractable characteristic in a formal sense, both the terms in an analogy of proportionality possess the analogue in a literal and unmetaphorical sense. Each has this analogue only proportionately to the nature of the analogates concerned. How Balthasar interprets this will become clear as we review his use of patristics.

Without the element of belief in the reality of a referent designated by theological language, the distinctively religious character of this speech is sought in vain. The syntactic character of theological discourse needs to be understood in terms of the linguistic community. The members of such communities have distinctive purposes and activities, different attitudes and emotions.

5. *The Theology of Karl Barth*, trans. John Drury (New York: Holt, Rinehart and Winston, 1971), p. 10.

## Introduction to Patristics

Balthasar's study of the Fathers under Henri de Lubac at Lyons was vital to the development of his thought. Whatever theme Balthasar broached, de Lubac noted, one sensed that "he has gone through the school of the Fathers of the Church—even when he mentions none by name. They have nourished and inspired him. . . . Their vision is his own."[6]

Balthasar has never studied patristics as an independent scholar. He has always claimed that study of the Fathers divorced from an attitude of belief is meaningless. This lack of a sense of academic objectivity has led some scholars to dismiss Balthasar's work on the Fathers as self-serving. I will demonstrate in later chapters that these critics are both right and wrong. They are right in criticizing Balthasar's lack of scholarly distance and concern for the establishment of the patristic text. They are wrong in assuming without a thorough study of Balthasar's work that his interpretation cannot illuminate aspects of patristic thought which traditional scholarship has ignored.

Robert Stadler, for example, has noted that one can understand Balthasar's life and work, especially his work on the Fathers, only in the light of his experience of the Spiritual Exercises.[7]

Werner Löser has also noted the traditional poles that focus Balthasar's patristic work. Friedrich Nitzsch (not Nietzsche) as early as 1865 distinguished between a dogmatic-historical interest and a purely historical interest in patristics.[8] Franz Overbeck likewise spoke of a purely historical interest and of pa-

6. Henri de Lubac, *H. U. von Balthasar* (Paris: Cerf, 1967), p. 200.

7. Robert Stadler, "Amour et vision," *Civitas* 20 (1964–65):605; cf. Werner Löser, *Im Geist des Origenes* (Frankfurt: Knecht, 1976), pp. 410–24.

8. Friedrich Nitzsch, "Geschichtliches und Methodologisches zur Patristik," *Jahrbuch für deutsche Theologie* 10 (1865):37–63.

tristics as "early Christian literary history": "Patristics, we can say, is nothing other than the earliest Christian literature which has been snared by a false theological concern." Löser pointed out that Balthasar's patristic work implies a fullness of knowledge obtained by purely historical research on the Fathers carried out either by himself or by other scholars. But one would miss the unique aspect of Balthasar's patristic methodology if one were to identify it with the usual scholar's approach.[9] Balthasar's own comment regarding his work on Maximus the Confessor may be taken as typical: "That which is given here is not a historically neutral, complete presentation of the life and work of this man."[10]

Is Balthasar's patrology simply a narrowly circumscribed support of dogmatic theology similar to that described by Michael Tetz? "The *theologia patristica* provides *testimonia* to orthodox systematics and works closely with biblical theology, whose task it was to have ready at hand the *dicta probantia*. So Patristics originally was a dogmatic-historical concern in theology."[11] Such a concern was typical of Catholic theology well into this century. Names of such practitioners come readily to mind: O. Bardenhewer, Johannes Quasten, and Bernard Altaner are probably most familiar to English or American readers.

Early in this century, however, a middle way was taken by scholars such as Henri de Lubac, Jean Daniélou, and others. Joseph Ratzinger expounded this *via media* for patristics between a purely historical study and a dedicated support for dogmatics.[12] This new way involves an objective historical

9. Cited in Löser, *Im Geiste des Origenes*, p. 9, n. 2.

10. *Kosmische Liturgie*, p. 12.

11. Michael Tetz, "Altchristliche Literaturgeschichte-Patrologie," *Theologische Rundschau, Neue Folge* 32 (1967): 3.

12. Joseph Ratzinger, "Die Bedeutung der Väter für die gegenwärtige Theologie," in Thomas Michels, ed., *Geschichtlichkeit der Theologie* (Salzburg/Munich, Kösel Verlag 1970), pp. 63–81.

and critical study of the theology of the Fathers guided by the question of their possible meaning for present-day theology. A historical-critical study which asks about this contemporary relevance summarizes Balthasar's approach. Yet he does something more. What that "more" involves leads us into the main body of this book.

Löser described Balthasar's method as "theological phenomenology":

> With this two things are said: first it is a matter of a phenomenological method. This concerns itself with the comprehension of forms. But forms are wholes, which are more than the sum of their parts. Historical forms cannot be comprehended, unless an extreme amount of exact historical-critical knowledge is brought to bear on them. Nevertheless the compilation of this historical information, which basically cannot be complete, does not present the "form." While science in the exact sense is analytic . . . the perception of the total form . . . is synthetic.[13]

Balthasar wrote in the introduction to *Origen: Spirit and Fire*:

> So, we have decided to make a selection, from all of his works, of what still makes sense today, and in such a way that out of the interconnection of these central passages the true face of Origen could shine forth as from a mosaic. . . . But in so far as this inner "spiritual bond" in Origen's thought is being sought out, we are obviously, already, placing ourselves beyond purely historical interest (as, to some extent, the Kösel editions have) and are erecting in the arena of intellectual investigation a statue for whose validity we are responsible.[14]

Löser argued that such a phenomenological procedure entails the will to let the uniqueness of the form appear and to perceive it objectively. My argument is that this is less a matter of phenomenology than a consequence of Balthasar's fundamental aesthetic theory. His entire focus is on "seeing the form."

13. Löser, *Im Geiste des Origines*, p. 11.
14. *Origen: Spirit and Fire*, p. 5.

He uses a particular form of experience. As Michael Novak observed, writing about God "means to write about experience, of a sort."[15]

Löser's second point is that Balthasar's method is also theological, a result of his Christocentric theology of grace.[16] Every individual stands inevitably in a definite relation to Christ, for Christ is the first, innermost, and ultimate ontological principle of creation. The relationship of the individual and his thinking to Christ determines his essential nature and constitutes his truth. The attempt to discover the relation of individual Fathers to Christ is the task of patristic scholarship as Balthasar sees and practices it, as he expressed in the foreword to *Présence et pensée:* "The central point of view which commands the choice and the grouping of ideas of each is not the concern to present that which from them would appear most able to interest or influence modern theology. We have not attempted any material transposition. Rather we wish to penetrate to that vital source of their spirit which directs the entire expression of their thought."[17]

## Building Blocks of Balthasar's Method

### The Positive Value of This World

In one of Balthasar's earliest papers, "Logos," which he gave before the members of the Literary Circle of the Vienna Academic Union, he stated: "There is absolutely nothing bad nor hateful in the realm of the contingent, for it lacks nothing. Nothing is removed from what should be there conceptually; rather it is full." Balthasar was then twenty-two years old; he

15. Michael Novak, *Confessions of a Catholic* (San Francisco: Harper & Row, 1983), p. 25.
16. Löser, *Im Geist des Origenes*, p. 11.
17. *Présence et pensée*, p. xi.

was already at work combining the aesthetic and religious parts of reality. The initial thrust involved walking a tightrope between aestheticism in the narrow sense and a puritan rejection of art: "Who affirms the higher does not have to reject the lower." He added, "Art moves from the concrete and is, if one will, a process of abstraction (if not logical). Religion on the other hand is concerned with the concrete *katexochen;* namely, fate and decision of the unique person."[18]

Part of Balthasar's fascination for Claudel was the way the French author valued this world. Balthasar's insight on the positive value of the world became fully developed in the *Theologik*. Przywara's influence on Balthasar also grew out of the significance of this world for the doctrine on the analogy of being.[19] Because this doctrine holds a central place in Balthasar's reading of Origen, it should be explained briefly.

Balthasar's valuation of this world comes in part from his thorough rejection of German Idealism. This rejection is important because Balthasar's method undoubtedly borrows heavily from that tradition; indeed, as I shall demonstrate in Chapter 9, he actually builds upon it. Przywara helped Balthasar restructure traditional Thomistic ontology. The basic principle is not the subjectivity of man as the place of the "unity of reality" (of God and world). The tradition tried to find that place in the *whole* of reality. Przywara characterized the human person as innerworldly and supraworldly. The former entailed the tension between existence and essence; the latter, the relation to the creator. This double character Przywara called the *analogia entis:* reality is analogous, simultaneously like and unlike divine being. It is like insofar as it "is," but unlike insofar as it shares any identity or necessity. This world could just as easily

18. "Kunst und Religion," pp. 363, 359, 367.
19. See Erich Przywara, *Analogia Entis* (Munich: Kösel/Pustet, 1932).

not be. It is and is valuable precisely because it exists because of God, who gives *Dasein* and *Sosein* ("being there" and "being what"). Thus analogy forms the foundation for the value of the finite. We can truly love this world because it is a reflection of the divine. The analogy of created being founds the necessity of transcending this world to the absolute transcendent reality of the divine. This world is a reflection of the divine. Therefore, its beauty, like the other transcendentals, one, good, and true, can function as a springboard to transcendence. Analogy becomes for Balthasar the only way to think about the relation between creature and creator and issues of nature and grace, reason and faith: "All comparison and relation of the creature consequently has its measure in a converse relation of God to the creature."[20] Karl Barth considered the Principle of the Analogy of Being the ultimate expression of Catholic thought and the absolutely convincing reason for not becoming Catholic.

Balthasar would disclaim having based his thought on this or any other principle. He even says modestly that were nothing original found in his work, he would be not surprised. But his systematic influence, like that of Karl Barth, is likely to be greater and deeper than the current eclipse of both seems to portend. Fashions that rule academia are not wholly absent from theology, and what today's glass of fashion reflects will not necessarily be tomorrow's concern.

However limited human thought about the absolute must of necessity be, in theological hermeneutics (the process of reflecting methodically on the dogmas of faith) the only possible way for man to gain insight is by some use of analogical method. Such use of analogy is more than an extension of historical method. It involves a form of analogical thinking,

20. "Analogie und Dialektik," *Divus Thomas* 22 (1944): 176.

which Ernst Troeltsch recognized as a "leaven that transforms everything, and finally shatters the whole framework of theological method as this has existed hitherto."[21]

In more modern terminology we might say that theological discourse involving analogical thinking refers to "metaphysical fact," that is, it functions on its semantic dimension as metaphysical language. The language of living religious belief is not used for the sake of a metaphysical argument, but questions of motivation can be bracketed in semantic considerations. Theological speech projects a model of significance which is drawn from a state of affairs as the key to its conceptual synthesis. This model includes the "spiritual" characteristics of personality.[22]

## Balthasar's Philosophical Position

Henri Bergson's critique of the inability of post-Cartesian thought—confused with what Bergson considered an inability of reason itself—to deal adequately with the philosophical fact of change foreshadowed a revival of classical realism, most evident in Neo-Thomism and interest in Aristotle. This movement erupted into an anti-Idealist preoccupation with the phenomena of change. Such an emphasis, however, could not fail to establish at least the possibility of a closer rapport with tradition.

Kierkegaard's critique of Hegel was a second manifestation of a growing classical trend in modern thought. Kierkegaard criticized Hegel's inability to consider the problem of individual existence; this critique introduced "existentialism," an em-

21. Quoted by Gerhard von Rad, "Typological Interpretation of the Old Testament," in Claus Westerman, ed., *Essays on Old Testament Hermeneutics* (Richmond: Abingdon, 1963), p. 23.

22. See Frederick Ferré, *Language, Logic and God* (New York: Harper & Row), pp. 163ff.

phasis on the uniqueness of the existing individual. Like the influence of Bergson, it could not help but bring the modern mind closer to viewing reality in a way strikingly different from many contemporary viewpoints.

The preoccupation among Neoscholastics before the Second Vatican Council with reviving the thought of St. Thomas Aquinas forced Balthasar to consider the problem of spirit in the world. Joseph Maréchal had done influential work on this problem. Przywara followed him, as did Karl Rahner and J. B. Metz. Rather than follow a strict Maréchallian line, as did Karl Rahner, Balthasar moved more and more in a direction corresponding to that of Gustav Siewerth, who stressed Aquinas's insight into the dependence of forms on being. In arguing that being is more than form, Thomas made his decisive correction on Aristotle. Being is the inexhaustible common act in which everything participates. Balthasar later stated that Siewerth was the most significant philosophic influence on his own later development. The two men were long close friends and colleagues. Another current philosopher who has influenced Balthasar is Ferdinand Ulrich.[23]

Balthasar attempts to integrate insights from such diverse thinkers as Plotinus, Eckhardt, and Cusanus. His integralism

23. For works illustrating the influence of Siewerth and Ulrich, see Gustav Siewerth, *Die Metaphysik der Erkenntis nach Thomas von Aquin. I. Teil: Die sinnliche Erkenntnis* (Munich and Berlin: Grünewald 1933); *Der Thomismus als Identitätssystem* (Frankfurt: Knecht, 1939); "Die Apriorität der menschlichen Erkenntnis nach Thomas von Aquin," *Symposion* 1 (1948): 89–167; *Thomas von Aquin: Die menschliche Willensfreiheit* (Düsseldorf, 1954). (The latter work has been extremely important in shaping Balthasar's emphasis on the movement of the will in every intellectual act.) See also Gustav Siewerth, *Schicksal der Metaphysik von Thomas bis Heidegger* (Einsiedeln: Johannesverlag 1959, esp. pp. 375ff.); Ferdinand Ulrich, *Atheismus und Menschwerdung* (Einsiedeln: Johannesverlag, 1966). One consequence of this influence has been to free Balthasar from the weight of Scholastic conceptualism.

becomes a modern paradigm for a synthesis similar to those achieved by Origen and Gregory of Nazianzen. Yet Balthasar avoids oversimplification. He notes, for instance, that a philosophy of history that does not consider the "mystery" of intelligibility and instead offers solutions is ridiculous from the start, just as is any philosophy that lays claim to a definition of *being* and *existence*. He maintains, however, that the problem of existence presupposes that a solution is possible. The helplessness of temporal existence grounds for him the consoling postulate of eternity. Such a postulate can even be found in Nietzsche's philosophy of "eternal return." Thus one has to classify Hans Urs von Balthasar as a philosophical eclectic. More often than not, however, he reverts to Platonic categories in a surprisingly fresh use.

Balthasar argues that created being is characterized by an inner tension, a nonidentity often described as the "real distinction" between essence and existence. He explains this tension by saying that creation is not its own existence but only receives it, or, in other words, never totally realizes its essence but is always in the process of becoming itself. This is what distinguishes creator from creature, a contrast greater than any possible similarity: *in tanta similitudine major dissimilitudo* (in so great a likeness an even greater unlikeness).

> It is a distinction not merely to our way of thinking, but inherent in the very being of things—*distinctio realis*, or at least *cum fundamento in realitate* [sic], which, taken seriously, leads to the first—and sets its stamp on the whole *life* of the finite being, and lies at the root of its structure as indicated by Aristotle; the tension between act and potency in its living, moving dynamism of charged potentiality and self-realizing actuality, and always a tension which is striving toward an end *entelecheia*.[24]

24. See *Word and Redemption*, p. 26. The life of the spirit may be conceived in the following categories: on the theoretical level it moves between the poles: potentiality—actuality: ideal—reality. On the practical level, between the poles: value—being; obligation—performance.

If entelechy implies that "ideality" and obligation are not excluded from being,[25] then the tension springs from some defect in being, causing it to extend itself. This constitutes the process of "becoming." Hence the life of spirit, for Balthasar, is vigorous only when it is constantly coming to itself, realizing itself. For man, there are two basic characteristics involved in this striving for self-completion: reception of the Word and love. The particular development of these human characteristics in the thought of Balthasar may be attributed to the work of Ferdinand Ulrich.[26]

## Principal Philosophical Concepts

Before we can summarize Balthasar's philosophical position as an interpreter of the Fathers, some fundamental concepts must be explained further.

### Transcendence

The terms *transcendence* and the *transcendental* are frequent sources of confusion. The basic implication is one of "going beyond" that which we perceive to a knowledge act. For example, if I see a straight stick partly inserted into water, my senses perceive it as bent. No matter how hard I may try to see it as I know it, the stick appears bent. In this attempt, however, I am "going beyond," "transcending" the visual representation. Such an attempt characterizes all knowledge. Normally "transcendental" knowledge has meant that form of knowledge which ascertains the metaphysical necessity of a proposition by demonstrating that negating the proposition entails contradiction.

25. Interest in the relation between existence and value is a major concern of philosophers of language. See, for example, John Searle, "How to Derive 'Ought' from 'Is,'" *Philosophical Review* 73 (1964):43–58.

26. Ulrich, *Atheismus und Menschwerdung*, p. 9.

The capacity for expressing the transcendent is linked to a potential for self-transcendence in individuals. So the analogous use of inherently ambiguous terms to express transcendence is linked to this self-realization—what Lonergan called *interiority*. To the extent that we are conscious of using an expression beyond its normal reference, because we experience that the term renders our aspirations at points of attainment or failure, we can be said to be using it properly.

Balthasar uses the term *transcendence* in at least four different ways: (1) epistemological: in this use it connotes a surpassing of the realm of awareness and some independence from it; (2) metaphysical: a surpassing of all sense experience, moving toward an "absolute other"; (3) anthropological: man's experience of his inability to influence the possibility of his existence; and (4) theological: an absolute, outerworldly freedom.

## Analogy of Being

I discussed this important concept in connection with the influence of Erich Przywara on Balthasar. Balthasar himself gives this concept its most inclusive definition in his book on Karl Barth. In brief, he understands by *analogia entis* the fundamental openness of the Christian to the *res*, not the *verbum*.

The analogy of being as such (and the analogy of the concept of being, "logical analogy") are founded on that community and diversity present in every existent as existing. If the univocal aspect of being is overemphasized, we come to an identification of finite and infinite being. If the equivocal element is exaggerated, a radical separation occurs between infinite and finite. The human mind attains to being only in individual things—but in such a way that owing to mind's transcendence, comprehension of being provides the permanent foundation for understanding particulars.

Balthasar indicated that "any attempt to set *act* over against *being* is absurd, inasmuch as Aristotelian and Thomistic thought picture real being as *energeia* or *actus*." Balthasar continued to point out that the attempt to establish an opposition between the analogy of being and the analogy of faith lacked any meaningful foundation: "To be sure, the word *analogy* itself has a purely analogous sense in the two terms. . . . This sense is justified, however, by the fact of creation; for in creation God determines the object of human reflection. It is rather arbitrary to restrict *analogy of being* to the relation established by creation and to set it in opposition to the highest relationship of being (the analogy of faith or grace)."[27]

The expression "concept of being" involves self-contradiction. An openness to the mystery of being is the transcendental prerequisite for any conceptual structure. The Greek Fathers and Augustine took the position that "natural" reason, by the very fact of being unable to comprehend God and in disclaiming statements about His essence, at least can know that He is and is this "is," experienced as incomparable with all we experience as "being" in the context of the world. In this sense Christ is the actual "analogy of being." Balthasar understood Barth's objection: "Karl Barth might reply that only the divine voice itself can make known to us the height from which it descends; otherwise, man could know and measure the distance that separates him and God prior to revelation."[28]

## Openness

Balthasar understands *openness* as a reflexive, illuminated self-awareness. It is more than incipient; rather, it is a perfected interiority. It is spirit illuminating itself (in the Scholastic sense of *intellectus agens*, "agent intellect"). While being spontaneous and autonomous as spirit, mind does not receive

27. *The Theology of Karl Barth*, pp. 295–96.
28. *Word and Revelation*, p. 142.

the sensible. It must have union with a corporeal principle, the "phantasm," to which it reverts in its act of understanding. For Augustine, mind is spontaneously receptive, so that the mind becomes a kind of dialogical light. For Balthasar, the question does not entail the mind's autonomy (Augustine) or heteronomy (Aquinas) of the spiritual act. Kant's alternative misses the secret of the mind's being. For certain recent thinkers such as Karl Jaspers, Martin Heidegger, Benedetto Croce, Martin Buber, José Ortega, and Rudolf Kassner, what is important is the fundamental experience that the light of being is not "at hand" like the immanent light of the "agent intellect." Yet the immanent light of the mind, its spontaneity and being-in-act, constitutes itself, its very transcendence to the world, and thus its openness.

## Truth

What Balthasar claims to be Aquinas's doctrine of *truth* orders many of his ideas. The third part of the trilogy expands on both the "truth of the world" and the "truth of God." Balthasar takes the basic tenet of this doctrine from the *Quaestiones Disputatae de Veritate* 1.2: *res naturalis inter duos intellectus constituta (est)*—a natural thing is constituted between two intellects (divine and human). With the situation of "the real" between absolute, creative divine knowledge and imitative, "conforming" human knowledge, the constitution of all reality is presented as a structure of interconnected archetypes and replicas. In this context Aquinas uses the concept of *measure*—which in this nonquantitative sense is ancient and presumably Pythagorean—of that which measures and is itself not measured (*mensurans non mensuratum*). Human knowledge as such is measured and not measuring—not, that is, the measure of the natural, though it is the measure of the artificial. This point becomes very important for Balthasar in distinguishing artifact and art.

The double-relatedness of things to divine and human intellect means there is a double concept of "truth of things." The first states their being-thought-created by God; the second, their intelligibility to man. Balthasar holds that this concept of truth as developed in the Middle Ages was perfectly correct in its own sphere. The Scholastic definition of truth as *adaequatio intellectus ad rem*, however, envisaged the theoretical aspect of truth as "understandable." The necessary connection between the true and the good as transcendental properties of the one being was admittedly considered, but usually from the standpoint of a mutual presupposition of objects of intellect and will rather than their mutual inclusiveness as transcendentals. Ultimately philosophy could not reach the supreme mode of understanding truth.[29] In Balthasar's view, man has a threefold relationship with truth: there is a horizontal relation to the coordinated being he encounters (usually called the "object of knowledge"); a relation of descent to the cosmos founded on openness (man's condition of immanence, of being spirit in the world), the traditional "conversio ad phantasmata"; and a relation of assent to the absolute. All three are aspects of one unique truth in man.

## Freedom of the Subject

Balthasar claims that we can speak of a freedom of the subject only in a very relative way, that is, in a way which does not violate the subject's fundamental receptivity. Even when knowledge transcends in the metaphysical sense, goes beyond the sensible, it must still begin with sense data. No subject can

29. *Word and Redemption*, p. 55.

think simply what he or she pleases. The subject does have a freedom of orientation and a freedom to reject what is unpleasant. Also, although many elements enter uninvited into the area of sense experience, the subject has freedom to sift them and to accept only those corresponding to personal interests. But this exclusion of much of what is impressed upon man points to a defect in the ability to know. At the same time a power of ordering, of choosing only those elements from the manifold that is presented, signifies an aspect of the freedom of the spirit.[30] "All the possible perversions coming from human freedom in interpreting being and its determinations attempt to remove a dimension of depth which allows it to be and remain a mystery in its revelation."[31]

For Balthasar spirit is that point at which man is absolutely free, the point of true autonomy. But this is a limitation. Hence we are faced with a paradox: man is absolute regarding freedom of self-determination, and yet he is not free.

Truth exists in the object in such a way that it is intelligible, is constantly unveiling and revealing itself. Yet the object remains truer and richer than any of its self-revelations. Movement in the act of knowledge is nothing other than the internal elucidation of being in which object becomes subject. An impetus to self-disclosure lies behind every manifestation of the object. This means that behind all spiritual elucidations is an abiding will toward self-disclosure and revelation. This comes close to being the key notion in Balthasar's system.

An existent thing has meaning if and only if it is both a presence to itself and a participant in another. Taken together these

30. This accords with the importance given to negative knowledge, that is, to the need of "not knowing" in order to be human.

31. *Theologik,* 1:xvi.

constitute the elucidation of reality. So the ultimate meaning of being is love. Love cannot suffer divorce from truth, for love is that aspect of truth which beyond all disclosure contains an ever new and more profound secret. A doctor, for example, is supposed to see revealed in the symptoms of the patient what the patient may suffer and may try to explain. The patient, lacking the medical knowledge, cannot say what is wrong. The special vision of the doctor from which the patient expects healing leads into the domain of real knowledge. What a subject cannot crystallize himself, he hopes to obtain through the mediation of another. The subject requires another—one who perceives the potential of the subject. The subject requires a lover. Balthasar holds that this is the mystery of the freedom of the subject. A lover keeps an ideal image of the beloved as the beloved's true being.

An existent denied the right of self-disclosure, that is, the right to truth, ultimately will perish, for love will punish this existent by ignoring it. A lover treats the present as if it were the future, a future actuality which only a lover can see in the beloved. And in the power of the lover's conviction the beloved finds the necessary dynamism for change.

Balthasar explains that this is the way to gain insight into revelation. There is not just knowledge and truth which reveal and disclose but also knowledge and truth which conceal and veil. Hence it belongs to the truth of a free being that a part of himself be entrusted to oblivion. The person must have faith.

In the same way that the graceful movement of a dancer must be grounded in a relatively free decision and capacity, so the grace of all being must be grounded ultimately in an absolutely free decision. It is because of this decision that the world is as it is. Ultimate freedom is the source of necessity. Balthasar developed these arguments in the first volume of *Wahrheit*. The

*Theologik* must be understood before parts of the *Theodramatik* and the theological aesthetics can be fully comprehended.[32]

## The Uses of Truth

Object and subject do not possess truth simply as freedom. Insofar as they have a *nature*, they move toward truth. The object is moved to self-disclosure; the subject, to openness. Witness to truth occurs as the intersection of nature and freedom. A man may not choose whether he wants to represent his knowledge accurately. Insofar as he is a being whose nature is self-disclosure, he cannot be arbitrary. Revelation of self to others in truth is not following an alien ordinance. It is the very law of being itself. And since it involves disclosure to a subject, the author of the disclosure must assume responsibility for the content.

Because the use of truth involves freedom, questions arise about the limits on its use. What rules, Balthasar asks, apply to the person who discloses himself and reveals his truth? When should he do so and to whom? What norms guide the recipient of the revelation?

Prudence involves application of principles to particular cases. Prudence judges each act of revelation. Since love is the meaning of the disclosure of truth as well as of its reception, love must contain the norm for particular uses of truth. Many propositions possess formal and irrefutable truth; but they lack that in terms of which all individual propositions obtain their truth: the truth of the self-revelation of being: "The truth of an Augustine or Plato can be transmitted by those who do not live inwardly in this truth. It shines through them in the same way

32. For example, the chapter "Freedom as Self-Movement," *Theodramatik*, vol. 2, pt. 1, pp. 192–219, and in *Glory of the Lord*, vol. 2, pt. 1, the exposition of the "expression" doctrine of Bonaventure.

that the sacramental grace of Christ can reach the recipient regardless of the worthiness of the administering priest. But this does not happen without a certain curtailment of the truth."[33] It may be disagreeable to hear or tell a certain truth. If spoken and received with love, there is no better communication.

We discover rules for the uses of truth in the relation between partial truth and the spirit of total truth. Every abuse of truth can be compared to a contractor who builds imperfect materials into a whole building (and thus undermines the whole). A person who would shut out part of the truth on the grounds of a particular philosophical position whose limitations are not seen or admitted abuses truth. Balthasar considers followers of Marxism or skepticism to fall into this category. Their error lies in drawing a line beyond which no truth may enter, in hardening a finite perspective. The abuse is not in what the person knows (only a fragment of the whole—all men know only a fragment), but in total satisfaction with the fragment.

## The Question and the Fourfold Distinction

Hans Urs von Balthasar's starting point for speculation is the question "*Warum ist überhaupt Etwas und nicht lieber Nichts?*" (Why is there anything at all, and not simply nothing?) No science asks this question seriously because a science always presupposes its object. Philosophers also do not commonly ask this question—or if they do, its importance is not always seen, either because philosophy chooses to begin with a

33. It is a characteristic trait of Balthasar to support a philosophical position with a theological argument rather than the reverse, the normal custom. This can be disconcerting, but it follows from the connectedness Balthasar sees between philosophy and theology.

description of reality or else it rushes headlong into the question about being-as-such. Balthasar states: "The question *why* there is any being at all is for modern people still just as elementary and primary as for people of every earlier period, and no science (which, to be sure, always begins thinking from what is on hand) can take this question away from them."[34] We shall see in a later chapter that this fundamental question of Balthasar's is really the one posed by the German Romantics and that his position is very close to theirs.

The analytical philosopher Milton Munitz took up this question in its Leibnitzian formulation: "Why is there anything at all rather than just nothing?" Munitz defended this approach against the philosophical analysts who would dismiss it as meaningless.[35]

Thomas Aquinas's teaching on the "real distinction" involves a philosophical position, but it accepts a separation of the *doxa* of the creator from cosmic order and beauty. The "real distinction" recaptures the "many" for the theologian.[36] The "de-essentializing of reality" demanded by Heidegger, which had been accomplished by Aquinas, follows upon the illumination of biblical revelation. Metaphysics must include reflection on the glory of the living God. Such reflection characterized all ancient philosophy. So the question about being

34. *Spiritus Creator*, p. 71. Balthasar continues: "The guilt shared by Christianity with its gnostic inside knowledge about God and his mysteries . . . does not excuse the inexcusable. On the other hand, the alliance between theology and (ancient) philosophy is problematic, and indeed not just because Christianity took over the envisioning of the invisible by way of the visible, or briefly put, the insight into the analogia entis (analogy of being), but most of all because it did not perceive the limits of philosophy as disclosed in theology and hence took up a false position in regard to philosophy."

35. Milton Munitz, *The Mystery of Existence: An Essay in Philosophical Cosmology* (New York: New York University Press, 1965).

36. *Herrlichkeit*, vol. 3, pt. 1, p. 365.

is not just about the starting point, but, as Heidegger saw, constitutes an abiding principle of thought. Preservation of primitive wonder about being forms the foundation of all philosophy. Balthasar attempts to outline four steps, each of which reveals more about the "real distinction" in the process of ascent to a "vision" of the *doxa*.

1. A question may perplex man about why he is surrounded by creatures similar to himself. Generations of men have rejected the answer that it is "pure chance." The importance of the other for self-disclosure and revelation is apparent in the first experience of the child that he has been brought into an environment in which he is known and loved.

2. The next step involves recognition that other persons also are *spirits* in the world. All similar persons participate in being but never exhaust it. Man's primitive wonder leads him to posit the existence of another in which beings participate. The fact that existence involves participation in an act of being can lead to the further insight that the fullness of being can be found only in a being fully present to itself. The divine epiphany occurs in the world, and this world must be approached first in a philosophical question about its existence.

3. Precisely in view of the relation (clearly seen by Aquinas, Hegel, and Heidegger) of being to its explanation in the being of man as spirit, it becomes impossible to grant responsibility for the variety of essential forms of the world to worldly being. Hence all explanations that see the totality of world-essence as simple self-unfolding of being fail. They do so whether they explain this unfolding as the unique implication of all essences in a static unit (Plotinus, Erigena, Cusanus, Böhme) or whether the being achieves existence dynamically as the non-subsisting idea of all essences (Johann Gottlieb Fichte, Friedrich Hölderlin, Friedrich Wilhelm Schelling, Georg Friedrich Wilhelm Hegel, the early Wladimir Solowjew).

The manifold and marvelous forms of the simplest natural beings, the infratomic structures, for example, betray an unconditioned and original power of fantasy for which a creating power must be posited. Mechanistic explanations (Descartes or materialism) become self-defeating in the same way as the theories of Schelling and Hegel, who see the forms of nature simply as steps of absolute spirit seeking itself. Mechanistic systems, Balthasar argues, cannot account for the marvelous freedom found in even the tiniest natural forms, including the puzzles of subatomic structures.

Not even Heidegger goes far enough, although Balthasar follows Heidegger closely. He values Heidegger's restoration of a forgotten *theologoumenon* (God in revealing Himself conceals Himself). This is not merely a Heideggerian insight, but is pre-Socratic, Plotinian, and patristic.[37]

4. The previous steps follow one upon another. Man finds himself in the world. The objective necessity of contingent spirit does not integrate itself. Yet all beings exist somehow analogously because they are integrated as participants in being. The third step—that being as a whole does not unfold its essential self (because a responsible production of forms presupposes conscious free spirit)—leads man to seek to resolve the distinction by finding a reason both for existence and multiplicity. From this the problem of a being discovered as self-presence moves from contingency toward necessity. This is insufficient to ground the distinction or to overcome it by means of an Hegelian synthesis. So man's questioning turns to the multiplicity of beings and refers contingent being to an ultimate freedom. This is a freedom of nonsubsistent being which

37. Ibid., p. 783. Heidegger has replaced the relation Being equals being-thing with the relation Being equals man (shepherd of beings). This latter relationship becomes so loaded for Heidegger that the original question, why something rather than nothing, disappears.

can be preserved only in its *glory* if grounded in a subsistent freedom of absolute being. The essential form is safe from the threat of existence only if it is related to an absolute power of imagination. If the ontological distinction must relate itself to the individual (as Plotinus argued), this distinction becomes a place of *doxa* (the revelation of the glory of being) in metaphysics.

## Theological a Priori of Metaphysics

If biblical revelation rests on the basis of a distinction between God and world, metaphysics must rest on the same basis. Balthasar likes to speak not only of an analogy of divine and created being but also of an analogy of divine, free, personal being and created, free, personal beings. God *appears* (in the Bible) as the free chooser. Man is free only to ratify or reject the choice. The relation between creature and creator builds no second story on top of other, natural relations.

Taking this choice seriously pushes man in a direction in which individual myths can be explained within the linguistic framework of being. Hence the individual cannot be allowed to sink into anonymity. Rather, he must elevate himself to that station where he can hear the call. The Word of God must be a word of being. For God the nonsubsistence of the *actus essendi* (act of being) is adequate to explain the kenotic word of the Cross. Man can understand this word only by noting the ontological distinction. Being itself is not the light; it gives witness to the light. Wherever in the history of Western philosophy being has been situated as the horizon of the cosmos, either it becomes itself the sphere of illumination (Aristotle) or the first emanation of that light that is the good, absolute self-diffusion of itself (Plotinus).

Man as such is an insufficient explanation of reality. What

good would a light serve if no one saw it? For what other reason could God be than for love? Any other approach to the absolute which ignores the ontological distinction ends by detracting from the absolute. So the basic act of metaphysics is erotic. A specifically Christian act becomes a response to the Word of God, which includes this new metaphysical eros.

The pursuit of truth is inseparable from the erotic quest for goodness. Love and thought must combine in a common act of wonder. Eros enables man to see because the vision of the eyes is grounded in the love seated in the heart.[38] So the pursuit of truth is the same as the search for ethical and aesthetic completeness, the search for self-realization. Balthasar sees this erotic movement as mimetic desire. This is the tradition of poets from the Renaissance to Goethe, Hölderlin, and Rilke, who return to the world of forms of ancient Greece as mediating cosmic splendor. Literature becomes a primary theological datum. Examination of Balthasar's reading of this literary tradition is our next task.

In outlining the history of this act of mimetic desire from Homer to Heidegger, Balthasar indicates that within the ontological distinction this desire must be both metaphysical and asexual—erotic in the Socratic sense. Virgil and Augustine had a keen vision of this distinction. Augustine in particular intensified the force of the decision for or against the light as it had been clarified by Plotinus. Heidegger represents but a recent attempt to find metaphysical eros in openness for being.[39] The next chapters present Balthasar's analysis of this act of appropriation in the classical and patristic traditions.

38. *Glory of the Lord,* 1:462.
39. *Herrlichkeit,* vol. 3, pt. 1, p. 379.

## Chapter 3

# The Classical Tradition, I: Literature

HANS URS von Balthasar has developed a theological aesthetics grounded not in a modern philosophical aesthetics but in a return to the great classical tradition. In this and the following chapter I will trace Balthasar's exposition of this classical tradition.

Before Plato gave up writing tragedies and began to write philosophy, Greek art had reached a climax in all areas. All that came afterward in the Hellenic world, in Rome, and later in Europe was inspired by antiquity. Balthasar claims that all great art is religious—that is, it is an act of homage to the glory of being. Etienne Gilson has defined this religious aesthetic: "In a created universe whatever exists is religious because it imitates God in its operations as well as its being."[1] For Gilson the artist's representational work is mimetic, a copy of nature. The aesthetic is founded on the analogy of the creative act. Gilson claims that when the Christian God took over as creator from Plato's Demiurge, art came to serve religion and not exclusively its self-appointed end of beauty.[2] Implicit in this claim is

1. Etienne Gilson, *Painting and Reality* (New York: Pantheon Books, 1957), p. 294.
2. Ibid., pp. 178–93.

a classical theory of *mimesis*. The standard view that grew out of Plato's theory via Aristotle's *Poetics* excluded an essential aspect of behavior from types subject to imitation, which René Girard calls "desire and, more fundamentally still, appropriation."[3] If someone imitates another who appropriates some object, conflict results. Plato does not explain the element of conflict in mimesis. He probably regarded it as self-evident. This mimetic desire is man's basic act of selfless receptivity.

All great art manifests a uniqueness of style, so for Balthasar art history witnesses Goethe's claim that all great art is religious. That art involves the gods was a given in ancient Greece. The artist drew his inspiration from the gods, and his task was to make the divine "appear." By praising Achilles, Homer praises the god who gave the hero his beautiful form. Homer reveals the divine splendor and inspires his listener to imitation.

Balthasar asks, "Is the Platonic mimesis of God already the play of a distributed role? Not in thematic clarity, which will soon appear."[4] This is, however, a foreshadowing of the central problem of role playing, and a key element in theatrical role playing is the *agon* or conflict. Balthasar notes that the Socratic Bion of Borysthenes (300–250 B.C.) expressly treated the concept of role. Man is given a role by the gods just as the playwright gives a role to an actor.

There was a time when the theory of mimesis was invoked to justify the alleged superiority of "classical" literature. This is no longer acknowledged as a valid basis for aesthetics. The resulting discredit has reinforced the tendency to regard these works as antiquated. To many the concept of aesthetic mimesis has become virtually meaningless. Again René Girard has argued:

3. René Girard, *To double business bound* (Baltimore: Johns Hopkins University Press, 1978), p. vii.

4. *Theodramatik*, 1:124–25.

The enormous emphasis on mimesis throughout the entire history of Western literature cannot be a mere mistake; there must be some deep-seated reason for it that has never been explained. I personally believe that the great masterpieces of our literature, primarily the dramas and the novels, really are "more mimetic" in the sense that they portray human relations and desire as mimetic, and implicitly at least—sometimes even explicitly, as in Shakespeare's *Troilus and Cressida*—they reintroduce into their so-called fictions the conflictual dimensions always eliminated from the theoretical definitions of this "faculty."[5]

Although mimesis is implicit in his aesthetic theory, Balthasar does not emphasize the concept. He would agree, however, that the great works of Greek literature are more mimetic than other works. All these great works share moments of mimetic revelation, a theophany of the divine. The argument of this chapter will be that Balthasar's reading of classical Greek poetry, lyric and dramatic, again demonstrates the importance of his thought for contemporary theology. He argues as well as any man that the corpus of Western literature demands recognition, in contemporary terms, as a text—something that differs from the translucence of other forms of communication through an opacity that demands not only a *reading* but a *reading into*. The characters in Homer or Sophocles recognize the same signs; the mystery that lies beyond them, that which is transcendent, concerns us all. The modern reader, critic or theologian, tends to look for his answers elsewhere, transferring the mystery to the signs themselves, questioning them rather than their possible reference.

Insofar as man aims to know divine being, he must strive to become divine himself. Thus the Greek mode of thought, whether in myth or history, is a philosophy of aspiration, a mimetic desire to establish man's identity with the gods, his

5. Girard, *To double business bound*, p. ix.

harmony with the physical world, and his unity with being as a whole. The underlying principle is that man's goals may be attained through some form of mediation.

Literary creativity describes the rhetorical act of substituting the infinite for the finite, memory for the present, the sublime for the ordinary. Balthasar triumphs over a paradoxical adherence to both a mimetic and an expressive theory of poetry. Like Giacomo Leopardi he posits a "poetic imagination" of man in which mimesis is primarily a rhetoricization or transposition of nature into language. He might reject this precise formulation, but what is implied underlies his method.

Reappropriation becomes the source of the sublime, a return to the state of consciousness in which men had to invent the meaning of the world because it was full of gods. This notion of poetry as dealing with the indefinite is consonant with most theories of the sublime from Longinus to contemporary aesthetic theory.

A discussion of Balthasar's sublime permits us to circumvent a typical critical impasse: the cul-de-sac of dichotomous critical pairs. Romantic writers tend to use classificatory dyads such as subject-object, mind-nature, and the like. The reader is ineluctably drawn to a passage from one state or pole to the other. The danger lies in the tendency to hypostatize these poles as mutually exclusive or to transfer from the domain of language to that of spatial-temporal loci.

Such binary poles may be useful if we examine the linguistic protocols characterizing each pole. In fact, it would be possible to borrow any number of binary pairs to describe the specific nature of the rhetorical transference of the Romantic sublime. What is paramount is the dynamic relationship of "subject" and "object," which occurs only within language and so is a rhetorical relationship.

We are faced today with the paradox that serious readers

claim to favor nonmimetic poetry, a poetry of withdrawal. The conclusion would be that readers want to follow the poet into his basement. Everybody wants to be alone together. In our age, which has evolved a mass culture and a mass media of communication, intimacy is better served than in the past. However aware earlier men may have been of the "I-you" situation, twentieth-century personalism is a phenomenon of the technological age. In the age of television, the vocal is in some ways regaining prestige over the visual, and it may be that we are approaching the end of the Gutenberg era. Speaking and hearing are not simple operations. Each exhibits a structure that mirrors the depths of the human soul. As man formulates his thoughts in words, a speaker hears these words echoing within himself and so follows his own thought as if he were another listening person. Conversely, a hearer repeats within himself the words he hears and so understands them, as though he were himself two individuals. Thus the poetry of withdrawal becomes a paradox. In this listening and speaking what is represented in poetic terms and what demands belief on the part of the reader is not that good things happen to a brave man, but that the fate of Achilles is Achillean; the epithets "godlike" and "astute" carry meaning only for those who know what they contain of Achilles' character. Heraclitus expressed this as "ethos [character] is destiny."

Homeric imitation, which the ancient critics called "mimesis," is not an attempt to copy from apearance. It springs like myth from the conception of figures who are all of a piece—who are whole even before observation. The mimesis of a scene such as the meeting of Odysseus and Nausicaa is not based on a clear description of the event but on an a priori conception of the nature and essence of both figures and their fates. Consequently, were Odysseus to have become involved romantically with the girl, it would have been a tragedy for both. Tragedy developed from epic, but it focused more and more on the moment of decision. This exercise of choice, of human freedom, becomes a central feature of Balthasar's *Theodramatik*. A man and his destiny are laid bare in the moment they are one, the moment of choice, the moment of doom. Manfred Lochbrunner in his excellent interpretation of Balthasar's theology understates the case when he writes, "The weight of suffering and the concepts of representation, sin, and sacrifice in Greek tragedy are elements which theology should not blindly bypass."[6]

Fictional domains underwent a long process of structuring, ossification, and delimitation. It is commonplace to remark that the most primitive epic and dramatic artifacts do not have fictive settings, at least for their primary users. The characters of these domains were gods and heroes, beings endowed with as much reality as myth can provide. In the eyes of its users, a myth is the very paradigm of truth. Zeus, Heracles, Aphrodite, Helen, and Oedipus were not fictional in any sense of the term. Not that anyone felt that they belonged to the same level of reality as the common mortals. To describe the ontology of societies that use myths, one needs at least two different ontological levels: the profane reality, characterized by ontological paucity and precariousness, and a mythical level, ontologically self-sufficient, unfolding in a privileged space and a cyclical time. Gods and heroes peopled the sacred space and lived in a cyclical time. This space was not seen as fictional; if anything, it was ontologically superior, endowed with a different kind of truth.

The ancient Greek viewed the cosmos as an epiphany of the divine and as an opening of man to this manifestation. For

6. Manfred Lochbrunner, *Analogia Caritatis* (Freiburg in Breisgau: Herder, 1981), p. 236.

man, the moral order emanated from the epiphany. From this same epiphany sufficient light radiated to enable man to support the difficulties and darkness of his limited existence. World order rested on a view of justice (*dike, themis*), which was of divine origin. Balthasar claims that in art and poetry the world reveals itself as *charis*, in which the *kalon* (the beautiful) in its metaphysical profundity becomes one with the good and the true. Plato's philosophical critique of the beautiful gave birth to an aesthetic teaching on the transcendentals which forever after marked Western metaphysical tradition. Theological criticism of this tradition resulted in a theological aesthetics—Balthasar's concern.

## Myth

Myth explains the mystery of the ultimate by placing that mystery in heroic or divine figures. A tragedy, for example, reenacts a myth and heightens the explanation by reinvoking the mystery it is constructed to explain. Failing to derive understanding from the mediation of a god, man does not give up on mediation: a wholly silent deity is no more conceivable than a wholly silent mystery. The same mystery may appear in many myths, and the same myth may appear in such diverse forms as a book of Homer, a digression in Pindar, a whole tragedy, or a scholion on Aristophanes. All these require a man to "speak" the *mythos* (word) in order to understand it.

The two-level ontological structure is a general feature of human culture, which accounts for both myths and fictions, and that circulation between the two levels has been and still is the rule governing relations between them. The two levels differ generally in weight and importance; one of them is felt as constituting the domain of immediate actuality; the other, which accounts for mythical or fictional projection, is accessible only through cultural mediation—legends, traditions, myths, epics, and the like. There is operative a conventional framing—an ensemble of devices both stylistic and semantic, which project individuals and events into a certain perspective, set them at a distance, and elevate them so that they may be easily comprehended.

Eventually epic stories lose their status as valid descriptions of a privileged territory; not that the territory disappears altogether, for it is too complex a structure, with too much exemplary value attached to it, for the culture to discard. The myths, or at least some of them, undergo a process of fictionalization.

## Homer

Balthasar noted, "Everything begins with the world drama on the bastions of Troy, where the heroes, representatives of mankind, fight for victory beneath the critical gaze of Zeus and the entire world of the gods."[7]

No work of world literature so constantly presents the thought of God in all situations as does Homer. The thought of divine power, presence, and universal action is everywhere. It is this sense of divine power and presence that Balthasar develops. For Homer the heart of the beautiful is less in harmony and proportion than in the immediate experience of human salvation, a salvation which without losing its proper form places the accent on charm (*kallei kai chariti stilbon*) (*Od.* 6.237) or on heroic magnanimity, the force of love or hidden virtue (for example, Eumaeus). Beauty radiates from the center and inflames everything. Men who live in such light and radiance are called "divine"—yet they are not elevated to the rank of gods. Man makes no attempt to measure himself against the

7. *La Gloire,* 4:65; *La Gloire* citations refer to *Herrlichkeit,* vol. 3, pt. 1, the French translation.

gods. When Telemachus perceives his father, Odysseus, beneath the transfigured form Athena gave Odysseus and takes him for a god, wise Odysseus says: "I am not a god; why do you compare me with the immortals? I am your father for whom you have groaned and suffered so many evils" (*Od.* 16.187–89). It is the business of the gods to elevate ephemeral man or to cast him down into slavery because, in Homer, man is one and his interior and exterior being are inseparable. Psychic gifts of inspiration and enthusiasm have a corresponding bodily manifestation. Hector under the powerful hand of Zeus blazes like a fire (*Il.* 15.523); Athena crowns the head of Achilles with clouds of gold and flames when he appears to the Trojans (*Il.* 18.205): "It is easy for the gods who possess the vastness of heaven to give to a mortal the splendor of beauty, the shame of ugliness" (*Od.* 16.211–12). When Athena disguised Odysseus, she revealed his true being as well as the form of his greatness. When Odysseus first appeared before Nausicaa naked and devoid of everything, the goddess clothed him in beauty, made him taller, and gave him gifts (*Od.* 6.229–35).

The relationship between Odysseus and Athena is marked by delicacy and respect but also shows a tender intimacy unequaled in ancient poetry. The relation portrays the hero and his protecting deity to whom he prays and in whom he places his trust. These divine-human relationships, and especially the care of Zeus, who more than the other gods carries the weight of his concern, constitute for Balthasar the key to the *Iliad*.

The concept of the epic hero is the core of one of the most powerful clusters of ideas that Greek culture has bequeathed to Western literature and art. It is also a target of major movements in contemporary theology and criticism, which seek to replace the person with the discourse of the person and to deconstruct the individual into mental categories, strategies of representation, and linguistic forms.

Homeric heroes act freely and responsibly as persons. No doubt *Ate* can cloud their actions; it casts a mysterious light of inevitability on every action. Agamemnon, for example (*Il.* 19.90ff.), blames *Ate* for the family problems. Priam reassures Helen that she is not responsible for the horrible war; the gods are (*Il.* 3.164–65). This may be a recognition of the force of Helen's beauty or an indication of the complicated consequences of Helen's actions.

In the description of Achilles' shield, forged in one night by Hephaistos, the adjective "beautiful" occurs repeatedly. Nor is it always clear whether the poet intends the adjective to apply only to the shield or to the represented scene. Form and content here become united because in a vision of the world that is both human and divine they are not separated. Balthasar calls this episode Homer's monogram, the representation of the force of his art. It involves a vision of the world elevated to the divine, but an undivided vision which the poet possesses as man and as inspired by the Muses. Balthasar observes that according to Aristotle, it was Homer, the father of tragedy, who opened "this zone of light for the West once and for all":

There above, composed and in need of nothing, the blessed gods, who nevertheless share decisively in the fate of humanity, who, as patron gods guide the heroes and their destinies, as counterforces impede and threaten them, until the threads of this heavenly play and counter play in a hidden plan of the "father of gods and men" inscrutably converge in the tapestry. There below the humans, demonstrated and represented in their natures by their heroes and kings: how they stand out in the zone of the gods' fate and still are not manipulated in it like puppets, but act freely and magnificently, in the full weight of their mortal uniqueness, but pray, sacrifice, trust in the divine guidance, fear the black "ate", rejoice in the light of success and fame; a play in which the eye of Zeus takes pleasure and which can be replaced by no feast of the gods.[8]

Homer's theophanies remained important for all posterity. They became exemplary not only for the event and the subject of the apparition but also and more importantly for the manner of the apparition—the rapport between man and god that bathes all in a scintillating light which the word *eros* cannot render any more than *philia*.[9] The Homeric gods convey the essence of the vision of glory and permanent value.

In Homer a divine spontaneity constantly impregnates the epiphany. The god wishes to appear, wishes to be recognized by one person and not by another. When Athena appeared to Odysseus in the house of Eumaeus, the dogs saw her and were frightened, but Telemachus, who was also there, did not see her and noticed nothing (*Od.* 6.155). "Who could with his eyes see a god going or coming, if the god did not wish it?" (*Od.* 10.573–74)

Balthasar argues that the Homeric poet knew this incarnation, this irruption of divine fire into human form which elevated man's natural beauty into divine glory. The poet knew this glory; gifted by the Muse, he described it and handed it on unchanged to the artistic tradition, even to ages that no longer believed in divine epiphanies. Balthasar finds an especially valid measure of this manifestation of glory in descriptions of the confrontation with death. Andromache, Hecuba, Priam, and Hector become great only at the moment of entering into the irrevocable shadow. What is important in the death march that Achilles makes from Book 19 to Book 22 is that he knows he is sacrificing himself, Odinlike, to the idea of himself. In

8. *Spiritus Creator*, p. 358.
9. Cf. *Od.* 7.201–5.

the indescribably beautiful meeting with Priam, Achilles explains: "Such is the way the gods spin life for unfortunate mortals, that we live in unhappiness, but the gods themselves have no sorrows" (*Il.* 24.524–26). We see two tendencies in Achilles' explanation to Priam. He does not dwell on the particular but rather sees in it the manifestation of a general truth. He cannot think of the human condition without at the same time imagining its opposite. He speaks assertively and mythologically. These tendencies—seeing the general in the particular, grasping one thing by contrast with its opposite, tracing human fortunes to the will of the gods, explaining the present by myth and proverb—endured as dominant forms of thought and style in archaic poetry.

Evoking Niobe and her inhuman suffering, she whose children Apollo had killed, Achilles invites the old king to a feast. The Homeric prince viewed himself as a possible god. This meant there was in archaic psychology a theory of the self as transcendent, as somehow divinized. A heroic aspiration to godhead was common in the ancient warrior, of which Achilles was the paradigm. He fulfilled the rigid demand: "How can I, mortal though I be, somehow vindicate my intuitions of likeness to divinity?" Yet mortal man remained aware of the distance. Death was the catalyst of the irreconcilables. In Book 12 of the *Iliad,* Sarpedon says to his kinsman Glaucus: "Good fellow, if we by fleeing this struggle and surviving, might always be ageless and immortal, neither would I urge you on to the glorifying war; since this is the case, after all, the fate of death awaits thousand-fold, whom no man's power can escape or avoid. Let us go, then, either to offer glory to someone or ourselves gain glory" (*Il.* 12.322–28).

The Homeric formulas that embody the epic are the fundamental elements to which Homer continually returns. The formulas and rhythms are the content as much as a composer's musical themes are his content. If the style is paratactic, the combination and repetition of formulas surpasses parataxis to create a world extremely rich in resonance and diversity.

## Hesiod

Homer situated the glory of existence in the exemplary confrontation of hero and his god. The question was then asked whether this model had any universal validity. Could the awareness of an encounter become an awareness of a state? Could everyman participate in the heroic condition? Could one actually conceive of a divine being under the form of a revealing god? These questions, Balthasar argues, became the concern of poets and thinkers from the time of Hesiod to that of Pindar.

The "Delian Hymn to Apollo" shows that the tendencies operating within the poetic diction of Homer continued within the Ionian tradition. Hesiod composed in the Ionian idioms, though at a more advanced stage.

The Muses gave Hesiod a poetic mission in the same way Amos received the mission of prophet. The authenticity of Hesiod's encounter with the "queens of Helicon" is witnessed by the abrupt manner with which they approach the poet:

> The Muses once taught Hesiod to sing
> Sweet songs, while he was shepherding his lambs
> On holy Helicon; . . .
> We know enough to make up lies which are convincing,
> But also have the skill, when we will,
> To speak the truth. (*Th.* 23ff.)

The beautiful song which Hesiod "learns" (*Th.* 22) is the song of the Muses, the marvelous concert of Olympus with which they praise "the gods according to their rank" (*Th.* 11–21) as well as "their origin." Hesiod sings of the birth of the gods and the cosmos as well as the works of man. Prometheus occupies the center of both poems, an image of the fragile position of man in the kingdom of Zeus. The concepts of *metron*, measure, and *sophrosyne*, prudence, self-control—important both for Greek life and art—acquire in Hesiod a profound theological significance (*EH*, 36–41):

> Come, let us settle our dispute at once,
> And let our judge be Zeus, whose laws are just.
> . . . . . . . . . . . . . .
> For we had already divided our inheritance, but
> You seized the greater share and carried it off,
> Greatly swelling the glory of our bribe-swallowing lords
> . . . . . . . . . . . . . . . .
> Fools, they know not how much more the half is than
> the whole. . . .

It is in this humble station—never presented as tragic—that the labors and the days unfold: the peasant year is given maxims: "Preserve a sense of right proportion; fitness is all important in all things" (*EH* 694). The terms for season are ambiguous, signifying at one time what is opportune, amiable, and beautiful. In the same way the "Hours" are goddesses who at one and the same time are responsible for cosmic order and erotic attraction. The terms "metron," "eukosmos," and "eukrines" have both an ethical and an aesthetic sense. For Hesiod such terms reveal the radical permanence of all beauty in the rectitude of life, especially in work. Balthasar says that one could easily discover a correspondence between the Decalogue and Hesiod's "rules for living,"[10] which include the commandment to pray morning and evening. Justice, daughter of Zeus, is shown to be linked narrowly to "the eye of Zeus which perceives and knows all" (*EH* 267–81). The Father is always Judge and in the style of the Old Testament rewards and punishes unto the fourth generation. This close liaison between Zeus and Dike prevents justice from being degraded into an ab-

10. *La Gloire*, 4:65.

stract, worldly principle. The mission the Muses gave Hesiod was to celebrate the ethics of a world in which gods and men ought to conquer, to struggle, and by courageous action learn to master obscurity.

## Lyric Poetry

Lyric involves a speaker in a particularized setting who carries on a colloquy with himself, or the outer scene, or an absent or silent listener. The speaker gives a setting that evokes a varied but integral process of memory, thought, anticipation, and feeling. This lyric resolves itself in the exchange of linguistic attitudes. Perhaps the uniqueness of the greater Romantic lyric lies in its experience of the rhetorical transference that constitutes transcendence, for this exposure suggests that transcendence belongs to language alone and thus puts into question the ontology of both subject and object. It is this desire to disrobe rhetorically that renders useless to some critics the notions of both mimetic and expressive theories of poetry. The sublime moment is located in the interstices between expression and mimesis. Again, such a view partially characterizes Balthasar's interpretation.

Balthasar calls Archilochus the angry man of antiquity and says it is strange that this early lyric poet encountered the Muses in a manner similar to Hesiod's meeting with the goddesses.[11] Archilochus sings of the gods:

> But the gods, my friend, to our woes
> Without cure have applied firm endurance
> As a remedy. Now one, now another
> Has this woe. . . . (13W, 45)[12]

11. Ibid.

12. *W* citations refer to Martin West, *Iambi et Elegi Graeci* (Oxford: Clarendon, 1971); *D* citations refer to *Anthologia Lyrica Graeca* (Berlin and Leipzig: Teubner, 1935). For contemporary analysis see A. W. H. Adkins, *Poetic Craft in the Early Greek Elegists* (Chicago: University of Chicago Press, 1985), pp. 36ff.

We possess thirty-six complete elegiac lines of Archilochus, a very small sample. It is large enough, however, to enable the reader to form some judgment of Archilochus as an elegiac poet and to regret that not more has been preserved.

Balthasar compares Archilochus to Villon in his straightforward attitude toward sexuality. Prayer is replaced in Archilochus's poetry by the cynical affirmation that Zeus is the most enlightened of the gods because nothing happens that he has not willed (80W, 84D).

Sappho, Balthasar says, lives only for love. Her epithalamia make mythical weddings actual and alive. But for the poetess herself, this festival means only renunciation and sadness. She renounces a girl whom she loves, but she preserves a mortal nostalgia. She desires "to die and see the lotus covered banks of Acheron" (95W, 97D). The erotic lyricism of Sappho reminds Balthasar of the Song of Songs: he cites "like the hyacinth which shepherds trample underfoot on the mountain, and it still blooms purple on the ground" (113W, 117D). Sappho noted "the man who is not beautiful is only ugly as long as one looks at him; the wise and good man is always beautiful" (48W, 49D). Nothing so enraptures as the beauty of another person.

Sappho initiates for Balthasar the "history of *eros* in the west." Its theoretical reflection becomes serious in Plato, even though it exists as *philia* in Homer and as cosmogonic eros in Hesiod.[13]

For Tyrtaeus, the poet of the Second Messenian War, whose songs accompanied the Spartans in their campaigns, courage and beauty are one and the same thing. Tyrtaeus reduces the individual to a cog in the Spartan state: "I would not say anything for a man nor take account of him for any speed of his feet or wrestling skill he might have. . . . Not if he had all splendors—except for a fighting spirit" (12W, 9D).

13. *Herrlichkeit*, vol. 3, pt. 1, pp. 43–72.

Solon saw the individual as a moral unit, bound inevitably to universal, divine justice. In a beautiful poem Solon describes how he freed the divine earth of Attica from the boundary stones that represented the foreclosures of the rich upon the poor. "But I cast my protection over both parties, and stood at bay, like a wolf among dogs" (Frag. 36W.26ff.). This concern for justice and order anticipates many issues of the tragedians, especially Sophocles, whose heroes assert their vision of the ground of a viable society.

Solon, for whom the beautiful is the expression of order and justice, wishes to proclaim this in the most sublime manner possible. I have noted that Balthasar argues that throughout antiquity ethics and aesthetics are one, as in Solon—only the various accents differ:

> But Zeus views the end of every affair and suddenly, just as spring clouds quickly scatter before the wind stirring the depths of the billowing uncharted sea, lays waste the fair fields over the wheat-bearing land, and reaching even to the highest heaven, the seat of the gods, makes the sky clear again to view, until the strong sun shines bright over the fat land and no cloud is seen again—even such is the vengeance of Zeus. He is not quick to anger, as we are, over each little thing. (13W, 1D.17–28)

Balthasar says these lines surpass the angry portraits of the prophets.[14]

## Pindar

The erotic ascent to the divine began for Pindar as it did for Sappho in the contemplation of the beautiful body—in Pindar's case, the glory of the conquering athlete. For Pindar the sole purpose of art is glory. Pindar's poetry combined the sound of the past with the vital concerns of the present in such a way that the present reembodied the past and was ennobled by it.

14. *La Gloire*, vol. 3, pt. 1, p. 69.

Balthasar observes that of the seventeen books of Pindar, we have only the four books of the victory odes. Yet these fragments allow us to state that they are a genuine reflection of the total corpus. We find in Pindar again the Homeric world of gods and men. Divine and human worlds are totally opposed, but the victorious man at the supreme moment of his transcendence is plunged into a divine light and only at that moment recognized as man. The presentation of great qualities is far more difficult to achieve when the subject matter has contemporary associations than when it is remote from us. One of the functions of myth was in the remoteness of its figures: "One is the race of men, another the race of gods, and from one mother do we both derive our breath, yet a power that is wholly separate keeps us apart, in that the one is nothing, while the other the brazen heaven endures as an unshaken dwelling forever. Although we mortals share some likeness either in mind or in nature to the immortals" (*Nem.* 6.1–7).

In the hymns of victory, everything, even the gift of a divine origin, converges on the supreme moment of final victory. In the victor, who remains a man, shines something of a divine incarnation. Platonic eros will eventually follow a path of spiritualization, abandoning the way of Pindar, that of glorification of the individual in the fullness of his *arete*, excellence. Hence Pindar's attraction for Balthasar is great because of his concern with the here and now.

In the unity of spiritual and corporeal excellence, total well-being radiates. The "fire" of glorification in which Pindar exalts is the convergence of the objective and subjective presence of the divine. To celebrate a victory is to be together (*koinon*) and to be friends (*philiai*). If the supreme expression of *charis* is the gift of the poet, this is made possible only by the *charis* of the victory itself—received from the hands of the gods and the Graces (*Ol.* 8.57–59; 14.6–8; *Isth.* 1.40–43):

It is right that, when the prize is won,
We should, with ungrudging thought, give
Him glorifying praise. For the wise poet
finds it easy . . . to say his beautiful word.

## Tragedy

Balthasar sees Greek tragedy as one of the most powerful representations of divine splendor. He claims that with the great tragedians Greek art attained its climax and then fell apart. He claims that great tragedy with its understanding of authentic glory finds ultimate achievement in the drama of Christ, and this is so total that afterwards no one can repeat the miracle.

In *Theodramatik* Balthasar argues that Greek tragedy was built on the foundation of ritual and the myth that explained the ritual.[15] It bends the myth back to its ritual origins. Tragedy displays human suffering to a deity, a *noumenon* that remains in the twilight between participation and avoidance. Consequently, it is with tragedy more than with Greek philosophy that Christians can converse. "It is tragedy that furnishes the golden key of the Christ event."[16] Tragedy is a mystery, played by believers for believing spectators. Its goal is to re-present glory that is both divine and humanly divine. The glory presented by tragedy is that of "mythic" man, the man whose deity has patterned an exemplary destiny, a man elevated and humbled, exalted to the supreme degree of pain. Since Christ fulfilled this destiny to the most perfect degree, no subsequent tragedy can be conceived or played. All later tragedy must reflect that of Christ. Balthasar mentions as examples Calderon, who shows Christ as the true Odysseus, Orpheus, Perseus,

15. *Theodramatik*, vol. 2, pt. 1, p. 42.
16. *La Gloire*, vol. 3, pt. 1, p. 81.

Eros, Apollo, Pan, and Shakespeare. Lear is the eternal father deprived of his power; the Duke in *Measure for Measure* is the central God advancing incognito and participating in suffering in order to reveal himself in the final act as judge of this world; Richard II is the man who suffers unimaginable humiliation.[17] Similar features are found in the tragedies of Corneille, Racine, and Schiller. Greek tragedy was born in liturgical celebration—the spring festivals of Dionysus.

Balthasar notes that the full weight of human existence is the foundation of Greek tragedy. "It is even the foundation of the philosophy that followed, which in the age of Greece is introduced by the tragic death of Socrates . . . later through the tragic death of Hermias, who died for the beloved beauty of philosophy." He goes on to mention Seneca and Boethius and ends with Kierkegaard, "the witness of truth in our times, who put the question, 'May one allow oneself to be struck dead for the truth?'"[18]

The tragic hero confronts the ultimate question of life in the largest terms, experiences the deepest sense of self in isolation and suffering, and refuses to constrict the greatness of his nature and ideals to suit conventions and any so-called norms. Suffering and death are chosen over submission or conformity.

In Greek tragedy action is secondary. Dramatic progress consists simply of unveiling a truth already present from the beginning. Man is made to appear before the gods in abject nakedness. Balthasar points out that the action in tragedy, as in Homer and Pindar, occurs in the immediate present and not in an Orphic or Platonic past or future. This immanence is seen for the final time in tragedy. Often it is explicit in the

17. This example should give pause to those who charge Balthasar with neglecting works of English literature.

18. *Spiritus Creator*, p. 349.

epiphany of a god in the prologue or epilogue. When Orestes kills his mother on Apollo's orders and is then pursued by the Furies, the solution is provided by Athena. Divine glory witnesses itself in the savagery of human sorrow and sacrifice.

The logos of a play is parallel with its mythos. The total sweep of the *Oresteia* or of the *Oedipus Rex* resists submission to Freudian or Aristotelian categories. By inventing what it represents on stage, tragedy transforms all the significations it includes in a way a liturgy does not. Not even the liturgical celebration of the mass can comment on what it re-presents. *Tragedy comments as it presents.*

The mythos comments on the mystery of ultimate forces by preserving the mystery it figures. The play reenacts the myth, on the ground of service to the figure of Dionysus, and it heightens explanation by reinvoking the mystery it is constructed to explain.

Balthasar stresses the importance of the mysterious image of the suppliant. In the *Iliad* we see in the first book Thetis as suppliant before Zeus and in the last book, Priam as suppliant before Achilles. Odysseus approaches Nausicaa, Arete, and Alkinoos, even Circe, as a suppliant. Orestes comes as suppliant to Athena. The aged Oedipus becomes a suppliant at Colonus. Balthasar reviews the surviving plays and finds this image in all of them. He cites as a typical supplication the words of Adrastus (*Suppliants*, 164–68):

> And shall not Zeus then be liable to the charge of
> injustice for condemning the child of the heifer,
> the child whom he once fathered. . . . No—
> may he from on high hear our supplication."

Tragedy involves a fall from an illusory world of security and happiness into a depth of inescapable anguish. A second condition is that the fall must concern us. Only when we are deeply stirred do we experience tragedy.[19] The protagonist must be fully aware of his situation and so suffer knowingly. To climb the heights of the divine and heroic, tragedy needs the masks; it could not present its own subjectivity.[20] The use of masks dates from an early liturgical practice. Later, with the great tragedians, real characters appear and the masks become devices that establish aesthetic distance, limited more definitely to the universe of space, for space separates; voice unites. As they evolve, the number and complexity of roles and of literary forms proliferate. The means of controlling and differentiating characters and forms have been developed as the tension between the vocal and the visual increases. For this tension the mask is the symbol, like later costume and makeup, a mitigated form of mask.

As this tension between visual and vocal balloons and with it the use of the truly dramatic character and the formalized separation of drama from life, there grows also, paradoxically, an awareness of the foundation in real human existence for dramatic character. The theater involves the projection of human existence onto a stage that interprets existence beyond itself for itself. Because existence knows itself as explained in this projection, it can recognize itself—in a limited experience—as a role in a larger play.[21] Greek tragedy portrays man delivered at once to the power—unknowingly or hostile—of other men or to the unlimited power of the gods. The suppliant can only invoke his powerlessness.

## Aeschylos

Aeschylos, who had fought at Marathon and probably at Salamis, identified himself with the new Athenian democracy

19. See Albin Lesky, *Greek Tragedy* (New York: Barnes and Noble, 1979), p. 10.
20. *Theodramatik*, 1:53.
21. Ibid., p. 20.

and envisaged it as a divinely established order. His participation in the Persian War confirmed his realization that human events are interwoven with the divine. He began with the *polis* in which gods and men live and work. As Balthasar writes, "In the drama of antiquity the *polis* was the essential point, in particular in its relationship to the religious; it is no different in most of the plays of Shakespeare and Schiller."[22] Here he searched for the meaning and justification of the divine in the world; he reached his insight into the unity of Zeus, *dike*, and fate.

It is by power that spirit conquers power, but as long as spirit is opposed to nature, it acts in a legalist, tyrannical manner. "I know that Zeus is hard, and that he holds the Law at his discretion" (*Prom.* 186–87). The conflict of power and spirit engenders a discord among the gods. Prometheus the Titan, who fought for Zeus, is punished by Zeus. Prometheus's confession that he is the enemy of the gods is a profession of faith in philosophy. The implications of "Titanism" for Balthasar are discussed in a later chapter.

In the trilogy the *Suppliants*, Aeschylos considers the resolution of the contradiction between virginity and fecundity, between the principle of Artemis and that of Aphrodite. The divine, whatever name one gives it, is shown to be at work in all the shades and contradictions.

The power of the somber, maternal earth is also the power of the dead. Balthasar says this is why in the "funerary sacrifice" of the *Oresteia*, Electra and Orestes, to gain the favor of their father's ghost following the matricide, strike the earth: "I pray to the earth and my father's grave" (*Choeph.* 540, 147–48, 489). The tragic event is brought about by gods and men. Man's inordinate desires conflict with an essentially divine order, which reveals to man his own limitation and gives

22. Ibid., p. 34.

meaning to his fall because his ruin testifies to the existence of order.

Power will struggle against power and right against right (*Choeph*. 461). The ultimate reconciliation of the ancient, feminine, hostile world of the Titans with the new Olympian order, which at the same time is a heavenly, cosmic, and political reconciliation, is also the work of Athena in creating the Areopagus. This is the supreme conclusion of Aeschylos. Balthasar agrees with certain other scholars, for example, Karl Reinhardt, that the transformation of the Erynes into Eumenides is entirely the work of Aeschylos. This change of avenging goddesses, this entry of the world of night into the glorious light of the Greek day, or moral, political, and aesthetic order, is without equal in world literature. The supreme effort of the myth consists in unifying the extreme tensions of the world. This unification is realized by a personal, divine act. Orestes receives a grace which founds in the same moment divine and human right. The order of the world is not a matter of philosophical synthesis. Everything tends to the glorious epiphany of the divine intervention, the unforeseeable revelation. By means of this divine action, all earthly beauty is an epiphany of glory, the same as that of Apollo on the western façade of the temple of Zeus at Olympia, where he appears in the midst of the wedding troubled by centaurs and restores order.

For Aeschylos the name of the creating god of unity is not a matter of importance: "Zeus, whatever be his name" (*Agam*. 159–61); what matters is his *khabod*, his *schechina*, which can designate not only abstract concepts—right, justice, order, retribution—but also, as in Pindar, the fluid light of divinity.

## Sophocles

Balthasar says that in Sophocles a reconciliation between man and God is possible because the deity shows himself accessible to contradiction and suffering. Destiny properly so-called is opposed to conscious error, such as the fault of Creon, but also to suffering voluntarily chosen. Sophocles shows us Athena in the prologue to the *Ajax* pointing out to her favorite, Odysseus, his enemy plunged in folly (*Ajax* 79). We are given a tragic situation pushed to its extreme: before a god a man is plundered by a god and made ridiculous. Ajax's humiliation by Athena is a particularly cruel, almost grotesque lesson of the gods.

Balthasar noted: "In the tragedies of Sophocles the accent is placed on the concealment and inevitability of divine right under which man ('Electra,' 'Deianeira') stands as the essential sufferer. Yet man is often displayed in subjective state of guilt (*hybris*) which is atoned through guilt decrees of the gods (in the *Ajax* the hero pays for his crime by death.)"[23] Oedipus, who swore he would find the murderer, finds himself. Oedipus discovers that he is himself the unwitting source of the trouble. Thebes is saved, and Oedipus, though blind and ruined, is on his way to an as yet undreamed salvation. The individual pariah becomes a deity. Heroic adherence to an absolute actually divinizes. His mysterious "death" is a translation. The *Oedipus at Colonus* is one of the greatest expressions of the heroic individual, with his intuition of the divine, reshaping and revivifying the world. The heroic paradox has become an unfathomable religious mystery. The mythic background is significant. In Laius the social and divine injunctions are intermixed and influence him to commit at least two sins: once in resisting the divine prohibition not to have children, once in thinking that he might be able to resist divine prohibition. In every encounter with such divine prohibitions, the role of the gods cannot be ignored. Jocasta voices a fundamental awareness. She says, "How many times have men in dreams, too, slept with their own mothers" (*OT*, 981–82). She speaks

23. Ibid., p. 425.

as if this truth were widespread and common, as though the desire for incest were common, when the injunctions of God and man prohibit it as a polluting calamity. If this mimetic desire is so common, why do the gods and men conspire to keep it quiet? If uncommon, why the conspiracy of silence? The myth shatters that silence. The consequences parallel those the action of the play rehearses and conspire to highlight the role of prophecy and the gods and thus make the play into a powerful affirmation of the truth of religion. Balthasar notes that for Sophocles the "fault" surges to the limit between time and eternity. This is not to say, as for example in Schiller, between necessity and inclination or between the noumenal self and the phenomenal self, the ideal self and the real self. Rather, it is a radical divergence between God and man. "The enigma of the demarcation between God and man" Balthasar calls the theme of tragedy. The chorus addresses Antigone: "Untouched by wasting disease, not paying the price of the sword, of your own action you go. Alone among mortals will you descend in life to the abode of death. . . . Yet even in death will you have fame, to have gone like a god to your fate, in living and dying alike" (821–22, 836–38).

What is the fascination of these plays that have inspired and produced imitations among the Alexandrians, Romans, and modern playwrights? Balthasar says it is not their horror. "Antigone is not horrible; what matters here is less a question of the rules of classical composition, the purely formal exigency of the language. . . . This power will only be explained in the case in which the poet mysteriously elaborates the domain of man so that he is elevated into the realm of the transcendent."[24]

> Numberless are the marvels of nature,
> But of all, the greatest marvel is man . . .

24. *La Gloire*, vol. 3, pt. 1, p. 101.

> this thing crosses the sea in winter's storm,
> making his path through the roaring waves.
> And she, the greatest of deities, earth—
> ageless and unwearied—he wears her down
> as the ploughs traverse from year
> to year and his mules churn up the soil. (*Antig.*, 332–41)

Creon and Antigone confront each other in irreconcilable conflict. Antigone claims she is fighting for the unwritten laws of the gods: "For me it was not Zeus who made that order. Nor did that Justice who lives with the gods below mark out such laws to hold among mankind. Nor did I consider your orders so powerful, that you, a mortal man, could over-run the gods' unwritten and unfailing laws. Not now nor yesterday; they live forever, and no one knows their beginning. So not through fear of any man's proud spirit would I be likely to neglect the laws" (450–59). Oedipus becomes a gift for Athens; "pious Antigone" (*Antig.*, 943) becomes a benediction for her race. These benefits are a grace. It is Greek *charis*, a beautiful act of love given gratuitously and reciprocally. Antigone, like Achilles, is moved to act by a perception of divinity in the midst of a corrupted society. The great achievement of Sophocles was in discovering an answer to a universal ethic—a true union of ethics and aesthetics. If man were to be the measure, let him "measure his course by the stars" (*OT*, 795).

Sophocles sees in man the divine reflection because of his willingness to welcome death as the will of the gods. The bruised, disfigured, humiliated body of Oedipus radiates a splendor that surpasses that of the most beautiful body and brings salvation to Thebes and eventually to Athens. Sophocles understands suffering and death as the media of transcendence because the encounter with the divine as totally other provides for true ecstasy.

Sophocles shared in the period of Athenian greatness. Despite expansion of Athenian power, life remained rooted in the *polis*. His work displays his awareness of the two elements: the uncurbed pride of human will and the powers that lie in wait to destroy man's *hybris*. Only in this way can we understand how the man whose good fortune was proverbial in Athens, whose serenity is reflected in the charming account given by his contemporary, Ion, in his *Epidemiae*, and whose charm won him the love of all men (*Vita* 16) could depict the most terrible suffering in his plays and create the most tragic figures of the Attic stage.[25] Did Sophocles conceive the divinely directed path through the world as did Aeschylos, in the form of an ever-renewed balance between guilt and retribution with wisdom as the ultimate aim? Is his Ajax a guilty man doing penance?

## Euripides

Balthasar suggests that perhaps the arc of tragedy, already stretched to the limit in Sophocles, could only break in Euripides. Euripides, after all, was a friend of the sophists. In his house was read the celebrated manifesto of human relativity: Man is the measure of all things.

Yet it was Euripides and not Aeschylos or Sophocles who set the pattern for European theater. Unfortunately, Euripides was understood through deformed prisms. Corneille and Racine read Euripides only in the Senecan version with its Stoic coloring. Goethe and Schiller read, studied, and translated Euripides. Goethe said, "Since Euripides nations have not had a single dramatic poet worthy to offer him his slippers." Schiller translated the *Iphigeneia at Aulis* and left out the final miracle. Goethe wrote an *Iphegeneia at Tauris* in the spirit of humanism which ignored the basic primitive theology with its

25. Lesky, *Greek Tragedy*, p. 95.

element of human sacrifice. The "sublimity" of German classicism does not correspond to what for Euripides was "glory."

In Greek tragedy after Sophocles fiction grew as the lacunae in the texture of the myths were gradually filled with new material. The relation between man and world changed. Individuals were no longer obliged to tradition, and conversely tradition no longer gave support. Man, confronted with antinomies, had to bear the entire burden of decision and responsibility.

After Sophocles there remained but one solution, a desperate solution, utopian and inevitable: that death be conquered by mortal man.[26] Nearly all the surviving tragedies of Euripides have death as their subject. Balthasar discusses this under four viewpoints: existence devoted to death; how the god finds himself behind such existence; how man is prepared to conquer death; and what is glory, fame, and beauty.

For Euripides man attains his credibility through suffering. In the *Trojan Women* scene after scene unfolds the devastating horror of individuals who have come to the limit of suffering. Hecuba, unable to speak, is like an animal. The children who still survive will either be put to death or taken captive. Hecuba wishes to throw herself into the flames of burning Ilion, but the way is barred. "On the way of death, who knows where the limits are? Who knows if living is what they call death, and death what they call living?" (Fragm. 833).

It is both true and false that in Euripides the gods are further away than in Sophocles. On one hand, they are immediately present as silent combatants. On the other, the gods remain uninvolved. Artemis and Aphrodite symbolize the struggle of the *Hippolytos*. The real problem, Balthasar argues,[27] is that the gods—even more than the philosophical idea of God—

26. *La Gloire*, vol. 3, pt. 1, p. 104.
27. Ibid., p. 110.

cannot partake of the suffering they inflict on men. Hippolytos addresses Artemis: "O Mistress, do you not see my miserable condition?" Artemis replies: "I see it, but tears are forbidden my eyes" (*Hipp.* 1395–96).

Euripides has imagined two ways of purifying the atmosphere of this oppression of increasing suffering: anger and love; vengeance and the gift of self. Both solutions are religious. The former theme is played out in the *Medea*, the *Hippolytos*, and the *Hecuba*; the latter, in the *Alcestis*, the *Heraclidae*, and the *Suppliants*. The vengeance theme often portrays the pathology of love. Phaedra, for example, plays the role of Potiphar's wife and avenges her unrequited love with her death. Medea, insulted when her husband takes a new bride, gains vengeance by killing the children. The most cruel vengeance is played out in the *Bacchae*. Dionysos repays Pentheus's slight by making him a sacrificial victim who is torn apart by his mother.

The second theme, that of the gift of self, is even more important for Euripides. The hero voluntarily sacrifices himself. Tragedy, enacted within a framework in which annual sacrifices preceded performance, carries reminiscences of sacrifice, the sacrifice of a man or of an animal surrogate. Moreover, in the sense that the audience experiences is emotionally purged by experiencing the representation of the sufferings on the stage, every tragedy symbolically reproduces a sacrifical pattern. Alcestis consents to die for her husband. Euripides here shows for the first time the heroism of a loving woman who decides to die for her beloved. Yet Euripides makes two important qualifications. The first is that the actual time of fulfilling the promise is deliberately left vague, and the action is further compounded by Alcestis exacting a promise of fidelity to her for the rest of his life. The second is that if the sudden decision to die confers on the act a heroic quality of grandeur, the final goodbye, coming much later, is an infinitely more sorrowful sacrifice.

The death of sacrifice, the death demanded by the gods, was a common motif in tragedy. But the theme of death inspired by personal love is new in Euripides. Macalie in the *Heraclidae* dies willingly, but, as she says, without being assured of a life after death (*Heraclid.* 547). She freely dies "for her race." Death is the issue—especially in a tragedy involving man and gods—in which the notions of mortal man and immortal gods meet, first by the contradiction inherent in the contrast, but next by the quasi-apotheosis through which an Alcestis, a Hippolytos, and an Oedipus may experience, become somehow divine after passing through death. Nothing is more characteristic of Odysseus, Oedipus, or the other tragic heroes than their humble receptivity to the will of the gods.

In the *Iphigeneia at Aulis* Agamemnon sacrifices his daughter. Even though in this play Artemis saves her and replaces the human with an animal, the role of human sacrifice is not denied. In the Old Testament the possibility and reality of human sacrifice is an underlying motif which points to that of Golgotha.

Physical beauty is a great gift. Helen was divinized because of her beauty, but it brought her only sorrow. Semele, who desired to see the glory of Zeus, was struck by lightning and reduced to ashes in spite of her beauty. Since those who sacrifice themselves have no thought of an eternal reward, their motive is *doxa*, glory. As in the Old Testament, glory is not a quality plastered on the exterior; it is that part of eternity dwelling in a human of supreme character.

Earlier I mentioned the significance of the image of the suppliant in Balthasar's theological aesthetics. The suppliant becomes a form of the unknown awaiting a theophany. Every mimetic desire of supplication evidences a duality—a part that claims to know and is impure, the part that cannot tell and is godlike—including those gods who are not content to remain figures of pure mystery.

Ritual, which begins as satisfaction of mimetic desire and ends as sacrament, is renewed in tragedy that describes and invites an excitation of comprehension through a myth. Aristotle's extremes of pity and fear are in *Oedipus Rex*, for example, the forbidden absolutes of mimetic sexual desire and murderous violence. That these are absolutes becomes clear in the vigilance with which Western society, which considers itself rational, still retains them. Greek tragedy, like ritual, is concerned with making transparent the role of the divine. But like the ritual, which is not the miracle itself, tragedy provides only a partial participation. We can take an example from the *Bacchae*. The Pentheus episode of the Dionysiac cycle constitutes an explicit representation of lynching. King Pentheus commits all kinds of impious actions and so becomes a wretched "fragment" that is radically eliminated by the bacchantes. His elimination fulfills the will of the god Dionysus and restores order to the city of Thebes. The Logos of the play becomes for the participant spectator an evidence of *being*, compelling him through understanding, and of *being there*, distancing him as a spectator. This double tension in the ritual corresponds to a psychological tension—awareness, repression. In tragedy that demonstrates this tension, the representation enhances mimetic desire.

Greek tragedy remains, in the complex forms of its presentation, an act of worship to Dionysus. Its artistic features tend not to make it the kind of "art" into which postindustrialization aesthetics would turn it. The empathetic moment comes into its own through the myth. A person does not suffer an erotic seizure but an approach of Aphrodite. The Logos may evoke problems in the mythos without either resolving the problems or dissolving the myth. The Dionysus of the *Bacchae* creates while he destroys; the Artemis of the *Hippolytos* impacably withdraws as she compassionately approaches. Aeschylos's vision like Euripides' doubt retains its own ambiguities.

This chapter began with the claim that Balthasar's reading into the Greek lyric and tragic poets revives a tradition that is important for today. Theologians and critics who focus strictly on the sense of a text and ignore a possible reference miss the understanding of the text. Logic does govern discourse but not the immediacy of Homer or Sophocles. The significance of a theological aesthetics has perhaps its most poignant formulation in a world after industrialization. Yet the special semantic strategy that invokes myth without managing transcendence has always existed. Xenophanes and Harvey Cox share a concern for secular structures. If the myth is merely an emotional algebra, then myths are assimilable one to another and their functions translatable into one another: Artemis into Aphrodite, Hera into Zeus. The myths in single details and in multiple complexes are repeated in different cultures. But this translatability of myth and its recurrence in other cultures does not argue for a single original form. Rather, these common features point out the element of mimetic desire that has a transcendent horizon. Claude Lévi-Strauss indirectly reinforces this conclusion with his theory of transformation that stresses the opacity of relation among details and their complexity rather than their assimilability one to another.

Nicholas Berdyaev formulated three epochs of divine revelation. The first epoch, which he identifies with God the Father, is the revelation of law when the divine natural force is revealed. The second epoch, revelation of the redemption from sin, is identified with Christ, the Son. Finally, the Holy Spirit reveals the dignity of man's creative nature. This third epoch began in the early Renaissance (fourteenth century with

Joachim di Fiori). In the twentieth century all three epochs coexist, but Berdyaev was most interested in pursuing the third. The promise of the early Renaissance to combine Greek classicism with Christianity, Berdyaev suggests, was doomed to failure because the Christian soul was already touched by "transcendent longing." Berdyaev says: "The aim of every creative act is to create another type of being, another kind of life, to break out through 'this world' to another world, out of the chaotic, heavy and deformed world into the free and beautiful cosmos. The aim and purpose of the artistic-creative act is theurgical." He added that the "final depths of all true art are religious. Art is religious in the depths of the artistic creative act itself."[28] A more recent critic has noted: "All art is religious in the sense that every work of art is a gift that not only has a special power to open us to *Being* but interprets *Being*."[29]

The classical tradition is the corpus of ideas and associations which are common to all Westerners and handed down from one generation to the next. It is, says Patrick Reyntiens, a "mental liquor still in process of fermentation and capable of survival through adaptation to circumstances and new stimuli."[30] Balthasar's theological aesthetics demonstrates the power of this process of adaptation.

28. Nicholas Berdyaev, *The Meaning of the Creative Act* (London: Victor Gollancz, 1955), pp. 234, 226.

29. F. David Martin, *Art and the Religious Experience: The "Language" of the Sacred* (Cranbury, N.J.: Associated University Presses, 1972), p. 161.

30. Patrick Reyntiens, "Art and Integrity," *Theology* 83 (September 1980): 336.

## Chapter 4

# The Classical Tradition, II: Philosophy and Religion

As long as Greeks expressed their relation to the universe in mythos, they could satisfy their striving for identification with the gods through the medium of ritual and saga. Thought was in the word (mythos) of epos and not in the discourse of reason (Logos).

Balthasar claims that this world of myth was also one of dialogue: of the personal deity who shed rays of glory on man, who dared play out his existence in this radiant light. All artistic creativity is rooted in this space. There was no fundamental theology of myth, but it was necessary to ask about the limits of understanding. Criteria for verification of argument had to be developed. The process of this development from the time of Plato has been called philosophy.

In *A Theological Anthropology* Balthasar explained this process briefly: "The illumination doctrine of Augustine could always be interpreted backward to Plotinus and Plato, and accordingly the concrete unity of the Logos in the trinitarian and Incarnate Son could be traced back to the unity of the Stoic-

Platonic, even Parmenidean, God. One could keep the former before his eyes and talk in the language of the latter."[1]

The world of philosophy attached itself directly to the antecedent world of myth. Balthasar argues that the unique question of philosophy always remains whether the light of reason can assimilate the glory of myth. He said that from the very start the answer has always been negative. Reason, which poses the question about being in its totality, is a "monological" act.[2]

Balthasar apparently sees a transition of great significance from the way men of the archaic and classical periods viewed "glory" to the philosophical concern with "the beautiful." In the transition from the mythical to the philosophical view of the world, the Logos tended to replace the gods and fate as the permanent ground of the universe. The Logos became the principle of being and, as rationalism progressed, it acquired powers of reason. Reason, which needs to assure itself of the value of its mimetic drive toward transcendence, toward the divine imperishable world, nevertheless should "bracket" methodologically the act of the adoration of God.

## Presocratic Forerunners

Philosophy did not start out that way. Parmenides, for example, in the first verses of his didactic poem witnesses an important event: a poet "doing" philosophy and in the process experiencing ecstasy. An ecstatic moment ravishes the thinker beyond the realm of appearance into the realm of thought and true being: "For the Sunmaidens had led him through the portals of night into the presence of the goddess of truth in her

1. A *Theological Anthropology*, p. 162.
2. *La Gloire*, 4:130.

realm of light" (*Way of Truth*, 28 B 1). Parmenides viewed the world of myth and asked what is this world and what can we truly know about it? His myth became the basis for an epistemological explanation of becoming. To account for experience, he reduced perception to a binary pole: light and night or being and nonbeing. These, he said, Eros originated and mixed into the appearance of the world.

If in Parmenides the transcendental movement splits the way of becoming from the way of being, his contemporary Heraclitus of Ephesus makes of Logos a union of opposites. The world of Heraclitus is generally understood to be in constant flux; yet the real question that troubled this thinker was how to establish permanence in the ever-changing world he experienced, the question of the one and the many. "To those stepping into the same rivers constantly different waters flow" (Frag. 12). Because he perceives in becoming the eternal harmony of opposites, Heraclitus transcends "the harmony of opposed forces like the bow and the lyre" (22 B 51). "Dike is strife" (22 B 80). "Strife is the father and ruler of all" (22 B 52). What is transcendent for Heraclitus is not divine but rather is the "proportion" or "harmony" subsisting and directing the process of becoming.

Heraclitus claimed, "The way up and the way down are the same." This is a paradox for a logic that imagines the climax to be some end at last attained. But for a vision whose imagination locates the presence and power of ultimacy closer to hand, it is a simple statement of a kind of experience.

Pythagoras provided the bridge to Plato. An arch stretches between his religious ethic with its Orphic doctrine of the transmigration of souls and his arithmetic view of the world. The teaching on arithmetic, geometry, music, and astronomy—which would become the medieval *quadrivium* and an important foundation for theology—constituted at the same time the nucleus of modern natural science.

Balthasar claims that this new world of philosophy provided three themes, which were to replace the world of myth. The first was a total reliance on the instrumentality of thought; the second, an ascending philosophical knowledge, or as Hegel expressed it, "In the principle of Greek Freedom is involved the self-emancipation of thought."[3] This would become in Plato the theme of ascending eros formally at odds with the theme of mythic theophany. The third theme, interlaced in the first two, was that of harmony or proportion in the most universal sense.

## Plato

The phrase *khalepa ta kala*—"the beautiful is difficult"—occurs five times in the Platonic corpus, each at an important point in the dialogue. We find it at the end of the *Hippias Maior*, where an attempt is made to define the beautiful; at the start of the *Cratylus*; in the *Republic*, where it introduces the initial search for the parts of the soul and again on the issue of the relation between philosophy and politics; and in the *Sophist*, at the supreme search for being.

Erich Auerbach gave a fine account of Plato's role in the transition between myth and philosophy. It is very similar to that of Hans Urs von Balthasar and deserves quotation:

> It was Plato who bridged the gap between poetry and philosophy; for in his work, appearance, despised by his Eleatic and Sophist predecessors, became a reflected image of perfection. He sets poets the task of writing philosophically, not only in the sense of giving instruction,

3. G. W. F. Hegel, *The Philosophy of History* (New York: Colonial Press, 1899), p. 268.

but in the sense of striving, by the imitation of appearance to arrive at its true essence and to show its insufficiency measured by the beauty of the Idea. He himself understood the art of mimesis more profoundly and practised it more consummately than any other Greek of his time, and apart from Homer he had greater influence as a poet than any other poet of antiquity.[4]

The death of Socrates, the witness for truth, is simply the final act of an inevitable tragedy that could only be produced by philosophy. Because the philosopher wishes truth without any conditions—and *aletheia* signifies reality just as it is—he divides men into two camps: those who are servants of truth and are obligated to it and those who accept a service of truth but do not wish any obligations toward it. They are those who pursue philosophy versus those who pursue poetry (*Repub.* 607b). The idea is presented in the dialogues with sophists (for example, Gorgias), but it is in the *Republic* that the issue is truly joined. Thrasymachus represents the point of view of the powerful with progressive brutality; next, Glaucon presents this view; and finally, Adeimantus, who cynically exposes the secret egotism of these devotees as a "moral interest" (*Repub.* 362e–367e).

Balthasar claims that the question of the degree to which Plato had idealized the figure of Socrates is of little matter. What counts is that the act of philosophy consists in the absolute dedication to truth. The basic choice is dedication either to truth or to self-interest. Truth is unconditioned and irrefutable (*Gorg.* 473b). Socrates could claim that by his service to the god, that is, by his witness to the truth, he has procured the greatest good for the state (*Apol.* 30a). "Because through his faith and love Socrates—perfectly and to the point of folly—

4. Erich Auerbach, "The Idea of Man in Literature," in Giles B. Gunn, ed., *Literature and Religion* (New York: Harper Forum Books, 1971), p. 268.

subordinated his existence to the *daimon* within him, he can be an intimation of Christ."[5] Within the personal soul and within the state the same principle of order reigns: the spirit should control the passions.

Plato repeatedly presents the "beautiful state" as a model (*paradeigma*), a design (*diagraphe*), a plan (*schẹma*), something "which is not totally and intrinsically impossible" (*Repub.* 502bc).

The philosopher is an expert whose expertise is excellence. This excellence consists in "health, beauty, and the good state of the soul" (*Repub.* 444d). These three intertwining concepts define objective justice. Philosophical inquiry from this viewpoint proceeds from myth and assumes the entire Hellenic tradition. Spirit is the possibility of perceiving what is revealed; it is the act of remaining open to reality at every stage. When in the *Symposium* this philosophical act is conceived as *eros*, Agathon should accept Socrates' decisive correction: he has overlooked the fact that as mimetic desire all love tends toward an object, confounding *eros* and *eraston*, subject and object (*Symp.* 199cd, 200ab, 204c). "Only when all of these things— names, definitions, and visual and other perceptions have been tested . . . only then, when reason and knowledge are at the very end of human effort, can they illuminate the nature of any object" (*Ep.* 7. 344b).

In various ways Plato had praised phenomenal beauty as a stage on the way to true beauty; it was through him that artists and lovers of art first began to reflect on the presence of the idea in the appearance of things and to long to attain it. Parmenides had separated the world into two halves: being and becoming. Plato used the same terms, but his spirit will not allow the element of the nonidentity of that which becomes.

5. *Glory of the Lord*, 1:184.

The world of becoming is the world of perception; the world of being is that of reason (*Tim.* 51d–52c). In every perishable or contingent being there remains something eternal and imperishable. This is a ray of immemorial "light"—the light being an image of something "more beautiful than beauty." "Both knowledge and truth are beautiful, but you are right in thinking of the Good as other and more beautiful than they" (*Repub.* 508e). How does one classify the beautiful in its unity with the good? The *Timaeus* furnishes the key concept: "Everything which is good is beautiful, and beauty does not extend without interior measure" (*Tim.* 87c).

In Plato's thought, for something to be it must be eternal. This does not mean that objects that come to be and pass away do not exist. Rather, they are not fully beings, because being must be eternal. Being is not the same as existence, but beings, that is, forms, most certainly exist. It is not an accident that the form of beauty is described as *auto o esti kalon.* Through the form, beauty, the beautiful particulars, come to be beautiful (*Phaedo* 100c).

Plato speaks of an "inconceivable and inaccessible beauty" (*Repub.* 509a). This goes beyond the term of Heraclitus (Diels 1. 22 B 18). Gregory of Nyssa echoed both when he spoke of the "unhoped for beauty" (*PG* 44.1037c).

Balthasar indicates that in this concept we are far removed from a simple a priori immanent reason. But what is the source of this light? Is it the return of a mythic revelation coming from beyond? Is it a mystical experience of union? Or is it only the empirical experience of the transcendental structure of knowledge? For Plato it is the ascending movement toward the idea, toward the light of the good, the principle of everything, which founds intuitive knowledge (*episteme*). So one cannot apply to Plato, as some moderns wish, the rigorous distinction between "scientific knowledge" and "mythical assertion." Four principal Platonic theses reinforce this claim: (1) the theory of knowledge as recollection, which is narrowly linked to the doctrine of immortality and rebirth; (2) the appeal to eros or daimon, to inspiration; (3) the assertion that is properly mythical; and (4) the esoteric manner of argument in which the dialectical method remains fixed. Balthasar develops each thesis with multiple citations from the texts.

In short, Plato's use of myth demonstrates that the age of myth is past, that this form of expression has become poetic. Yet inspiration, eros, and myth do point to a supreme reality.

## The True Dimension of the *Kalon*

The *kalon* contains more than is evoked for us by the word "beauty." The *kalon* is the just, the good, that which is adapted to being, what gives it its integrity, its health, and its salvation. The question can be asked: is the good the same as the beautiful? Is not the beautiful simply a superficial appearance, or is it really something essential? The *kalon* in any case is coextensive with being; it is a transcendental. The *Symposium* portrays the ascent of the beautiful body to the beauty of soul and to beauty in itself.

When Socrates asked Hippias if he knew what beauty was, Hippias replied by giving two examples: (1) of beautiful young girls—but are they beautiful of themselves or only by the vision of a being of the same nature? (2) shining gold, but only if applied as in the case of the eyes of Athena in Phidias's statue; the "fitting" is beautiful, but only in relation to something else and not to itself; in appearance but not in essence (*Hipp. mai.* 293e–294a). The good as such is beautiful (*Symp.* 201c); one who has attained the beautiful has attained the good (*Symp.* 204de). The three concepts which the biblical book of Wisdom takes up and which become fundamental for Augustine define the Platonic doctrine of beauty: measure, number, and weight (*Laws* 757b).

Balthasar phrases the great question of Platonic aesthetics: does the divine dominate the soul by imposing its law upon it (this will be the Augustinian hierarchy), or is the measure between God and world the same, only aggrandized like that between soul and body? This will be Plato's solution. The mature works know a *mysterium* of the beautiful. "The beauty of a thing is produced by nothing other than by the original beauty or by a presence of this Beauty or by a communication" (*Phaedo* 100d). While the *mysterium* of an ineffable presence is manifested in the order of the world, the state, the human being, the observer obtains such satisfaction that the *mysterium* is forgotten. He becomes absorbed in a mathematical daze in which the "sage" (in the *Epinomis*) discerns or contemplates immediately the divinity of being (*Epin.* 978ab–982ae).

The explication of *kalon* by *dikaion*—as the sum of all the excellences—justifies the critique of poets that ends the *Republic.* It exacts from man the supreme task: to suffer for the true, the perfect beauty, to the point at which all visible beauty has disappeared (*Laws* 859d–860a). The most beautiful and the greatest among the harmonies will be called the greatest *sophia* (*Laws* 689d). It is no longer a question of a mimetic desire for wisdom (*philosophia*) but of *sophia* herself, which is identified in the cosmic and human spheres.

This is the extreme point of an ethical aesthetics immanent in the world, where the divine as well as the human appears in a supreme identity of the same vibrant harmony. This is the birth of a philosophical aesthetics of the grand style, which has influenced all Western humanism in antiquity, the Middle Ages, and modern times. It is an aesthetics that tries to interpret divine glory in the direction of a human "sublime" or provisionally returns to the same, a cosmic sublimity. All learning, *mathesis universalis,* is called *sophia,* wisdom. The original astonishment, the first philosophic act, no longer bears on being; rather, there is a profound neglect of being—and the act looks to the stars (*Epin.* 986cd).

## Religion

The long period after Plato and Aristotle witnessed an attempt to give the term "religion" the meaning of a synthesis between philosophy and myth. Myth has always been alive, and even philosophy, as Balthasar noted, turns to myth when it reaches the limits of reason. The mythic cult that survives agrees with this tendency in the same way that philosophy comes to encounter the rational justification of the cult. It is in this search for meeting that one must see the proper character of religion. One dreams of building a bridge, beginning from both banks at once. Even if the sections of the arch progress toward each other, they never join. The essence of religion in the Hellenistic age—and of all religion to the extent that it distinguishes itself from true myth and from authentic philosophy—is similar to such a bridge because it is syncretism.

When Varro edited his seventy-six books of the *Logohistorikon,* each philosophical problem was expressed by a mythical or historical image, as indicated by the titles: "Orestes, *de insania,*" "Maris, *de fortuna,*" and so on. It is clear that the image comes to the aid of the concept. It is the same with the tripartite division of religion into mythical, physical, and civil proposed by Augustine.

Balthasar notes that in addition to the coordination of religions revealed by Hellenistic philosophy and again by the political needs of Rome, the "civil" religion of Varro made common cause with the "physical" religion and opposed "mythical" religion. This process leads in Hegel's words to the destruction of art.[6] Canonical beauty in art proceeds from the domain and the epoch of mythical revelation; it alone is ringed with glory. Graeco-Roman art, even when an expression of official religion, could only copy faithfully—or more often not so faithfully—the archetypes of a lost Greek world. But these copies lack the archetypal éclat of mythic glory. If philosophical religion lacks images, mythical religion pours itself forth in a torrent of images, arbitrarily combined.

## The Philosophical Pillar

Balthasar says that "religion" rests on two dogmas: the *theion*, an immanent active principle (in Stoic tradition) and the *syngeneia* (*cognatio*), the relation between human and divine spirit. These two dogmas transcend individual philosophical schools and are part of the common store of philosophical thought. For them to become axioms of philosophy required the step from Plato to Aristotle. In the *Peri philosophias* Aristotle described the rapid development of philosophy up to his own time, much as he described the development of tragedy in the *Poetics*. Aristotle was fully conscious that with him philosophy had reached its goal (Frag. 1, Rose). Aristotle attributed to the heavens the quintessential reality, that which subsumed the four elements of the cosmos, and this was the constitution of the stars and of divine intelligences (Cicero, *Acad.* 1.7.26). It is the same with the soul, which participates in eternal motion and is called *entelecheia*.

Aristotle's world is a cosmos, an ordered world in which all parts are well situated within a whole, each part constituting a

6. G. W. F. Hegel, *Vorlesungen über die Philosophie der Religion II*, *Werke*, vol. 12 (1832), p. 141.

wholeness of its own in proportion to all the other parts. This is true not only of Aristotle's theory of the beautiful but also of his physics, ethics, and metaphysics. In general, it proclaims the Greek aesthetic approach to reality. The world is like the plot of a tragedy, "complete in itself as a whole of some magnitude. . . . Again: to be beautiful (and for that matter, to be, which is to act toward an end in view), a living creature, and every whole made up of parts, must not only present a certain order in its arrangement of parts, but also be of a certain definite magnitude" (*Poetics* 1450b, 25–36).

Cicero explains the beauty radiating in the world on the basis of his source, Posidonius, as unity in multiplicity, an organic law (*De nat. deorum* 2.39–60). In the *De Mundo*, which probably dates from the first century B.C., the cosmos appears from the same source as the most radiant glory before all because it is perfect equilibrium, established in God, of all parts and their contraries (97a 28s, 397b4, 400 b28). It is the same with the Stoics, among whom aesthetic *thaumazein* is constantly absorbed in the ethical order.[7]

Aristotle opened anew the way to this religious sense. For him nature was marvelous, even in its "least noble parts" (*De part. anim.* 1.5). Balthasar calls Cleanthes' Hymn to Zeus the most beautiful prayer of antiquity. Such Stoics who recognized their program not as a step beyond but behind myth interpreted their philosophy in the light of myth and allowed it to issue in an authentic prayer.

The prayerful act is one of wisdom, because it is simply the truth; one of ethics, because it is a submission to the norm of all good; and one of aesthetics, because the cosmic order sovereignly returns everything which is measured to its sovereign

7. See *Stoicorum Veterum Fragmenta*, ed. Heinrich von Arnum (Zurich: Weidman, 1903–5), 1:114.

measure. Just as Aristotle contemplated the stars with mythic eyes and as a moralist begged the goddess with a mystic fervor, Cleanthes, the Stoic pantheist, prays to the universal Spirit with a mythic religiosity; the philosophy of identity is necessarily projected into myth to be religion. Neoplatonism will be the last attempt to preserve in a systematic fashion the glory of reality, which is more and more hidden in the thought of identity. But this attempt will occur in the core of an englobing unity without the power to radiate the true glory.

## Dialectic

A pious pantheism can quickly turn into an impious atheism. If the religious factor became in Stoicism a modality of ethics, it became in Neoplatonism a modality of mysticism, but this modality was less able to avoid a dialectic of identity. Stoic philanthropy is founded on the identity of essences.

### The Mythical Pillar

Two ways now open. One looks back to Hesiod, Pindar, and Aeschylos, and this way leads to the tragic proofs of the divine that gnosis places in God. The other way is attached more narrowly to philosophy and is entailed in the concept of revelation: divine absolute being reveals and conceals itself. This becomes the way of Neoplatonism.

The two dogmas of the foundation of a mythology projected onto philosophy are, first, that there exists a revelation which is an irruption of a light from on high and second, that this revelation presupposes a hierarchical order of being. The new Christianity would retain much of what is authentic in the mythology of ancient Greece. It would struggle with gnosticism over the meaning of true revelation and even longer with Neoplatonism.

The God of myth was surpassed by the God of the philosophers. The primary emergence of being into an immortal divine world and a mortal human world set inappropriate limits on the divine and its power and freedom. In Plato the divine "surpasses reality in sublimity and power" (*Repub.* 509c) but cannot be presented as personal love.

Balthasar observes that the idea of God cannot be completed because it requires two points of departure, the two pilings for the arch. Purely philosophical or civil religion cannot exist; it must depend on the mythical, where alone there can be prayer and sacrifice.[8]

Pindar could reflect the glory of being in the splendor celebrated at a great victory. Plato, going beyond Parmenides and Heraclitus, had comprehended the totality of being and situated everything in the light of the good: that is, the truth, which includes the integrity of the *kalon*, has been given new focus. Whoever wished after Plato to place a tension in absolute being would have to prove that the idea of absolute good could not be preserved otherwise.

Because mythic thought is founded essentially on particulars, when gnosticism strives for universality, gnostic religion succumbs inevitably to *hybris* in its most intolerable form because it is most contradictory. One could thus interpret gnosticism as a multiple form of the objectivization of impressions, conditions, and existential desires of the human soul. Quasi-biblical themes appear in a neutralized setting in both Porphyry and Iamblichus.

The *De mysteriis* is a good example of the immediate identification of myth and philosophy. Hegel later made the same attempt and integrated all forms of dialogical faith in the monological knowledge of reason.

8. *Spiritus Creator*, p. 22.

If this had been the only contribution of antiquity, Christianity would not have had such a long struggle to obtain an understanding of glory. It could have installed the missing arch and so completed the bridge.

Balthasar repeats his profound conviction that one can agree with Karl Barth that Christianity is not a religion, with Kierkegaard that it is not a philosophy, and with Bultmann that it is not a myth. "But God would not have become man if he had not entered interiorly and positively into contact with these three forms."[9]

In the midst of the turbulence of Rome two prestigious figures, each in his own way, indicated a possible way out of the labyrinth of the pre-Christian world: Virgil and Plotinus. Without Virgil the great national epics of the Western world would not have been born: those of Tasso, Camoens, and Milton. Through the eyes of Plotinus the Cappadocian Fathers and Augustine read their Plato. Plotinus inspired Boethius, Scotus Erigena, and Thomas Aquinas.

## Virgil

Balthasar appreciates the consummate magic of Virgil's poetry, its purity of feeling, and the spiritual and political rebirth it betokens. The peasant's son from Mantua combined a deep attachment to the Italian soil with the highest sense of culture.

Virgil has appealed to all as the seer and sorcerer of popular legend and as a storehouse of antiquarian lore and the epitome of learning. His privileged status throughout the Middle Ages was assured almost by accident. His *Fourth Eclogue* was read as a prophecy. Virgil designed it for such reading, and his mysterious lines were interpreted to support imperial claims in the

9. *La Gloire*, vol. 3, pt. 1, p. 201.

early Christian centuries. The most famous and influential interpretation was Constantine's official recognition in a Good Friday sermon of the poem as a prophecy of the coming of Christ, which Eusebius appended to his life of the emperor. Constantine's allegorical interpretation canonized Virgil, so that, in the words of T. S. Eliot, he became "a liaison between the old world and the new."[10]

Macrobius forged an even more permanent link in the perpetuation of the "Christian" Virgil. In a passage of the *Commentarii in Somnium Scipionis* Macrobius started a tradition of Christian allegorization that would last well into the Renaissance. The *Aeneid* was a source book, in Macrobius's view, of all philosophical and scientific truth. Bernard Silvester may serve as an example of this allegorization. He construes the wanderings of Aeneas as an exemplary tale of those who pursue wisdom by erroneous paths. Underneath the hexameters of Virgil's epic lies the odyssey of the human soul imprisoned in the body.

This tradition forms the horizon for what is perhaps the most important encounter in Western literature, the meeting of Dante and Virgil in the first canto of the *Inferno*. It is hard for the modern reader to appreciate that Dante recognized Virgil as his true master, whom he knew intimately from his diligent study of the poet.

Virgil uses philosophy, religion, and myth, but he surpasses them. Virgil is not a Greek but a Roman. Neither ideas nor myths interest him very much. He is involved with solid reality:

10. See Harold Mattingly, "Virgil's Fourth Eclogue," *Journal of the Warburg and Courtauld Institutes* 10 (1947): 14–19; W. H. Roberts, ed., *The Nicene and Post-Nicene Fathers of the Christian Church*, 2d ed. (Grand Rapids: Occidental, 1952), 1: 561–80; T. S. Eliot, *On Poetry and Poets* (New York: Farrar, Straus, and Giroux, 1943), p. 63.

nec sum animi dubius, verbis ea vincere magnum quam sit et angustis hunc addere rebus honorem: sed me Parnasi deserta per ardua dulcis raptat amor.

(I am not ignorant of the difficulty of winning with words a triumph, and so to crown with glory a humble theme. But sweet desire hurries me over the hard wastelands of Parnassus.) (*Georgics* 3.289–92)

In Virgil's arcadia, in his pure world of poetic and aesthetic symbols, we are far from Greek aesthetics. The aesthetic claim to be made for the *Georgics* is that this poem is the first in which description is the primary source of the beautiful. Consider, for example, the following prose passage: "In summer they wend their way to pasture at daybreak, because then the grass, being dewy, is sweeter than that of mid-day, when it is drier." This passage is from Varro (2.2.10–11). Virgil takes the same scene:

> But when the west winds call and the exquisite warm season
> Ushers them out, both sheep and goats, to glade and pasture
> At the first glimpse of the Morning Star, let us wend away
> To the far fields, while the morning is young, the
> Meadow pearly, . . . .

In Virgil the description of the beautiful scene is what matters and the didactic content almost hides.

Whereas the *amor* which in Lucretius is all-powerful ruler of the world (*De rerum nat.* 1.10–20), in Virgil this daimon is very different: *omnia vincit amor, et nos cedamus amori* (*Buc.* 10.69). The delicate heart of the poet participates intimately in every joy and sorrow, in every glorification and destruction. It is a strangely chaste and reserved love. If Athena was the protectress of the Greeks, the anagram Roma-Amor was not without value for Virgil. In the *Georgics* the arcadian shepherd has become a wise Italian laborer: *si te digna manet divini gloria ruris* (1.168; cf. 199–203).

We find in Rilke's *Sonnets to Orpheus* a similar theme, Orpheus's descent into the underworld, which Rilke intends to use to illustrate the encounter with life's greatest mystery, death. Virgil and Rilke share a common vision. It is not the folly of Orpheus's looking back which caused him to lose Eurydice and ultimately to bring on his own death. Orpheus had to die to symbolize the function of the human *vates*. In this sense Virgil used Orpheus as both climax and conclusion of the *Georgics*. The same "obedience to an inner direction" that guided Rilke may have led Virgil to end his poem with this traditional element.[11] The legend of death and of eternal life is transformed in the *Aeneid*. The vision Virgil had of himself as *vates*, one who brings knowledge of the divine ("sacra fero"), helps us understand that the glory which bathes the entire poem radiates from a "yes" to life, a "yes" proffered consciously and which is a reply to the supreme "yes" emanating from being.

Virgil repeatedly presents the reader with both a divine and a human perspective on the action which forces the reader to attempt a reconciliation. A dynamic is established between the human and the divine. Using devices of expectation and allusion Virgil invites the reader to experience the manifestation of the divine in the course of Aeneas's heroic development. Jupiter's splendor is the ground of the fate that sends and accompanies Aeneas as his ethical norm.

The *Aeneid* is the first work in the spiritual history of Europe that is both ethical and aesthetic at the same time. The idea came to Virgil to consider Rome, not in her being but in her becoming, not in her possession but in her desire, not in her power but in her submission and renunciation. Virgil dis-

11. See Louis Roberts, "The Orpheus Mythologem: Virgil and Rilke," *Texas Studies in Literature and Language* 15 (1974):882–91.

covers a strange new heroism. Contrary to the Homeric hero, he is no longer a plastic figure whom one can exhibit. There is in Aeneas, in his actions, in his gods, a quality that has no visage, no color. It is this pale heroism which Virgil dares offer to the Romans so preoccupied with success. Through it Virgil elevates his own people, even Caesar. A parallel with Abraham and the people of the Old Testament is unavoidable. Abraham and *pius* Aeneas make sense only from the viewpoint of faith, hope, and obedience, a sense located in a distant past. Abraham is the father of all believers; Aeneas is the model of all Romans (*Aeneid* 8.729–31). The feeling of hope frees Virgil from the obligation of presenting the actual time of Augustus as an unsurpassable *eschaton*.

*His, ego nec metas rerum, nec tempora pono: Imperium sine fine dedi* (For there I place neither boundaries nor periods. Dominion without end I have given.). The figure Virgil can dress as Rome (Roma—Amor), in which is recognized the place beyond myth, philosophy, and religion, presents in the ethical-aesthetic domain an analogy with the Bible without being at the same time an anticipation or a replica of revelation. Yet here a new fact is inscribed in the heart of the mysterious preparations for the birth of the child. This child will not be truly human unless he has his historic horoscope, his *kairos*, which contributes to defining his fortune. Rome was foreseen as matter and content, but matter and form are relative notions. Balthasar says it is necessary to consider three issues: the mission insofar as the form of life is characterized by obedience; the mission insofar as it is *fatum*, willed by the gods; and the mission insofar as glory involves humiliation.

First, to be sent from Troy to Latium constitutes a mission. The issue is really a commandment: "Do not fear to obey the orders of your mother and do not refuse to follow her counsels" (*Aeneid* 2.605–6). The hero leaves to his son an example of courage and patience, of true obedience, but not necessarily of goodness (12.435–36). The idea that a man should pursue a sacred mission is absent from earlier epic. Ascent through labors to apotheosis was a familiar theme, but before Virgil it had never been tied to an earthly career.

Second, the mission is *fatum*. Aeneas was conscious of his mission. It was revealed by the prophecy of his divine mother and the word of his father, as indicated repeatedly by oracles and partial prophecies: *iussa deum cogunt* (6.461); *Jovis imperium* (5.747); *fata deum imperiis suis* (7.239–40); *jussis ingentibus urget Apollo* (7.241); *praecepta jubent* (6.632); *Coelestium vis magna jubet* (7.431). *Sic placitum:* "Such is my will" (1.283), says the father of gods and men. Between god and men is established an ineffable relation of love of which it is better not to speak and of which the greatest moment is that—as in Homer—when the gods reveal themselves and man in the ardor of his desire stretches his arms out to them (1.402–10). The mission in part is already known to poet and audience, for it is Roman history past and present. In the tragic episode of Aeneas and Dido is inscribed the historical struggle of Rome and Carthage as well as the victory over Cleopatra, who, after Actium, commits suicide as did Dido. In the encounter of Aeneas and Dido in the underworld the structural and verbal patterning contains thematic implications that reach beyond the direct perceptions of the former lovers to touch upon a tragic paradox, the radical conflict between private values and public duty. Even more it is the history of the struggle between the eternal seduction of the Orient and the mission of Rome to the West. The missions are considered and appreciated in their geographic and geopolitical dimensions as later they will be in Claudel's *Soulier de satin*. What Virgil glorified was political—the empire. The union of religious currents that he exploited aimed at more than that. The glory of Rome is transcended into another glory, which remains unknown. Roman *pietas* is defined as perpetual readiness to hear and respond to the divine Word spoken in the language of being.

Third, Aeneas is forced to present himself to the inhabitants of Italy as a "deserter from Asia" (12.15), as a suppliant, just as he had presented himself before Dido (1.519). A destiny has been pronounced over Troy; the gods have fled the temples and deserted the altars (2.350–52).

The Aeneas who occupied Italy is very different from the Aeneas who fled burning Troy with his family and household gods. By his own account his actions on that tragic night of Troy's disaster were not heroic or brilliant. His major gift, *pietas*, carried him through the crisis. Anchises was the real leader; Aeneas had to learn by suffering. The encounter with Dido could not be the same as Odysseus's meetings with Circe and Calypso, for Aeneas was to become the symbol of the glory of Rome in a way that neither Achilles nor Odysseus could be for Greece. The character and fate of *pius* Aeneas, who fought his way through temptation to his destiny, were new elements in the heroic vision.

Aeneas is thus, Balthasar wrote, "the highest approximation to the true source-point of religion: existence as calling to a future work and complete docility (on condition of painful renunciation) in the hands of the gods; not for nothing did the Christian West place its religious poetry under the sign of Virgil."[12]

## Plotinus

Plotinus is the philosopher who understood Plato's intentions even better than the Master (Plato). His main interest is the Absolute One, which he equates with the Platonic good.

12. *Spiritus Creator*, p. 25.

In his philosophy Plotinus assumes the values of myth and religion. But he does not do so in a sterile manner, as in the religious syncretism already met here, but, like Virgil, by making a passionate return to the origins which knew not the divisions of today. He went back beyond the dualism of myth (as revelation coming from God) and of philosophy (as thought coming from man). For Plotinus being itself is divine, and its total revelation is so magnificent that it surpasses in glory all particular myths. Plotinus is not a disciple but a founder. He thinks in a way at once rigorous and reflexive. Like Virgil he is a man "exceptionally pure and simple," who lived a celibate life at Rome. Afflicted with an incurable disease and abandoned by his pupils, he died alone. His subsequent influence in Europe and in the Arabic countries was immense. Through him the heritage of antiquity was handed on to the Fathers of the Church: Gregory of Nyssa, Augustine, Dionysus, Maximus the Confessor, who joined his struggle in interpreting being theologically. The Scholastics received philosophy colored by Plotinus from Boethius and John Scotus Erigena to Albert the Great, Bonaventure, Thomas Aquinas, Eckhardt, Dante, Nicholas of Cusa, John Gerson, Marsilio Ficino. Giordano Bruno, Shaftesbury, and Herder followed him; and Hegel recognized him as one of his predecessors. Today Plotinus is often interpreted in the direction of Hegel, in the hope of obtaining a speculative justification for his system. According to Balthasar, "Just as Idealism had its roots in Plotinus and Augustine, so, too, did Thomism itself, at least when it sought to grow beyond strict scholastic requirements and develop a universal perspective."[13]

In most Plotinian texts the good is identified with the One, and beauty is relegated to second place because it is less true,

13. *Glory of the Lord*, 1:104.

that is, it has less of reality. The standard is not the beautiful but the real. What was Plotinus's view of the relation between the real and the beautiful?

In *Enneads* 1.6.6. Plotinus notes that beauty is the being of what is real, that its opposite is the ugly, that is, the first evil, and that we should identify good and beautiful and the good and beauty. He says in line 25 that beauty, which is to be identified with the good, is the first principle; next comes *nous*, which is to be identified with the beautiful. So the first hypothesis is called beauty; the second, the beautiful.

Nevertheless we read in 1.6.7, in the description of the ascent to the good, a claim that anyone who has seen it knows that it is beautiful. In passages describing the ascent of the soul, Plotinus is influenced by Plato's *Symposium*, in which the beautiful is the aim of the philosopher's quest. When the soul rises to *nous*, it will say that the ideas are beauty. Beyond the ideas it will be in the realm of the good, which radiates the beautiful before it.

Since the One is formless and the source of beauty, it is only to be expected that as compared with the beauty of the intelligible world it will be different in kind and that whereas the individual forms are beautiful and the intelligible world has beauty, it, the source of beauty, will be beauty above beauty, the begetter and maker of beauty.

Plotinus contemplates the glory of the cosmos with astonishment. One finds in him an aspect of the later Plato, of Aristotle, and especially of the Stoics. One finds an eternal spirit in which the act of thinker and the object of his thought are identified. It is the Aristotelian deity: *noesis noeseos*. At the summit of this spirit reigns an ineffable mystery. All beauty in the world is only a sign coming from the mystery and returning to it.

Whatever Plotinus's solution to the problem of death and

suffering, there is never a moment's doubt about the total harmony of the divine cosmos. Balthasar notes that Plotinus's use of a theater image gives an initial "aesthetic answer" to the problem of how particulars come about. Particulars must be different and ordered to form the most beautiful whole.[14] If one wants to speak of a fall, one ought always to maintain also the opposite aspect of an ascent. Among the divine hypostases of the One, intelligence, and soul, distances could create a relation of superiority and inferiority. "We are not separated from being; we are in it; and it is not separated from us" (6.5, 1, 25–26).

The sovereignty of the absolute is guaranteed, and his "manifestation" into the world appears as the epiphany of his own internal necessity or, on the contrary, as that of his perfect sufficiency (liberty). The deity is absolute transcendence and absolute immanence. In this Plotinus, like Virgil, represents an irreversible *kairos* in which the direction of thought remains suspended and philosophy faces a crucial choice.

This decision appears in his doctrine of intelligence. Intelligence is pure, essential thought. There is an irreducible priority of object to subject, but what is thought does not exist outside of thought and in this sense "before" it. This is true only for sensible perception. Intelligence is one with its projections (5.4, 2, 46–48, 50). There exists total reciprocity of thought and being, but this reciprocity does not suppress the otherness that is constantly presupposed and surmounted. In this theory of the double unity of thought and being, Plotinus wishes to see the sum of philosophical tradition: the Platonic world of ideas is given its due but so are Parmenides, Heraclitus, Empedocles, and Aristotle. Plotinus's doctrine is an objective idealism or a realistic idealism that bases all being in a

14. *Theodramatik*, 1:133.

logic in which it is originally thought by an archetypal intellect (5.6, 6, 20).

In most texts the good is identified with the One, and beauty is relegated to second place because it is less true, that is, it has less of reality. We noted that in 1.6.6 Plotinus cites beauty as the being of what is real. When the soul rises to *nous* it will say that the ideas are beauty. Beyond the ideas it will be in the realm of the good, which radiates the beautiful before it.

Since the One is formless and the source of beauty, it is only to be expected that as compared with the beauty of the intelligible world it will be different in kind and that whereas the individual forms are beautiful and the intelligible world has *kallos*, it, the source of *kallos*, will be beauty above beauty. It is the begetter and creator of beauty.

Every being is beautiful because it is form and because it involves intelligence. The One is beyond being and intelligence, form and beauty, inasmuch as the One is the source of all. The form "being," however, is nothing other than the individual form of the thing. Intelligence and being are secondary; they are the reflection of an original principle that appears as the form of the beautiful, of knowledge, and of love.

Plotinus, building on both Plato and Aristotle, was able to ask about the source of the distance between the eternal and the temporal: "Instead of just setting one order off against another as original and copy (Plato) or as eternally moved and unmoved (Aristotle), Plotinus asks about that movement which has caused the distance between the eternal and the temporal."[15] Platonic and Aristotelian eros is immanent in movement, but as "longing upwards" through *conversio*, it acquires the sense of a return home to a lost origin. Time is the existential distance between departure and return, but distance within

15. A *Theological Anthropology*, p. 21.

the same continuum. Thus time for Plotinus is the measure of the distance from the One. In this context Plotinus became an important source for Balthasar's theology of history.

Augustine translated Plotinian eros into Christian *desiderium*. Intelligence and being are always present, always manifest to those who have eyes to see and show themselves as the place where eternal beauty rests. *Theoria* is needed to find the unsurpassable glory that radiates from the depth of intelligible being. Modern philosophical aesthetics will take this way inasmuch as it distinguishes itself from a theological aesthetics. The *theoria* is the act and mirror of a total opening into the contemplation of being as *noema*, an act lost in contemplation but also an act of a return to self, a reencounter of the self in the object. Plotinus's Greek inheritance rendered him capable of discovering in being itself a divine epiphany.

All his life Plotinus remained stupefied at the marvel of being that surpasses all reason. The ascent toward the identity of *nous* is useful for the knowledge of the One, but it is useless to the same degree (5.5 (32), 6, 20–21). What Plotinus searches for with such desire and for which no name is adequate is ineffable beauty or that which is beyond beauty (6.7 (38), 32, 33). These notions are fundamental in Plotinian aesthetics. The One is elevated beyond beauty; this is a constant assertion in Plotinus. Beauty is posterior to the One and comes from it as the light of the day comes from the sun (6.9, 4, 10–11). By it is discovered the ultimate structure of the beautiful. It has its true reality in the domain of *nous*, which is the kingdom of the form, of the reciprocal transparency of subject and object, of difference and identity. But it has its truth only as an epiphany of the mystery of being, then as indication of this mystery. It is a reality radiating horizontally, but the radiance that makes this reality splendid comes vertically from on high. This is the structure with which Balthasar began *The Glory of the Lord*, volume 1: form and splendor. The two aspects become in Plotinus an anatomy of the beautiful, but for him beauty can exist and be understood only in the superbeautiful, the realm of "glory." The structure of the beautiful is inscribed in the formal structure of the doctrine of God.

Plotinus takes up the figure of Odysseus in the treatise *On Beauty*: "This would be better advice: 'Let us fly to our beloved country.' What this is is our way of escape; how do we find it? We shall put out to sea, as Odysseus did, from the witch Circe or Calypso—as the poet says . . . and was not content to stay though he had pleasure of the eyes and lived among much sensual beauty" (1.6 8, 16–21).

The Greek tradition reveals itself in Plotinus. Being is beautiful because it is the revelation of the divine. Beauty is consequently interiorly structured in the form of radiation, brilliance, and harmony. The ontology and formal aesthetics of Plotinus remain open to a pure philosophy and a conscious theology, and it is in this opening that we find his *kairos*. Christian theology adopted his body of thought for the doctrine of the Trinity, for example, the *nous* becomes the Logos, the Verbum, and the relation between the world and the soul furnishes an analogy for understanding Christ. This Plotinian doctrine was transmitted by Pseudo-Dionysus, through the ninth-century translations of Hilduin and Scotus Erigena. Erigena is particularly important because he brought together both Augustinian and Dionysian traditions. When Christian thinkers took over this framework for use in their explication of the faith, they had to make two changes. They had first to condense the subordinationist hierarchy of divine hypostases in Plotinus into one supreme principle in which the three Persons within the divine nature were coequal, distinguished only by relations, not differing levels of perfection. Second, the single God was identically creator of the world through knowledge and free act of love, exercising providence over each individual creature. The Platonic world of ideas became incorporated indirectly into the one supreme divine nature.

The mythological-mystic translation of the relation between the free person and the fated role in Plato and Plotinus—both know that they were trying to approach the ineffable—clearly demonstrates how closely one approaches the secret source of what it means to be human.[16] Western man needs to recapture the archetypal experience of being that he originally had in Greece. Like the individual, the entire culture must reappropriate this experience if it is to survive.

In this and the preceding chapter we have reviewed Balthasar's interpretation of the classical tradition. It constitutes the ground of his theological aesthetics. The next two chapters consider the development of this tradition in Balthasar's reading of the Fathers of the Church.

16. *Theodramatik*, 1:234.

## Chapter 5

# Resurrected Patristics

NOTHING HARMS understanding as much as the failure to account for context. An exploration of the patristic study of Hans Urs von Balthasar must consider not only his philosophical presuppositions, the subject of Chapter 2, but also his understanding of some presuppositions inherited from the classical tradition and shared by the Fathers. In emphasizing the importance of patristics in Balthasar's theology, we must remember that he himself did not ask for any particular new emphasis on the Fathers: "What is required is neither an enthusiastic revival of one thing or another nor pure historical research, but that kind of Christian humanism which goes directly to the sources to discover what is alive and truly original—and not to a school of thought long since dried out—in a spirit of joy and freedom so that one can weigh the true value of things."[1]

Balthasar's use of these sources illustrates both his method and his originality. His patristic studies serve his goal of promoting tomorrow's theology. The understanding of the faith delivered to the Fathers lies as the core of the church's mission. It cannot escape the difficulties inherent in the process of tradition.

1. *Word and Redemption*, p. 21.

Important movements in the church have been marked by a return to the sources. Concern with the church of the early centuries led the Tractarians, and Cardinal John Henry Newman in particular, to a study of the writings of the Fathers. Seventeenth-century theologians had drunk deeply at the well of patristic theology; the followers of the Oxford movement did the same. The theological vision of that movement was in large measure a rediscovery and reinterpretation of patristics. Newman wrote in the *Apologia* that the "broad philosophy of Clement and Origen carried him away." Balthasar's writings demonstrate this same concern.

## Preliminary Concepts

Just as preceding chapters concentrated on a few concepts of central importance for Balthasar's philosophy, so here a similar selection of concepts important in Balthasar's reading of patristic sources is presented.

### *Theologia*

By *theologia* the Greeks understood not a subject of academic study but a way of speaking about the divine associated more with the poet than the philosopher. For Plato *theologia* was akin to *mythologia*, narratives about the gods. Aristotle in turn ordered the three kinds of "theoretic" philosophy into *mathematike*, *physike*, and *theologike*.[2] In this order "theology" was that branch of "theoretic" philosophy concerned with the divine. The Greek Fathers in general and the Alexandrians in particular considered this "theoretic" study Christian *gnosis*.

Today the word "gnosticism" is often used loosely to express any attempt to think abstractly about faith. Balthasar's inter-

2. See Plato, *Republic*, 378e–379e; Aristotle, *Metaphysics*, 1.1026a.

pretation of gnosticism must be distinguished from a contemporary usage that facilely equates it with a simple attempt to raise consciousness—as some feminist ideologues would argue. The issue is of importance because the late Karl Rahner accused Balthasar of gnosticism.[3] For the Alexandrians, "gnosticism" was *theologia*, a collection of speculations about nonempirical matters together with "inside information" about how the soul, fallen and imprisoned in matter, could obtain a privileged return ticket to the supramundane world. Clement of Alexandria, whose thinking resembled that of the Stoics, speaks of genuine Christian "gnosis" as insight coming from moral self-discipline and freedom from the passions. So the Christian, the true "gnostic," obtained union with the divine rather than some esoteric knowledge. This union reflects an influence from the theory of mimetic desire elaborated earlier in the chapters on the classical tradition.

Balthasar observes that both Clement and Origen view the complete Christian as a "gnostic" who truly understands his faith in the evangelical sense. Such understanding is not reserved for the intellectually gifted but simply accords with the objective act of faith. The opposition between "believer" and "knower" highlights the difference between the Christian who bases belief on authority and the Christian who strives to appropriate the content of faith and so sees the essentials of the faith.[4] This is a fundamental point in Balthasar's theological aesthetics. It is a continuation of the teaching on mimetic desire and appropriation considered earlier, and its larger implications will be discussed later.

Alexandrian "gnosis" within *theologia* can be misunderstood in two ways. It is seen in a Hegelian light as elevation

3. This issue is discussed in the Epilogue.
4. *Glory of the Lord*, 1:137.

to the idea of the absolute, or it is seen as "rational exposition of the faith." The Alexandrian Fathers neither intended nor used the term in either sense. They included a different term, *theoria*.

## *Theoria*

More important than the concept of *gnosis* for an understanding of Balthasar's patrology is his appropriation of and appreciation for the concept of *theoria*.[5]

In the Greek mystery religions such as those of Eleusis, the initiate would be brought to an inner state of ecstasy and his attention focused on something literally *seen*, a ritual performance to which only the initiated were admitted. The root of the Greek verb *theorein*, "to see," brings this direct visual sense to the forefront. Possibly for the Pythagoreans and certainly for Plato, *seeing* became identified with the internal and intellectual act of vision—a metaphor we still use to indicate the immediate grasp of an intellectual point: "Oh, I see!" The concept *theoria* still maintains its connotation of the ecstatic revelation of a spectacle, connected with a more abstract idea. We saw earlier that for Plato the appreciation of an *idea* becomes the appreciation of the "seen abstract form."

It is significant in this context that a comparison of poetry with painting was attributed to Simonides, for it has something in common with stories about the invention of memory. According to Cicero, this latter discovery rested on Simonides' discovery of the superiority of the sense of sight over the remaining senses. The equating of poetry and painting assumes the superiority of the visual sense. Both poet and painter think

5. *Theoria* is a richer term than the English derivative, "theory." It connotes the action of "seeing" as well as what is "seen" intellectually. See Dorothy Emmet, "*Theoria* and the Way of Life," *Journal of Theological Studies*, n.s., 12 (April 1966): 38–52.

in visual images which the former expresses in poetry and the latter in painting.

Unlike Aristotle, Plato believed that there is a knowledge not derived from the senses. Plato held that there are latent in memory the forms or "ideas" of the realities the soul knew before its descent into the world. True knowledge consists in fitting the impressions of the senses to the form of the higher reality of which the things in the world are reflections. The *Phaedo* develops the argument that all sensible objects can be referred to certain types of which they are likenesses. Man has not seen or learned the types but saw them previous to this life, so that this knowledge is innate in the memory. So true knowledge consists in fitting the imprints from sense impressions on to the basic form or idea to which the object of sense corresponds.

Socrates seems to have combined in *theoria* charismatic moral quality with a capacity for endurance in contemplation, which was compatible with a conviction for calling into question every possible opinion including his own. The practice of such an ascetic life was considered both moral and intellectual discipline. In the *Phaedo* Plato expresses this way of life in the extreme form of "practice of dying." In the *Republic* it is said to involve a "conversion," a "turning round of the soul." In the *Thaeatetus* it is a turning away from the world to enter upon an "imitation of the god" as far as possible.

The Fathers inherited this tradition and were confronted with the issue of "imitation of God." They assumed that the way of life meant by *theoria* was one of perfecting the powers of contemplative insight—and this was the way of metaphysical eros. Gregory of Nyssa, for example, followed the Greek notion of the contemplative life as an asceticism of virtue in pursuit of perfection—an integral wholeness, a humanness, and not just moral impeccability—which issues in *theoria*. Gregory united Platonic thought with the Pauline image of the

Christian athlete. "Seeing God" meant for Gregory actual participation in the divine life. Along with Origen, Gregory of Nyssa became one of the most significant Greek Fathers in shaping Balthasar's thought. Balthasar's stress on both the immanence and the transcendence of participation may be traced to this source.

## The Beautiful

Balthasar firmly believed that the religious thought of Plato had cast a shadow over the spirituality of all succeeding centuries. Plato hungered after the absolute. He wanted to attain a "beauty" that was not beautiful under one aspect, nor beautiful only at a given moment, but remained always and absolutely beautiful. Since this "beauty" was one among many names for supreme reality, what Plato sought to attain was the divine. After Plato many of those who felt the same hunger followed in his footsteps.[6]

Balthasar's theological aesthetics begins with "beauty," an insight that is the heart of the classical world, its myths, philosophy, art, and literature. That which appears in the beauty of natural and created forms is the glory of being, *der Glanz des Seins*. It speaks of the mystery of that which transcends and yet inheres in all existents. Consequently, aesthetics is not just one department of knowledge, which in relative independence of others constitutes a relatively autonomous discipline. When one sees the beauty of a person, a work of art, or a sunset, one is confronted at the same time with the mystery of its otherness. This sense of the wonder of beauty, Balthasar believes, is at the root of all serious metaphysical endeavor.

6. For development of this process, see André Jean Festugière, O.P., *Personal Religion among the Greeks* (Berkeley and Los Angeles: University of California Press, 1960).

Werner Jaeger argued that the idea of God as the principle of nature first appeared in Greece with the pre-Socratics.[7] The idea of God as guarantor of justice and cause of all events of human life is much older. I noted in Chapter 3 that Balthasar stresses that this idea is found in Hesiod and is portrayed magnificently in Pindar (for example, "Isthmian V") and with incomparable power in Aeschylos.

Patristic writers did not hesitate to address the *beautiful* as a theological category. Whereas the later Scholastics used "transcendental beauty" as a basis for their approach to a theology of creation, deriving the beauty of this world from its creator, the Fathers saw beauty as a pure transcendental and in the light of its radiance built their theological systems. Because this is precisely what Balthasar has done, he may be said to be a direct descendant of the Fathers.

## Overall Influence of Patristics

Before singling out Origen as a particular example of patristic influence, a summary picture of the overall impact of patristic thought on Balthasar's theological aesthetics may be helpful.

The Christians of the later Roman period felt a documented need to relate to the religious culture of the time.[8] In their thinking about the incarnate Logos, men began to use the terms *sophia* or *gnosis*. Following the Logos was interpreted as overcoming the passions in good Stoic tradition. Philo had already fashioned a synthesis between the Greek "imitation of

7. Werner Jaeger, *The Theology of the Early Greek Philosophers* (Oxford: Oxford University Press, 1947).

8. See, for example, Wayne A. Meeks, *The First Urban Christians* (New Haven: Yale University Press, 1983).

God" and the biblical "walking the way of God." The Greek Fathers studied Philo.

Balthasar notes that it is difficult if not impossible to say where in the patristic theology of the Alexandrians and Cappadocians Platonic and Stoic elements are used for the sake of expression and where Christian thought is made to serve contemporary theory. The same thinker can exhibit both trends at the same time. Beneath the often far-reaching appropriation of Platonic and Stoic elements lies a genuine theology.

In addition to such attempts to relate Christian thought to prevailing philosophies, there is in the history of Western culture a long line of "systems" stretching without a break from Heraclitus to Kierkegaard and Hegel, the obscurity of which is not wholly accidental. Such systems do not attempt to unfold a simple exposition for the profane but to explain mystery as it reveals itself, to explain *how it appears*. Several Greek Fathers must be placed in the midst of this tradition: Gregory of Nyssa, Gregory Nazianzen, Dionysus, and particularly Clement and Origen of Alexandria. The place that the "God who speaks" held in their thinking is very different from God's place in contemporary thought. For these Fathers, the Word which was heard and the Logos which was understood were what mattered. Balthasar says they view this as the mystery symbolized in John the Baptist and repeated throughout church history. A temporal sign always precedes the eternally given.

Balthasar notes that a great number of theses found in patristic theology require contemporary development. Many of the ideas initiated by the Fathers eventually were adopted and then considered unsuitable for a later time. After the Middle Ages the Fathers were so thoroughly excluded that today only a few scholars have any understanding of the extent of patristic theology.

## Origen

Origen remains the most outstanding teacher known in the Eastern church. Balthasar began his major work with the statement, "It is all but impossible to overestimate Origen and his importance for the history of Christian thought. To rank him beside Augustine and Thomas simply accords him his rightful place in this history."[9] He was a contemporary and possible classmate of Plotinus. For two centuries he was a controversial figure who eventually was condemned as a heretic. This condemnation shattered his influence. Only a small part of his massive scholarly production survives in the original and somewhat more in the Latin translation of Rufinus. Unfortunately, Rufinus often softened the effect of some of Origen's teachings.[10] Origen studied under Ammonios Sakkas, the porter turned philosopher, whose school produced two of the greatest thinkers of late Greek antiquity: Origen the Christian and Plotinus the exponent of Neoplatonism.

For Origen (and for the theological aesthetics of Hans Urs von Balthasar) the study of theology begins with an extended review of all accessible philosophers and poets. Their opinions about the divine are described, compared, and examined for their continuity of truth. The intermingling of philosophy and Scripture gives rise to the system of Origen's *Peri Archôn*. His title was probably intentionally ambiguous, since it can be translated either as "On Basic Principles" or "On Primoridal Matters." Origen accomplished first the task which all later systematic theologians set for themselves: to present a Christian view of the world in harmony with the educated thought

9. *Origen: Spirit and Fire*, p. 1.

10. For example, *De Princ.* 1.3, 5; and cf. Jerome's more faithful version in the *Letter to Avitus*, *Ep.* 124.2.

of the age. Origen's attempt is impressively complete. The sources of his system lay in the traditional ideas of his time: God, the Logos, providence, freedom. The eternal drama of the world displays the consequences of the interaction of these ideas.

Origen immersed himself in the thought of Plato, the Neoplatonists, and the Pythagoreans. These studies were important because they gave him a sound knowledge of the methods and the boundaries of thought and feeling which passed for learning at the start of the third century.

As early as Plutarch we find traces of this learning with its Platonic tinges. Key notions are the separation and distance between God and the world, the existence of intermediate beings, detailed discussion of the problem of divine providence and justice, the assertion of immortality and personal responsibility of the soul, and the doctrine of man's participation in the divine.

Because Balthasar prefers to see Origen as synthesizer rather than as systematizer, Balthasar must disengage from Origen's synthesis its truly formal structure. Balthasar insists that his own study is historical rather than merely dogmatic.

Origen, Balthasar notes, assumed extreme standpoints in the fashion of Secrétans or Sartre.[11] The creature is identical with (limited-choice) freedom, and so all souls in the state of preexistence are essentially alike and receive their proper nature on the basis of their decisions. Origen argues forcefully for the inseparability of reason and freedom.[12]

If the relation word equals Logos is central in Origen's thought, Balthasar observes that Christian Bigg must be given credit for calling Origen's "sacramental mystery of nature" the

11. *Theodramatik*, 2:197.
12. *De Princ.* 3.1.1–3; cf. *Contra Celsum*, 4.3.

"all embracing law" of his system.[13] Balthasar attempts to unfold this sacramental view of reality. He stresses that we must grant the word *mysterion (sacramentum)* the lack of specific meaning it had at the end of the third century in various Alexandrian formulations, whether in gnosticism, Philo, or Neoplatonism.

Before he takes up an analysis of the "science of *mysterion*," Balthasar concentrates on its formal character. Origen considered initiation into theology to be analogous to obtaining privileges that enabled one to penetrate the meaning of Scripture and so become capable of carrying divine secrets without spiritual harm. In this sense Origen is a "gnostic." Origen's God, however, is described as light and fire: fire to cleanse and purify and light without shadow in the beauty of glory.

Balthasar asks: "How should we interpret Origen? It will not do to go in the intellectual direction, since the distinguishing qualities of the spiritual senses imply a great deal more than mere paraphrases for the act of spiritual cognition. Nor can we go in the mystical direction, as Karl Rahner wants . . . because then the opposition between the specifically mystical mode of experience and that of ordinary living faith would have to be explained in a totally different manner."[14]

Behind a possible esoteric danger lies a rich Platonic heritage, the fruit of Origen's studies. The Spirit breathes where he will: "Behold at the confluence of Christianity and Platonism axioms which by participating in traditional gifts could elaborate a new gnoseology. The theory of ideas, a dangerous temptation for impersonal noeticism, still shares in the priceless assistance of these initial intuitions. It assures directly the fundamental analogous character of the concept of truth, ordered

13. *Parole et mystère chez Origène*, p. 12.
14. *Glory of the Lord*, 1:369–70.

hierarchically according to the degrees of being."[15] Balthasar's analysis includes the following steps: (1) If the "truth" of an existent is its idea, and if the league of ideas is spirit, then man "climbs" the ladder of being in the way that the "truth" moves from a condition of being relative (matter) to a state of being absolute (spirit).

(2) The fact that the Spirit is the "locus of ideas" provides Origen with a double advantage. The Spirit has, on one hand, an intrinsic relation (that of his own truth) and participation in spiritual being, and, on the other, will be "true" to the degree of its actuation. Origen's favorite symbol involves the movement of transcendence in the individual being like a jet of water reaching the clouds, a bounding upward toward eternal life. In viewing man as one who strives "upward," Origen does not break with the tradition that begins with Irenaeus and stretches to Gregory of Nyssa. Origen emphasized the relation found in the church between the "simple" (those still striving) and the "knowers" (the perfect). Those who "know" are those who have the mind of the church. They have allowed their own consciousness to merge with that of the church and thus represent in themselves the very essence of the bride.[16]

God, the ultimate unity and original source of all existence, is incomprehensible and inconceivable to unaided human reason. Apart from recognizing God's omnipotence, the human being can only make negative or indirect pronouncements about the divine. For Origen the prime predicate is incorporeality, an assertion that contradicted not only Stoic views but also the popular conception of the laity. Origen changed the positive insight that God was the ultimate cause of everything into the striking view of the absolute goodness of God, who created because he wished to manifest goodness and love.

15. Ibid.
16. *Church and World*, p. 145.

Origen taught that the concept of time could not be predicated of the divinity and that in addition to the horizontal division of phenomena in a temporal sequence there was a vertical division that takes account of a series of causes and effects independent of the concept of time.[17] Hence the Son was eternally begotten by the Father just as radiance is always produced by light. Only to the extent that we know the Son do we know the Father.

Three groups of symbols explain the mystery of ontological compenetration of creature and creator. The first is that of the senses in their active potency to receive light, sound, smell, and taste; second, the image of "nourishment"; third, images built around "marriage." Regarding the last group, Origen sees every element of nature ordered toward its "idea" as a bride is ordered to her bridegroom. The movement of any existent toward its ideal is the progress of the truth-in-act. The Christian necessarily progresses through interpersonal contacts and relationships.[18] Man can choose an idol or an ideal. This is his only option. This choice is the core of Origen's esotericism. Balthasar claims that if Origen's God is not total "darkness," Origen still sees the essential incomprehensibility of the divine. According to Origen, the five senses are the consequence of the fall and scattering into the realm of matter of an original and abundant capacity to perceive God and divine things. These divine things can never be reduced to a mystical unity without modes, but, rather, they possess a fullness and a glory that transcend the distant reflection and likeness (C. *Celsum* 4.74). We shall see that Balthasar resurrects many of these symbols for his theological aesthetics.

Balthasar first illuminates Origen's metaphysics and then demonstrates synthetically the structure of *mysterion*. Then he

17. See Origen, *De Princ.* 1.2.2.14.
18. See *Parole et mystère*, p. 29.

establishes the identity of this theoretical structure with the structure of the sacraments and shows their relationship to be that of the "total sacrament" to the individual sacraments.

For Origen the three sensible manifestations of the Logos (Incarnation, church, Scripture) are inadequately distinct. Christ lives in three substantial modes: individual body, the body of the church, and the body of the faithful. These manifestations intermingle in Origen's thinking—and not without reason. The manifestation of the Logos in Scripture has an affinity with the manifestation of Logos in the individual. The reason lies in the historicity of the drama of the redemption. For Origen the historical life of Jesus contained in Scripture is symbolic, ordered to an ontological and exemplary preparation of the church. The individual's life, a spiritual combat directed by the psychic sense of Scripture, becomes more and more spiritual, for the spiritual life of Christ and of the individual is lived only in the church, the complete Christ.

Scripture has a very special role. It includes both a vertical and a horizontal dynamism. Participating vertically in literal, psychic, and pneumatic levels, Scripture conducts man's ascent to God. it acts as instrument of elevation. Scripture is the word offered historically, which itself makes history. In this sense it moves from a horizontal, literal stage (that of the Old Testament) to the symbolic stage of the New Testament. The third and final stage is the eternal gospel. This notion became a skeleton of Balthasar's theology of history: "Scripture is the Logos objectified and made the norm for all ages by the Holy Spirit in the context of the Incarnation. According to Origen it is the body of the divine Son *in so far as* he is the Logos, the truth-word."[19]

If Scripture is history in act, it is necessary to read it "histori-

19. A *Theology of History*, p. 100.

cally." Thus to possess the New Testament, one must possess the Old Testament and recapitulate the history of salvation. In effect, the sanctity of God is revealed *ex fide in fidem*—from the faith of the people of the Old Covenant to the faith of the people of the New.[20]

Scripture makes the incarnate Logos present in the same way that the Eucharist makes present the historical body. So Origen admonishes the Christian to approach the word in Scripture with the same reverence with which he approaches the body of the Lord in the Eucharist. Balthasar criticizes Origen for equating the application of philosophy to Scripture with handing over the Word to torture. An implied identification of scriptural word with the Word can lead to absurd confusions if carried too far.[21] Balthasar does say, however, that the "immeasurable fruitfulness" of the allegorical "method can be unfolded only when the Bible is understood in its immediate relationship with the incarnation and the same laws of understanding are applied to both."[22]

The scriptural word is not so much itself a sacrament as an aspect of the total higher reality that underlies each particular sacrament and is called *mysterion*. Once it is understood that *mystery* is the basis of the primal sacrament, it will be easier to understand how the particular sacraments came to be.

According to Origen, the source of all salvation is the humanity of the Redeemer. The hypostatic union is the exemplary cause of all grace-bearing union with God. If he had not become man, we would never have "known" God. In the Incarnation God becomes "tangible." The pagan cult of heroes shares in the idea that the flesh can become a temple of the

20. Ibid., pp. 74–75.
21. See *Word and Redemption*, p. 61.
22. *Origen: Spirit and Fire*, p. 11.

divine.[23] In virtue of his body, God wants to save man by "touching him" and in that moment of contact impart grace. It is the way of Jesus, who wished to heal by touching the sick.

The double relation of participation in the world (noted in the Incarnation—a transcendence without admixture and an immanence up to a blurring of the frontiers) guarantees the sacramental character of the *mystery* that is the church, for Christ mediates between God and the world. In this connection Balthasar notes that Adolf von Harnack once thought he could find no trace in Origen of a synthesis between Christ's sacrifice and the liturgical celebration of the mass. In an astonishingly rich display of texts, Balthasar demonstrates that Origen did indeed see such a relation. Therefore Tertullian and Cyprian were not its inventors as Harnack maintained: "Not only was Origen the first to place the idea of a prolonged sacrifice of Christ in full light as the center of a theology of the mass, but he also enunciated the relation between this sacrifice and the liturgy."[24] Balthasar does ask whether the mystery of the cross finds a real place in Origen's system: "Is his wholehearted idea of the following of Christ perhaps a too ascetical business, a necessary training for perfect gnosis? And is this not also the case in the struggle against devils on behalf of Christians taught by the *Didascalia*?"[25]

Throughout the ages, the theology of the church has been a spiritual exploration of the letter and so a reflection of the glorified Christ, the beginning of the transfiguration of the world. The domain of the Word, even in the humble sign of the letter, is a sacramental reality that precedes any particular sacrament. Its materiality is immediately the efficacious sym-

23. *Parole et mystère*, p. 80.
24. Ibid., pp. 91–92.
25. See *Church and World*, p. 97.

bol of the essence of the Word among us. Balthasar compares Origen and Augustine schematically:

| ORIGEN | AUGUSTINE |
| --- | --- |
| Logos | Christ-Church |
| Christ-Word-Sacrament | |
| Sacraments | Word-Sacraments |

Augustine's scheme became traditional, but Balthasar seems to favor Origen's. The parallelism between Word and sacrament rests on a theory of signs as visible words and of words as spiritual signs.

Balthasar convincingly argues that much of what is considered *avant garde* in modern sacramental theology had been developed by the Alexandrians. Origen, for example, had a theology of the Eucharist that displays the humanity of Christ as the primoridal sacrament within which we find the dynamic relations among the elements of the mystery. In Origen's Platonic interpretation, presence and spiritual manducation become equivalent to a real presence and a real manducation. This unique category contains diverse elements, one of which is the real presence and the other the sacramental manducation. The sacramental "mode" is symbolic in relation to other types of presence and manducation but is essentially truer (more spiritual), signifying the material symbol, bread and wine. This could exist by virtue of a metaphysics of matter which defines its essence in terms of a relation to its meaning (the spiritual) as, for example, a flag is composed of bits of colored cloth and yet its reality is something more than just the different bits of red, white, and blue cloth. A further consideration is that the identification of Christ and Verbum in no way prevents distinguishing the natures: Verbum and God-man. Matter remains matter but receives something divine.[26] In the Eucharist, bread remains bread but is still somehow divine. Among its qualities we note an exemption from any spatial relation, participating fully in the "ubiquity" of the Logos.

This idea corresponds with other Alexandrian notions. A human being by definition is one to whom God has spoken and who is so constructed as to be able to hear and respond. Alexandrian theology, which derives the rational character of creation from the presence of the Logos, agrees with such modern philosophers as Wilhelm Dilthey, Martin Heidegger, and Wilhelm Kamlah.[27]

Balthasar compares Origen and Hegel. The concept of elevation appears as the central nerve of both their systems. The key to Hegel's dialectic is the recognition of his term *Aufheben*, which, as he says, "is one of the most important concepts of philosophy. *Aufheben* has a double meaning in language, inasmuch as it signifies to preserve or *retain* and at the same time to leave off or *put an end*. . . . Thus the *Aufgehobene* is at the same time a preservation which only lost its immediacy but was not thereby annihilated."[28] Both Origen and Hegel view a restitution of the world in God, of the material in the spiritual, of symbol in truth. But Origen gives the movement toward restitution a mythical expression; Hegel gives it a wholly intellectual construction.[29]

26. *Parole et mystère*, p. 106.

27. Dilthey, Heidegger, and Kamlah all see a significance in the derivation of *Vernunft* (reason) from *vernehmen* (to perceive). Buber and Ebner could also be named here because they find the essence of creation in its capacity for the word. See *Word and Revelation*, p. 26.

28. Hegel, *Wissenschaft der Logik* 1:113–14.

29. The ultimate significance of this comparison awaits Balthasar's completion of the third part of the triology, the *Theologik*. See also *Herrlichkeit*, vol. 3, pt. 2, pp. 909ff.

Hans Urs von Balthasar claims that we are indebted to Origen and Karl Barth for the two most coherent outlines of a theology of the Word, not the *Logos nudus*, but *incarnandus* and *incarnatus*. The Logos upholds creation, is its justification, and shows itself in historical revelation as the ultimate meaning of creation. It is to misunderstand Origen to subordinate the Incarnation to a universal, neutral presence in every created reason, as though Origen modeled his Logos on Plato's Demiurge. Balthasar concedes that Origen has no understanding of reason apart from its serving as an organ for hearing the word: "In the midst of you there stands one whom you know not" in the sense of the presence (*parousia*) of the Logos in the midst of every man's reason. Yet his attitude to heresy and non-Christian philosophy makes it clear that Origen did not wish to subordinate the historical revelation of the Word to a neutral presence. For Origen the center of world history is the process of redemption, to which he devotes unremittingly all his energies: "Individuals encounter the Word as person and spirit: It is this characteristic which imparts to the whole of Origen's theology a dynamism enabling it to penetrate through every external cover, every rite, institution, and external historical circumstance to the spiritual truth, so that he almost comes to view the envelope of the 'flesh' as purely phenomenal in 'letter,' 'sacrament,' and 'institution.'"[30]

Balthasar says we cannot solve the question of Origen's fine balance between judgment and grace by the shibboleth of *apokatastasis*, a term rightly applied to pantheist systems of later disciples such as Evagrius and Bar Suadili. They forced the Hellenic principle of decline and restoration to prevail, even in the history of salvation. For Origen, who was scrupulous about the exact interpretation of words in Scripture, the term

30. *Word and Redemption*, p. 136.

had a more restricted meaning. Balthasar revives this meaning in his Theodramatics.

Certain of Origen's positions became the source of Balthasar's own views, for example, the theology of history. The next section of this chapter will examine Origen as this wellspring for the theological aesthetics of Hans Urs von Balthasar. He remarked, "Origen remains for me the most congenial, the most spacious interpreter and devotee of the Word of God. I am nowhere so comfortable as in his presence."[31] It was Origen's continual concern for the Word that made Balthasar feel at home in Origen's works.[32] Even in its formal aspects, Origen's thinking focused on the Word, the "flash" and reflection of the veiled beauty of the Father. In the anonymity of this Word Origen's voice is included: "In this sense there has been talk of the pronounced *theologia gloriae* of the Greeks in general and of Origen in particular."[33] The discovery of the agreement in content and form, style and object in Origen's work meant for Balthasar that he had found the true core of Origen's thought.

## Origen's Importance for Theology of History

Balthasar claimed that it was scarcely possible to overvalue the importance of Origen for the history of Christian thought. Harnack had argued that it was through the work of Origen that the decisive hellenization of Christianity occurred. Balthasar does not reject this thesis outright; instead, he divides the inheritance from Origen into three parts. The first covers Origen's heterodox views, especially subordinationism in the doctrine on the Trinity, the separation of the roles of the divine

31. *Origenes Geist und Feuer*, p. 81.
32. For example, *Theologik*, 2:141, 167, 243.
33. *Origen: Spirit and Fire*, p. 8.

Persons, the teaching on the Incarnation of the Logos in every stage of being, the mystical interpretation of original sin, and the teaching on the ascent of the soul. In all these doctrines Origen was strongly under the influence of Plato, so that each of these doctrines became an explicit development of Platonic philosophy of identity. Balthasar summarizes, however: "Only in penultimate things is Origen 'heterodox.' In ultimate things he is catholic."[34]

The second collection encompasses a formal attitude rather than any particular material content of Origen's thought. The attitude is separable from the content: "An ultimate chasm, often scarcely palpable, separates here content and expression."[35] This attitude is what marks Origen's system a "theologia ascendens."

The third collection, which, like the first, did not become part of tradition, is the element of love of the Word. Origen's most valuable insights may be read in the light of this love. Of these Balthasar again selects three. First is the insight into the essence of Scripture as the great sacrament of the real presence of the divine Word in the world: "The church is for him the great total sacrament which continues the 'sacrament' of the Body of Christ, preserves in itself the 'sacrament' of the scriptural word, and activates the sacraments . . . as its distinctive marks and functions."[36] The second is the teaching on the spiritual communion of the Word, and the third is the meditation on the passion of the Word. So Balthasar sees mysticism of the Word as the basis of Origen's thought. This threefold division of Origen's work allowed Balthasar to make a different judgment from that of Harnack: "The religious world view of

34. Ibid., p. 20.
35. "Patristik, Scholastik und wir," p. 86.
36. *Origen: Spirit and Fire,* pp. 20, 21.

Harnack lacks the concept of a WORD living on and continuing to give witness in the church as its Body. This explains why he falsely formulated what he rightly sensed."[37]

Balthasar does argue that through Origen's influence elements crept into theology which are not truly biblical in the form they assumed. Balthasar here refers to the danger of "spiritualism." To the extent that the stress falls on "theologia ascendens," there is improper Hellenic influence on the history of theology. This means that Greek philosophy was leading the development of doctrine rather than Scripture.

The sacramental theology of the Logos, however, is Origen's great contribution. Tradition neglected this gift. Balthasar has tried to restore it and implicitly to restore Origen to his proper place.

## Origen's Theology of the Logos

Balthasar interpreted Origen's teaching on the Logos symbolically. The sacramental character of the presence of the Logos is the object of chapter II of *Parole et mystère chez Origène*. According to Origen, men live removed from spirit and dedicated to the corporal and material, from which derives their sinfulness and consequent need of salvation. In the Incarnation the divine Logos assumed this situation in order to return man to the original state of unity with the spiritual. The Incarnation of the Logos produced a symbolic presence in the world, first, as a limited human; second, as the Church; and third, as the sacred Scriptures.

Insofar as every creature is an expression of the Logos of God, it exists in a symbolic relation with the creator. In the Logos this relation is the product of the Incarnation. Since in general the body of every created rational being is its expres-

37. Ibid., p. 6.

sion, Christ assumes this form also: "The Word become flesh is therefore its own unique symbol: as creature symbol of its divinity; as bodily nature, symbol of its spiritual being."[38]

In Christ a divine Person became man. The infinitude of the divine obtains therein its precise expression in that the body of Christ surpasses the limits of a finite human body and extends to the limits of spiritual creation. The symbol of this mystical body of Christ is the visible church.

To the extent that the eternal Logos in its difference from Father and Holy Spirit became incarnate, a third mode of presence resulted: the Logos is present in the world as sacred Scripture, within which the body-spirit image is repeated: the Scripture is the presence of the Logos in the companionship of letter and spirit.

Jesus Christ the individual man, sacred Scripture, and the church are symbols of the one present Logos. The three modes of being present belong together in this total reality Balthasar names "mysterium."[39] Balthasar proceeds to derive the individual sacraments from the primal sacrament: "One could say that the place which the treatise 'de sacramentis in genere' assumes in modern theology was taken in Platonic theology by the treatise 'de sacramento generico (concreto)'. . . . The idea of participation (in opposition to a specification of an abstract generic idea) demonstrates that the possible and the real expressions in no way exhaust the actual genre or class."[40]

I noted earlier that Balthasar compares Origen with Hegel. He notes that when casting a critical glance over this theological synthesis, one is tempted to compare it to that of Hegel. The idea of *Aufhebung* appears to be the nerve of both systems. Both authors are unclear on this point: the elevation of

38. *Parole et mystère*, p. 36.
39. Ibid., p. 51.
40. Ibid., p. 99.

the world into the divine, of material into spiritual, of symbol into reality, is the reconstitution of the original condition. "Origen gives to this circular movement an entirely mystical and imagelike expression: Hegel, a completely intellectual reformation. But the basic idea is the same."[41] The tearing away of the soul from union with spirit, sin, appears in Origen simply as one moment within the enclosed circle of eternity. The equality of beginning and end leads to an endless movement of the eons. As long as the end is not richer than the abstract oneness of the beginning, completion must be sought in the infinite number of movements of creation. Their origin is the choice of evil.

Balthasar argues that Gregory of Nyssa was the first to succeed in thinking of motion and rest together in the triune God. Origen, who preceded Gregory, approaches Gregory's synthesis, but he does not reach it. To this extent Origen remains close to an idealist view of the world: "In him as in Hegel something of the Greek *daimon* continues to live, for whom opposition and its beauty have an absolute meaning, for whom consequently world and God remain in a secret but tragic opposition."[42]

Every intellectual idealism has yielded to this *daimon*, the incapacity of man to overcome this opposition and change it into a positive value. There is in Origen something of this idealistic world view, but he continually manages to overcome its most disastrous consequences. Balthasar's interpretation of Origen is therefore controlled by the question whether and in what way Origen is a thinker of the analogy of being.

Löser noted that Origen more than any other Father of the Church affected Balthasar's philosophical and theological

41. Ibid., p. 113.
42. Ibid., p. 114.

thought, especially the theology of the Logos in all forms. Balthasar, nevertheless, was not blind to Origen's faults and explicitly pointed them out along with their attendant dangers. Just how deeply indebted Balthasar is to Origen and other patristic sources will become clear in the next few chapters.

## Chapter 6

# Gregory, Evagrius, Basil, and Augustine

BALTHASAR'S GUIDING idea of "concrete universality," of "received fullness which is given to others," assumed historical, bodily form from his reading of the Fathers. In the previous chapter we reviewed the influence of Origen. This chapter focuses on some other major patristic authors who influenced the theological aesthetics of Hans Urs von Balthasar. The second volume of the *Theologik* particularly reflects this influence. In his words, the choice, apart from intrinsic excellence, is based upon their historical significance: "In the main we have chosen official theologians, so long as such were available, who were able to treat the radiant power of the revelation of Christ both influentially and originally . . . but after Thomas Aquinas theologians of such stature are rare. Now it is primarily laity."[1]

## Gregory of Nyssa

Balthasar published a translation of Gregory of Nyssa's "Commentary on the Canticle of Canticles" in 1939 under the

1. *Glory of the Lord*, 2:15.

title, *Der versiegelte Quell*. He provided in his *Présence et pensée* an extensive introduction to the translation which can be considered a summary of his major study of the thought of Gregory. This book was published in 1942 but was essentially complete before 1939. With this study Balthasar provided a new impetus to research on Gregory of Nyssa.[2] What appealed to Balthasar was Gregory's balance of system and life, idea and existential drama. Balthasar faults scholars who consider Gregory unoriginal.[3] True, the influence of Plato and the Stoa is unmistakable. Gregory tries to mediate between the positions of Irenaeus and Origen on original sin, and his mystical theology rests on both biblical teaching and that of Plato and Philo. Thus Gregory would be simply a disciple of these masters. Balthasar asks, however, what great intellect does not stand in such a line. Does not Thomas mediate between Aristotle and Augustine and Kant between Leibniz and Hume? Balthasar sums up the question of originality in Gregory of Nyssa by stating that Gregory's originality can only be seen dramatically. If his work is viewed statically it can appear to be merely a collection of contradictory propositions. In Gregory love of God is an "*erotikon pathos*." Balthasar observed that Gregory had already provided an answer to Rilke's "pathos of longing." This notion assumed a central position in Balthasar's *Theodramatik*.

Gregory, in competition with the Stoics and Plotinus, traveled the farthest in developing the notion of limited freedom. Gregory found numerous expressions for the "royal value"

2. Marguerite Harl, for example, wrote, "The year 1969 presented every indication to recall that two works had given an initial impulse to our studies in France; a quarter century earlier, that of H. U. von Balthasar, *Présence et pensée* ("Ecriture et culture philosophique dans la pensée de Grégoire de Nysse," *Actes du colloque de Chevetogne*, September 22–26, 1969 [Leiden: Brill, 1971], p. ix).

3. See *Der versiegelte Quell*, p. 7.

(*PG* 44.136C) of human freedom, the quality that makes man divine. This divine-human similarity, however, because it can give rise to evil, is limited. Gregory is more pessimistic than his predecessors.

Balthasar's general intention in his study of the Fathers was always to penetrate to that basic intuition which formed the expression of each one's thought. Balthasar finds in Gregory's work basic decisions that remain important today and are similar to Balthasar's own positions. Two prominent and fundamental issues are highlighted in *Présence et pensée:* the relation of nature and grace, which is seen in connection with the teaching on the analogy of being; and the teaching on the difference between essence and existence.

According to Balthasar, Gregory of Nyssa understood the relation between nature and grace differently than did the Scholastics. Gregory avoided the hypothesis of a *natura pura*. The actual world is from the very beginning supernaturally elevated. At the same time Gregory preserves the freedom of the order of grace.

This theme orders the structure of *Présence et pensée*. The book has three parts: Part I is the philosophy of becoming and of desire; Part II, the philosophy of the image; Part III, the philosophy of love. The first two parts contain the philosophy of the incomplete movement of man's ascent to God. Part III considers Gregory's theology of God's descent into the world. The point of departure in the two first parts is the God-seeking soul and in the third, the man-seeking God.

Balthasar considers Gregory's perception of the difference between essence and existence a great achievement. It was a consequence of Gregory's struggle with neoplatonism. The basic difference between the thought of Gregory and that of the Neoplatonists is that Gregory allows no mediating steps between God and creation. Neoplatonism, especially Plotinus, views the One as the origin and end of all being. Spirit proceeds from the One. Spirit expresses being. Spirit is the place of the ideas, object of knowledge. He is separate from the One. The soul accords with *nous*. Matter is entirely formless. As I observed in Chapter 4, there were mediating stages between Father and world. Gregory of Nyssa portrays the triune God in whom there is no trace of Eunomian subordination, as standing over against the world.[4]

Balthasar argues that the world of ideas shatters into three parts. What in Plato was formally divine recedes to superessential deity, but the absolute oneness of thought, will, and accomplishment in God forbids a distinction between thought and intentions of God and his action and being. What was spiritual in the world of ideas is attributed to the world of pure spirits, the angels of Christian theology. Gregory, however, places these spirits on the same level as human souls. Finally, that which was noetic, universality and necessity of concepts, is attributed to the soul insofar as the soul is an image of the infinite.[5] Gregory cannot accept a One which is beyond being. One and being are identified, but being as existence is opposed to essence. Existence is the actuality of all essence.

For Plotinus human knowledge is directed primarily to the ideas; the unknowable One remains beyond this object. For Gregory of Nyssa human knowledge is ordered to supreme being. Gregory makes no differentiation between God and the ideas. God is being and not something behind the idea of being. In the sixth homily of the "Commentary on the Canticle of Canticles," Gregory notes that the "bride" after finding the object of the search recognizes that "in not knowing what He is comprehends that He is."[6] Such comprehension in-

4. *Theodramatik*, vol. 2, pt. 1, p. 199.
5. *Der versiegelte Quell*, p. 10.
6. *Gregorii Nysseni Opera*, ed. Werner Jaeger, 4:183.

cludes a sense of presence. In the eleventh homily Gregory writes: "Now is the bride surrounded by the divine night in which the bridegroom approaches but does not appear. How then does something approach in the night which one does not see?" A certain perception of the presence (*aisthesis tis tes parousias*) is the answer.[7] This perception grows with each new attempt to comprehend the divine conceptually. Thought is ordered to being but attains it only in the act of judgment.

Löser notes that this aspect of Gregory's system explains why Balthasar called his study *Présence et pensée*. Balthasar wanted to highlight the manner in which Gregory avoided the potential danger in the Neoplatonism of his time.

A second purpose in Balthasar's study of Gregory of Nyssa was to make explicit what Balthasar saw as implicit in Gregory's work: a theory of mystical knowledge of God, which Balthasar saw as the meaning of the image of the "versiegelte Quell" (sealed well) (Cant. 4.12). The image of the eternally flowing well illumines the entire philosophy of becoming in Gregory. Its being "locked" is a figure for Gregory's symbol. In the philosophy of love, both elements coalesce into a higher synthesis in which the philosophy of becoming and the philosophy of the symbol do not disappear but remain elevated.

The philosophy of love, which reflects the synthesis of rest and motion, image and object, is grounded in a revolution of the motion. Balthasar summarizes: "It is no longer a question of how the soul attains the divine (and so of philosophy) but of how God has managed to approach the soul (and so of theology). The resolution for the mystical philosophy of Plotinus and the Stoa, for the philosophy of becoming and of the symbol only the incarnation of the Word accomplishes."[8]

7. *Der versiegelte Quell*, p. 84.
8. Ibid., p. 20.

## The Philosophy of Becoming

The basic ontological category of created being is that of *diastasis*. God, who is being, differs in that there is no distinction. In the area of created being *diastasis* means space and time. Gregory stressed temporality more than spatiality. Temporality means the horizontal process of "being on the way" from a starting point to an end. Balthasar claims that this aspect demonstrates that Gregory's concept of time does not spring directly from Greek philosophy of time and so differs from that of, say, Heidegger.

*Diastasis* characterizes not only material being but also created intellectual being. Limited intellectual being can be described only in paradoxical statements. It is in temporal motion but does not chase a temporal goal; it is limited and limitless at once. Material being depends on God as the source of its being; intellectual created being relates itself beyond this aspect to God as goal. In the movement of limited spirit toward God as its origin and goal the Neoplatonic notion of the ascent of spirit to the One is both reflected and transformed.

From the ontological analysis of created being Gregory develops a corresponding theory of gnosis. Balthasar explains this theory in two steps. First, he compares Gregory's teaching on knowledge of the world, man, and God with Stoic teaching. The Stoic ideal of knowledge is rationalistic. Man is capable of comprehending the object of knowledge. Gregory agrees that this is possible so far as material objects are concerned, but human knowledge of God is impossible. God is thus the object of a mystical knowledge.

In the second step Balthasar analyzes Gregory's understanding of this mystical knowledge of God. He asks what is the meaning of this "perception of presence"? The answer is that on this level, according to Gregory, the knowledge of God that is possible for limited spirit is identical with the limitless desire that transcends every fixed image and concept. The limitless longing that abandons every fixed image is the form of the *aisthesis tes parousias*, which is a consequence of the philosophy of becoming. Gregory's works are filled with images for this ascending knowledge of God. This is an especially "dark way," and so Gregory can rightly be said to be the first Christian theologian to speak of the "mystical night," the "shining darkness of God."[9] Balthasar found Gregory's attempts to elucidate the process of "seeing," "perceiving," impressive; and they are reflected in the theological aesthetics. He wrote: "The same feeling comes with Gregory of Nyssa's 'ineffable splendor' as a description of God, so awesome that it daunts any hope of grasping it entirely with the mind, let alone of putting it into words."[10]

## The Philosophy of Symbol

Gregory developed his philosophy of becoming from his analysis of created being. The philosophy of the symbol offers a way out: "If it remains true that the creature can never possess God, could one then not embark on another way and ask whether within the analogy itself God can *be* in a definite way."[11]

The Greek notion that the soul is somehow divine consists in participation in the divine. Spirit, intellect, and love of man are moments illustrating this participation. Being thus an "image" of the divine means being related and entails both a Stoic and a biblical motif. According to Gregory, man is a "mikrokosmos" in body but an image of God in soul. The relatedness

9. Ibid., p. 17.
10. A *Theological Anthropology*, p. 265.
11. *Présence et pensée*, p. 77.

of the image with the original, of man with God, is the ontological basis for the philosophy of the image.

The process of presentation, desire, and "perception of the presence" in the philosophy of becoming were psychological acts. In the philosophy of symbol they become real aspects of human nature. The *aisthesis tes parousias* now has the form of the "relation" of the human soul with the divine. In the philosophy of becoming the world as a whole or its parts were the content of the presentation. In the philosophy of image the soul itself is this content.

## The Philosophy of Love

The Incarnation of the Word of God means the opening of the closed world of man. Balthasar reviews Gregory's theology of the Incarnation thoroughly. The uniqueness of this theology lies in the manner in which Gregory explains the relation of the Incarnation to the world of man as a whole: "The solution for the philosophical mysticism of Plotinus and the Stoa, for the philosophy of becoming and the philosophy of symbol is provided by the Incarnation of the Word." Balthasar then notes that another basic teaching of Gregory's becomes essential, "the teaching on the ontological, yes, physical unity of human nature. According to Gregory the true bearer of the image of God is not the individual soul but the one, unique human nature of which individual men are only expressions and presentations. Christ, in becoming an individual man assumed this general human nature and at the same time made it divine."[12] All men stand in immediate communion with Christ and so are open to the stream of divine grace. The Incarnation is finally complete when the totality of human na-

12. *Der versiegelte Quell*, p. 20.

ture becomes open for the grace of the Incarnation, when out of the body "Adam" becomes the mystical body of Christ.

The space in which individual assimilation to Christ occurs is the church. The church as bride is the true subject of the following of the "bridegroom" Christ. Individual men are assimilated through baptism and Christian life and thereby become *anima ecclesiastica*. In this process occurs "knowledge of God through love." Balthasar says Gregory's teaching leads to the expression of the mystical knowledge of God as knowledge of God in the following of Christ in the church. This is what is ultimately meant by the image of "versiegelte Quell."

Balthasar interpreted the unity of the incarnate Logos with humankind in the sense of the so-called "physical doctrine of redemption." Balthasar claims that Gregory of Nyssa held that Christ in the Incarnation assumed an individual human nature and thereby entered into physical contact with human nature as a whole. Through this contact Christ transmitted grace, resurrection, and divinization. To be globally effective, the Incarnation presupposes the essential unity of humankind. The individual participates temporally and spatially in the one, universal, actual nature of man. God directly creates humanity and by doing so, and in a mediated manner, individual human beings. Humanity is the one actual human nature which is the image of God.

The entrance of the Logos into such a humankind has a "social content." The presence of Christ in humankind that through sin has lost the unity of being an image of God brings to this humanity redemption—restoration of its being an image of God. The Resurrection signifies the temporal point at which this redemption is accomplished. But Christ's saving work is completed at the end of time, when all men have become united with the body of Christ. Balthasar claims that it is against this theory that Gregory's theory of *apokatastasis* needs to be understood.[13]

Adolf von Harnack in the second volume of his *History of Dogma* (pp. 166–67) explained Gregory's doctrine on the unity of human nature as thoroughly Platonic. The universal idea "humanity" was what the Logos assumed. Gregory of Nyssa thus appears as the theologian who gave a philosophical foundation to the "physical doctrine of redemption" of Irenaeus, Athanasius, Hilary, and others. For the unity of human nature forms not only the basis of the universality of the body of Christ but also in this sense is the basis for the automatic, physical spread of original sin and salvation. This is the central concept of soteriology and the basis for the *apokatastasis*.

At the time Balthasar interpreted Gregory of Nyssa in this manner, few scholars had studied the matter. Careful study of the texts, however, has shown that Balthasar erred in his exegesis.[14] Nevertheless, Balthasar's contribution to the study of the works of Gregory of Nyssa will remain important in the sense that he along with de Lubac initiated the renewed effort to understand Gregory.

## Evagrius Ponticus

Although the work on Gregory represented by *Présence et pensée* may now seem a bit dated, Balthasar's contribution to work on Evagrius will remain significant because of its originality. Balthasar published two studies of Evagrius Ponticus.

13. *Présence et pensée*, pp. 109–10.

14. For example, Reinhard Hübner has corrected Balthasar on the "physical theory of redemption." For this correction and others by such recent scholars as Ernst Mühlenberg, see Werner Löser, *Im Geiste des Origenes* (Frankfurt: Knecht, 1976), pp. 112ff.

The first, *Metaphysik und Mystik des Evagrius Ponticus* (1939), offers a brief overview of Evagrius's thought; the second, *Die Hiera des Evagrius* (1939), is a critical edition which presents a reconstruction of two biblical commentaries: Evagrius's "Commentary on the Psalms and the Proverbs" and a collection of fragments from the Commentaries on Genesis, Numbers, Kings, Canticle of Canticles, Job, and the Gospel of Luke.

Balthasar's argument is that the *Hiera* which Palladius mentions in his list of writings of Evagrius (*Historia lausiaca* c. 86, *PG* 34.1194A) includes scriptural commentaries "to which no one has given any attention."[15] Balthasar thus made available a text of the Commentary on the Psalms and the Proverbs and demonstrated that a large number of texts that were attributed to Origen and others were actually the work of Evagrius.

Balthasar had argued on the basis of the doctrine contained in the texts. Twenty years after Balthasar published his edition, Marie-Josèphe Rondeau discovered in a tenth-century manuscript (Vaticanus graecus 754) the text of Evagrius's Commentary on the Psalms. This discovery confirmed the correctness of Balthasar's edition. Evagrius, according to Balthasar, followed the gnostic-symbolic direction of Origen.

> The clear, gnostic direction finds its purest expression in a form which again displays its greatest and most powerful development: in the desert monk and follower of Origen, Evagrius Ponticus. We have attempted to present . . . the inevitable logic of his thought that without concern for the visible hierarchical church and the community of the mystical body prescribes a radical abstraction from the senses and an idealism which nearly approaches Buddhism, of pure, absolute knowledge as the way of salvation: Origen the gnostic is reduced here to his formula.[16]

15. "Die Hiera des Evagrius," p. 87.
16. *Wendung nach Osten*, pp. 35, 36.

Evagrius follows "Origenism" completely. Balthasar claims that any position of Evagrius is a fanatical development of this aspect of Origen's thought. Evagrius turned the fluid system of the Alexandrian into an ultimate, mathematically sharp and precise system. Balthasar follows the direction Werner Bousset set in seeing Evagrius as an "Origenist."[17] Again Balthasar's interpretation of Evagrius as more "Origenist" than Origen has been upheld by the discovery of the original *Kephalaia gnostica* of Evagrius, which contain an unabridged treatment that smacks of Origen.[18]

The skeleton of Evagrius's system is as follows: God as original unity; creation of the kingdom of pure, bodiless spirits; fall of these spirits; fall as occasion for creation of the cosmos, which is not bad but in which every spirit receives a body according to the degree of the "fall"; asceticism to overcome the shell of the body; and return to unity in the *apokatastasis*.

A vast gulf separates God and creation as well as spirit and bodily world. God is without opposite and timeless. Creation is the place of opposites and time. Originally pure spirit existed and at the end will exist again. Now all created beings are spirit-body: angels, men, devils. Each differs from the other through the relation of spirit and body. The climb back, the way to bridge the gulf, is denial of the body. Balthasar argues that Evagrius in this system is more Buddhist than Christian.

17. Wilhelm Bousset, *Apophtegmata. Studien zur Geschichte des älteren Mönchtums* (Tübingen: Kerle, 1923), pp. 281–341.

18. André Guillaumont, *Les six centuries des Kephalaia gnostica d'Evagre le Pontique*, Edition critique de la version syriaque commune et édition d'une nouvelle version syriaque, intégrale avec une double traduction française (Paris: Gallimard, 1958). Guillaumont credited Balthasar on the correctness of his interpretation. See also Francis Refoulé, "Evagre, fut-il origéniste?" *Revue des Sciences philosophiques et théologiques* 47 (1963): 398–400.

Evagrius stands on the pre-Christian step of denial of the world. His theory involves pantheism and total idealism.

The recovery of the *Kephalaia gnostica* meant that certain strains in Balthasar's interpretation of Evagrius needed correction. Balthasar had available for his study few texts that bore on Christology. The *Kephalaia gnostica* contain a complete exposition of this aspect of Evagrius's thought which Balthasar had neglected. Balthasar also claimed that Evagrius did not teach that the bodily world was the result of a second act of creation but was only the situation of the fallen soul. Again the complete text shows that Evagrius did hold that the bodily world was the result of a second creation. In addition, Balthasar assumed that for Evagrius God and human spirit were identical in the act of mystical experience. The new texts display that Evagrius did think more analogically than Balthasar's interpretation allowed. Thus Balthasar's argument that Evagrius was more Buddhist than Christian requires modification.[19]

## Basil

After completing his studies in Constantinople and Athens, Basil was baptized in 356 and began a life of asceticism. Basil equated the decision to become a baptized Christian with the necessity to follow Christ existentially. This was possible in the fourth century because baptism might be delayed until old age and because the notion of a more perfect following of Christ in religious life as a monk or nun was not widespread. Christians lived in close community with their bishops.

Balthasar concerned himself with the *Regulae Morales* of

19. See Heinrich Bacht, "Pachomius und Evagrius," in *Koptische Kunst: Christentum am Nil* (Essen: Villa Hügel, 1963), pp. 142–57, and Löser, *Im Geiste des Origenes*, pp. 125ff.

Basil. The genius of Basil lay in his ability to use Platonic metaphysics and Stoic ethics to express the ascetical demands of the gospel.[20] Basil's leaning toward ethical integralism is particularly Stoic, for Basil denies a difference between mild and mortal sin. Basil's concern was for the church, which he saw as split and full of discord. The "rules" were to help restore unity and provide the proper atmosphere for the Spirit to direct Christians according to the will of Christ. Alongside the basic theme of ecclesiastical reform Basil stressed individual morality, which led to an emphasis on personal responsibility and a teaching on judgment. Balthasar cites the teaching on the face of the judge that streams forth divine light which illuminates hearts and "we will have no other prosecutor than our own sins made present by this light."[21] Stoic and cynic ethics were baptized by Basil. Balthasar viewed Basil's teaching as containing the idea of the twentieth-century secular institute. Balthasar took as a central question from Basil whether there could be more than one form of the Christian life.[22]

## Augustine

Although Origen remained his favorite patristic author, Balthasar repeatedly turned to Augustine. As early as 1936 he published a selection from Augustine's *Enarrationes in Psalmos*. Six years later another selection of texts appeared from the sermons, under the title *Das Antlitz der Kirche*. In 1955 Balthasar provided a foreword and notes for an edition of the *Confessions*. In 1960 he published a translation and introduction to Book 12 of *De Genesi ad litteram (Psychologie und My-*

20. "Die Grossen Regeln des Heiligen Basilius," p. 52.
21. *Theodramatik*, 4:444.
22. "Die Grossen Regeln des Heiligen Basilius," p. 46.

*stik)*. In 1961 Balthasar edited a selection of texts from the *De Civitate Dei* together with a lengthy introduction, *Die Gottesbürgerschaft*. The next year appeared the aesthetic study of Augustine in *The Glory of the Lord*, volume 2, part 1.

In these major studies as well as many minor citations in other works Balthasar ignores the usual picture of Augustine as the symbol of religious subjectivity and pictures him as "man of the church," arguing that Augustine's later work, especially the sermons, would justify this interpretation.[23] Augustine exemplifies a goal of the theological aesthetics: "Augustine's path, which we call his conversion and which comprises many stages, is, less than all the other exemplary 'turnings', one from 'aesthetics' to 'religion'; rather, in its crucial articulation, it is one from a lower to a higher aesthetics."[24]

Balthasar studies Augustine in three major areas: ecclesiology, the theology of time and of history,[25] and aesthetic and mystical theology.

Augustine's repeated statement that Christ is head of the body of the church demonstrates that like the Greek Fathers, he assumed not only a moral but a physical unity between Christ and church. Augustine's strong emphasis on the actuality of this unity brings him to a "christological pantheism."[26] The Incarnation is necessarily (though not hypostatically) union of God and the human body. But the body-head image is not the only one Augustine employs. He also speaks of the bride and bridegroom in which the accent is placed on the distance between Christ and church. Balthasar sees the core of

23. See "Kleiner Lageplan," p. 219, and "Psychologie der Heilegen?" *Schweizer Rundschau* 48 (1948): 3–11.

24. *Glory of the Lord*, vol. 2, pt. 1, p. 95.

25. This study may be found conveniently compressed as Chapter 1 of *Das Ganze im Fragment*.

26. *Das Antlitz der Kirche*, p. 15.

Augustine's ecclesiology in his attempt to determine the limits of the church. In volume 4 of *Theodramatik,* Balthasar pulls together a number of texts from Augustine which focus on the relation of Christ and church. He summarizes with a text from the *Confessions* (345): "Only in God is the meaning of the cross realized." The text unites the elements of sacrifice, Eucharist, and church.[27]

Balthasar presented the interpretation of Augustine's theory of time in *Das Ganze im Fragment* in two parts. The first involves a presentation of the content of the last four books of the *Confessions.* The second is a systematic interpretation of the teaching on time as such. Balthasar argues that the concept of the time of creation in Augustine accords with the analogy of being. Temporality is the basic quality of created being as such and so being created and being temporal are positive acts. Yet the experience of time in Augustine includes experience of the time of sin and time of grace. Augustine's conversion was the experience of this duality in time. The time of sin is under the shadow of death at every moment. The time of grace does not affect the time of creation and does not simply replace the time of sin. Man can die in a state of grace.

Balthasar sees the last books of the *Confessions* as containing Augustine's reflections on the ontotheological dimension of the individual experience of time. The twenty-two books of the *De Civitate Dei* contain a translation of the meaning of this experience into ecclesiastical and world history. Balthasar stresses that Augustine presents not the history but the historicity of the kingdom of God on earth and provides the existential presupposition and conditions for this historicity. The basic tendency in Augustine is to view the two kingdoms as those of *caritas* and *cupiditas.*

27. See *Theodramatik,* 4:444.

Balthasar approaches his study of Augustine's philosophical and theological aesthetics with the assumption that Augustine's theology presupposes the analogy of being. Limited being exists as matter and form, which participate in unlimited light. Augustine's early works, especially the *De vera religione*, develop this theory. Balthasar argues that this most simple light of God, original truth, is also original beauty; but what then is the relation to the multiplicity of number? Must not the key to the entire aesthetics of Augustine lie in this very relation of light and number?[28]

The theological aesthetics of Augustine developed further from that early phase. The philosophy of numbers reappears occasionally. The aesthetic basic relation of transcendence and immanence of the original beautiful assumes Christological significance through the doctrine on the Trinity. Balthasar described the stages in this development. Augustine's psychological image of the Trinity in the created soul forms the completion not only of his metaphysics but also of his aesthetics. This theory magnifies the justification of the beauty of all being because the interior vitality of being as such in this approach receives its fullness, which neither hierarchical order alone nor the dynamism of eros can supply.

As Augustine argues in Book 12 of *De Genesi ad litteram*, man achieves knowledge and even knowledge of God through three hierarchically ordered ways of knowing: bodily perception, presence in the imagination, and the insight of reason. Human knowledge is a part of all three. Augustine maintains the dualism of spirit and senses. Yet Balthasar claims that Augustine's aesthetics preserves the teaching on the analogy of being: "Augustine was constantly aware of the always greater

28. It is necessary to read the section of *The Glory of the Lord*, vol. 2, pt. 1, dedicated to Augustine, to appreciate Balthasar's careful analysis.

dissimilarity between God and his creatures, and indeed right to the end (in the struggle against the Pelagians) continued to become increasingly aware of it." Just as Augustine "saw the temporal void as the medium of beauty, he now sees Christ's *kenosis* as the revelation of the beauty and the fullness of God: 'the path itself is beauty.'"[29] The beauty is only a dynamic striving toward a unity that cannot be realized.

Augustine's rejection of manichaeism ended in an aesthetic justification, for the incomplete character of evil and even imperfection contribute to the beauty of the whole. Balthasar indicates that it is from this aesthetic justification and not primarily from Scripture that proceed the shadows emanating from Gottschalk, John Calvin, and Charles Jansen. Augustine developed his doctrine in the light of the intellectual currents of his time. He fell victim to certain Neoplatonic strains, which colored certain aspects of his theology.

Balthasar demonstrated that in the case of Irenaeus, Clement, Origen, Gregory of Nyssa, Augustine, Maximus Confessor, Bernard, and Thomas Aquinas the teaching on limited freedom, the condition of self-possession (*autexousion*), was never considered an absolute but rather was always open to the unlimited absolute.[30]

29. *Glory of the Lord*, vol. 2, pt. 1, pp. 139, 123.

30. Balthasar states that his argument shows Augustine's response to Plotinus on the issue of free will and clarifies the overemphasis of misinterpretations (e.g., Luther and Jansenius) on only partial aspects of Augustine's thought that upset the balance of his work (*Theodramatik*, vol. 2, pt. 1, p. 212).

## Chapter 7

# Benedict, Dionysus, Maximus, and Others

IN THIS chapter we continue the brief review of Hans Urs von Balthasar's study of the Fathers of the Church. In previous chapters we examined Balthasar's interpretation of Origen, Evagrius, Basil, and Augustine. Here we consider his study of Benedict, Dionysus, Maximus the Confessor, and John of Skythopolis. The argument, as Balthasar summarizes, is that "if Greek thought from Plato to Plotinus has an essentially aesthetic religious structure—for the cosmos is experienced as the representation and manifestation of the hidden transcendent beauty of God—then it is no sacrilege, but rather a fulfilment, if Christian theology, following Philo . . . takes over this aesthetic and metaphysical schema."[1]

## Benedict

A survey of themes involving the Gospel of John led Balthasar to examine the influence of that gospel on the rules of St. Benedict. In 1975 he published an essay, *Les thèmes johan-*

1. *Glory of the Lord*, vol. 2, pt. 1, p. 154.

*niques dans la Règle de S. Benoît et leur actualité.* Again a major concern is the analogy of being. Because Benedict rarely cites the Gospel of John, it would appear that there is little Johannine influence. Balthasar argues that although there may be little manifest influence, Benedict in his rules is thoroughly subject to the spirit of the fourth gospel.

The rules belong to the literary genre of the "master rule."[2] The master rule, however, presents a very closed ascetic system. It promotes a rigid life of denial and promises a richly described paradise as reward. The Benedictine rule depends on the master rule and repeats many of the suggestions for mortification. Yet a major change has occurred. Benedict's rule focuses on Christ, and the ascetic life is secondary—a service of Christ.

Balthasar stresses the following points which move the rule from simply a promotion of asceticism to a practical Christology. First he cites the mention of "our holy Father Basil" (*Göttliches und Menschliches im Räteleben* 73.5). Then he notes, "In Basil, originally, there is no differentiation between Gospel and Rule; rather there is a clever attempt to see the living rule of the Christian life in the biblical text."[3] Second, he claims that toward the end of Benedict's rules we find a growing influence from Augustine. Third, he argues that there is an explicit opening to living tradition and Scripture.

Benedict adapted his "rule to the spirit of Augustine and Basil, and through these two included the spirit of John. On the other hand he left it open to the entire Gospel as a rule of life and that meant concretely: open to the mystery of Christ.

2. See Albert Génestout, O.S.B., "Die Magisterregel—eine würdige Grundlage der Regel des hl. Benedikt," in K. S. Franke, ed., *Askes und Mönchtum in der alten Kirche* (Darmstadt: Wissenschaftliche Buchgesellschaft, 1975), pp. 327–48.

3. *Göttliches und Menschliches im Räteleben*, p. 4.

Thus Benedict is necessarily confronted with the ultimate and deepest interpretation of this mystery, with that of John."[4] Important themes in the rule for Balthasar are the *stabilitas* ordered of the monk, the struggle of life against darkness, and the relation between abbot and monk.

Balthasar sees in the Gospel of John the deepest and most comprehensive exposition of the mystery of Christ. This interpretation was a direct result of his work with Adrienne von Speyr, and, as noted earlier, the "Community of John" and the Johannesverlag signal the importance of Johannine theology. The central significance of the love of the cross can be seen in Balthasar's commentary.[5]

## Dionysus

Dionysus remains the only important figure in the history of theology, or for that matter, in the history of intellectual endeavor, who has been able to hide his identity.[6] He probably wrote early in the sixth century. The problems of his identity and the time of his work have led scholars to argue that the prefix "pseudo" should accompany his name: Pseudo-Dionysus. Some scholars want to deny originality to his writing and say it all comes from Plotinus, Proklus, and the Alexandrian and Cappadocian Fathers. Others argue that he was simply struggling with the Neoplatonism of his time. Finally, still others claim that because the language is esoteric, it is artificial and does not spring from authentic personal experience.

Balthasar presented his interpretation of Dionysus as one of the twelve studies in volume 2 *The Glory of the Lord*, *Studies*

4. Ibid., p. 5.
5. E.g., ibid., pp. 404ff.
6. *Glory of the Lord*, vol. 2, pt. 1, p. 144.

*in Theological Style*. In many other places, however, Balthasar presents citations or summaries of the argument of Dionysus. He considered Dionysus "a man of the very first rank and inevitable effect."[7] Rather than adopt a negative attitude regarding Dionysus, Balthasar stressed the positive. So what is unique becomes apparent only with the recognition that Dionysus totally submerged his personality in his mission. The chosen name, "Dionysus," became a figure for the meaning of his work. He chose the name not to promote confusion between himself and the Dionysus mentioned by St. Paul but to give expression to his similar task.

Balthasar claims that the work does not lack originality. Dionysus did not have merely an apologetic goal. His language is not artificial. Instead, he chose a method and manner of expression that accorded with what he wished to communicate—the divine mystery. The theological form of the *corpus dionysiacum* is not only external but internal form: language such as no one before or after ever spoke. Balthasar argues that in the opinion of Dionysus, eros captures the sense of the transport of man's being better than *agape*, and this constitutes for Dionysus an aesthetic as well as a soteriological statement.[8]

Balthasar interprets the thought of Dionysus as a prominent development of the stream of Origen's teaching, which Balthasar termed "symbolist." Balthasar sees Dionysus completing a logical, Neoplatonic process. "Appearance" is to be taken in the aesthetic sense of sharing and "Logos" in a Greek viewpoint as becoming visible in reality (and not as Maya or phantasmagoria)—always as "appearance of the non-appearing." For Dionysus the category of participation includes the structural laws of the analogy of being. That in which creatures par-

7. *Göttliches und Menschliches im Räteleben*, p. 147.
8. *The Glory of the Lord*, vol. 1, pt. 1, p. 122.

ticipate is "precisely that in which they cannot participate; were this not the case, they would not participate in the divine."[9] The creature does not participate in the sense of Spinoza as accident on a substance, but necessarily has the ontological difference (*zwischen Sein und Seiendem*) in itself. Balthasar believes that the liturgical, hymnic, sometimes poetic language of the Areopagite is a "more exact expression for the vision of the divinity of God than what most of theological definition about God is able to say."[10]

Balthasar's characterization builds on the work of René Roques, who distinguished four theological methods in Dionysus: symbolic, affirmative, negative, and mystical.[11] Balthasar narrows this categorization to three: theological symbolism, theological eidetic, and theological mysticism. Theological eidetic embraces Roques's "positive" theology, and Balthasar considers theological mysticism as the negative. Balthasar's intention is to indicate that these methods entail the analogy of being. It is a theology which avoids Neoplatonism and Hegelian idealism. He writes in *Theodramatik*, volume 4, that if the "ideas of the Areopagite are essentially 'divine acts of will' (*theia thelemata*), what could the divine idea of the individual be other than the definition of what he must be and must accomplish in Christ?"[12] "The theology of the Areopagite was seen and used for a thousand years and longer and is one of the basic forms of the church's theology. He remains with Augustine *the* classic representative of theological form in the West."[13]

9. Ibid., pp. 189–90.
10. René Roques, *L'Univers Dionysien*, trans. Balthasar, in ibid., p. 181.
11. See especially Roques, "Denys l'Areopagite," *Dictionnaire de spiritualité*, 3 (Paris: Aubier, 1957), pp. 244–86.
12. *Theodramatik*, 4:359.
13. *Glory of the Lord*, vol. 2, pt. 1, pp. 207–8.

## John of Skythopolis

Balthasar corrected the mistaken attribution of the scholia to the *Corpus Dionysiacum* to Maximus the Confessor.[14] Bernard Altaner started Balthasar asking whether Dionysus needed such justification.[15] In 1940 he began the process or removing the scholia from the work of Maximus.[16] He demonstrated that the scholia were the work of John of Skythopolis. Because confusion existed in the manuscripts, Balthasar had to find criteria for distinguishing the work of Maximus from that of John.

He found the first tool in the Syriac translation of the scholia which Phocas bar Sergius had produced in the middle of the eighth century. Balthasar argued that this incomplete translation represented the work of John of Skythopolis, who had developed in his introduction an exact statement of what he intended to do in his commentary. Balthasar argued that following this statement of intention would be another criterion for distinguishing the work. John planned to demonstrate the apostolic age of the author, his faith, and especially his attempt to translate the profane philosophy of the Greeks into Christian and orthodox doctrine; defend the author against the charge of heresy; and explain his interest in Greek civilization and culture, especially history, poetry, and philology.[17]

With the help of these criteria Balthasar succeeded in de-

14. *Patrologiae cursus completus* Migne (*PG*), 4; Karl Krumbacher, *Geschichte der Byzantinischen Literature* (Munich: Pustet, 1897), p. 63: "Pseudo Dionysus was introducted into the Greek church by Maximus; he brought the Areopagite into harmony with the traditional teaching of the church."

15. Alois Stuiber, *Patrologie* (Freiburg: Herder, 1966), p. 521: "An extensive meaning attaches to his (Maximus') orthodox interpretation of the Dionysian writings."

16. "Das Problem der Dionysius Scholien," *Kosmische Liturgie*, p. 644.

17. Ibid., p. 653.

monstrating that a number of the scholia that were not included in the Syriac translation were also the work of John. Balthasar noted that a complete differentiation could be accomplished only by careful study of all the manuscripts.

A leitmotif of Balthasar's thought, as we have seen, is that the limitation on created being is not negative. John of Skythopolis developed the unique and positive aspect of the finite in the areas of Christology, teaching on the soul's relation to the body, and in eschatology. John avoided any possible pantheistic interpretation in his well-developed cosmology. A large part of his work involved taking what was best from Greek tradition and explaining it as Christian inheritance. It is little wonder that Balthasar found John so congenial.

## Maximus the Confessor

Maximus was born A.D. 579/580 in Palestine, the son of a Samaritan father and a Persian slave. At the age of ten he was placed in a monastery (St. Chariton), where the abbot Pantoleon replaced his name of Moschion with Maximus. Pantoleon also indoctrinated the youth with the teachings of Origen. When the Persians conquered Jerusalem in 614, he fled to Chrysopolis near Constantinople. Eventually he went to the monastery of St. George in Cyzikus (Erdek). In 632 he was in Carthage and later may have been back in Palestine. From 641 to 645 he lived in Hippo Diarrhytus. In July of 645 at Carthage he debated Pyrrhus on the question of monoetheletism. Eventually he came to Rome, and in 649 Pope Martin I conducted the Lateran synod with his guidance. He was captured in 653, taken to Constantinople, and tried. A final trial was held in 662. As an old man, now eighty-two years of age, he was found guilty and maimed in hand and tongue. He died shortly thereafter at Lazien.

Despite his predilection for Origen, Hans Urs von Balthasar has devoted his patristic studies more thoroughly to Maximus than to any other Greek Father. The major work, *Kosmische Liturgie,* that was first published in 1941 and redone twenty years later witnesses this concentration. Balthasar for all his work, highlights the uniqueness and originality of the thinker under consideration. The work of Maximus has usually been seen as a collection of different kinds of material which lacked unity.[18] Balthasar's concern for the importance of Maximus related to his understanding of the global nature of the man who bridged the thought of East and West. Because of the great need for building such bridges, Balthasar felt to ignore Maximus was a great injustice.[19]

The major difficulty in presenting Maximus as an original thinker is that his "Gnostic Centuries" contain ideas that cannot be harmonized with the rest of the corpus. Balthasar seized on this problem. He points out that the "Centuries" breathe the spirit of Origen, the Origen of the *Peri archôn*, the *Commentary on John,* and the *Homilies.* Balthasar argues that the thought of Maximus underwent a crisis and that Maximus suffered a change, possibly during a stay at Alexandria. The impact of being in the city of Origen may have for a time put out of balance the teaching of Chalcedon and the philosophy of Aristotle in Maximus's mind.

This solution was regarded as facile. Polycarp Sherwood, for example, argued that Balthasar "has noted the first group of *Gegenmotive* 1.1–10. He has not noted however that such a group of 10 sentences is a variant of the century form used not

18. See, for example, Marcel Viller, "Aux sources de la spiritualité de S. Maxime: Les oeuvres d'Évagre le Pontique," *Revue ancienne et médiéval* 11 (1930): 156–84; Ireneaus Hausherr, "Ignorance infinie," *Orientalia Christiana Periodica* 2 (1936): 351–62.

19. *Kosmische Liturgie*, pp. 47ff.

infrequently by Maximus." Sherwood went on to state that this section "may well have once stood by itself as a concise summary of Maximus' philosophico-theological position in the fact of the Evagrian and Origenist error."[20] If Sherwood is correct, Maximus provided a framework for understanding the sentences from Origen and Evagrius.

In his second edition of *Komische Liturgie* Balthasar took account of this criticism and abandoned the theory of crises. Instead he argued that the issue involved all the work of Maximus. For example, Balthasar repeatedly stressed the influence of Evagrius on Maximus.[21] As noted earlier, it is unfortunate that in the second edition Balthasar did not take into account the Version S 2 of the *Kephalaia gnostica* of Evagrius.

The work of Maximus "has in all its dimensions synthesis as inner form."[22] The synthesis is of oppositions which remain intact, namely, those of the Christianity of Chalcedon and the world-view of Maximus. Erich von Ivanka took a very different view. He argued that Maximus's basic idea was of a universal union of all being and forms of created being in the incarnate Logos.[23] Sherwood claimed that the "divine intent, on which the whole thought of Maximus hangs, terminates in the mystery of Christ, in the *personal* union of the human and divine nature in the incarnate Logos."[24] In this view, Maximus and his monoethelite struggle would tend to remove the rational

20. Polycarp Sherwood, *An Annotated Date-list of the Works of Maximus the Confessor* (Rome: Anselmiana, 1952), p. 35.

21. "His position is partly determined by Evagrius, who for him is more the theologian and mystic of the direct ascent over all forms to the formlessness of God than the keen mystical psychologist of experience" (*Glory of the Lord*, vol. 1, pt. 1, p. 282).

22. *Kosmische Liturgie*, p. 19.

23. Erich von Ivanka, *Einleitung zu Maximus der Bekenner, All eins in Christus, Sigillum* 19 (Einsiedeln: Johannesverlag, 1961), p. 6.

24. Polycarp Sherwood, "Survey of Recent Works on St. Maximus the Confessor," *Traditio* 20 (1964):435.

aspects of that nature. For Sherwood the confrontation with Origenism provided the opening into the thought of Maximus, whereas for Balthasar it was the confrontation with monotheletism. Balthasar did not understand Origenism in the same way Sherwood did. Lars Thunberg considered both viewpoints and concluded that under certain conditions they could be united. Von Ivanka and Sherwood, he noted, saw the key to Maximus's vision in the union of divine and human nature in the incarnate Logos. Balthasar is also correct when he stresses the unique significance of unity and difference.[25] Thunberg agreed with Balthasar in stressing Maximus's faithfulness to Chalcedon and Constantinople in both cosmological and anthropological considerations. Created natures and human "synthetic" nature find fulfillment in union with God through Christ, not in spite of diversity but as its true manifestation.

Balthasar began his analysis of Maximus with the question, how did Maximus, caught between two-person teaching and one-nature, conceive of two natures in Christ? To avoid monophysitism he had to stress the freedom of the synthesis. To avoid Nestorianism, the solution had to be actual. Next, Balthasar studied the terms Maximus used. Following Leontius of Byzantium, Maximus used *ousia* in a sense different from that of Aristotle. For Maximus the term meant either the highest and most general category or else *physis* in the sense of a particular nature. *Hypostasis* then meant the act of having *ousia*. So Maximus could hold that the unity of divine and human nature in Christ was a pure hypostatic unity. The union of

25. Lars Thunberg, *Microcosm and Mediator: The Theological Anthropology of Maximus the Confessor* (Lund: Aalen, 1965), p. 462, states: "Von Ivanka and Sherwood are right in regarding the union of human and divine natures in the incarnate Logos as the key to Maximus' vision, and as the divine intent which he claims to have discovered through the mystery of Christ, but precisely for this reason von Balthasar is also right in stressing the proper balance of unity and diversity."

body and soul in man is a natural synthesis and consequently not just the product of a divine decision. The synthesis in Christ, however, is not natural but free and in this sense purely hypostatic. Balthasar states that Maximus thus came close to the solution of the Thomist school first enunciated by Capreolus and renewed by Maurice de la Taille.[26]

The hypostatic union had its supreme paradox in the suffering and death of Christ: ultimate expression of the finitude of human nature and at the same time supreme freedom of divine nature. Maximus in his argument with Pyrrhus granted the moments of freedom and will to nature; Pyrrhus did not. For Maximus personality meant the act of being ordered to nature; for Pyrrhus it was something irrational, beyond nature. So for Maximus there could not exist a spiritual nature without freedom and will.

Maximus saw the goal of creation and redemption in the union of all created being in the incarnate Logos. The Logos is the core and source of all synthesis of cosmos and history. Balthasar urges that scholars recognize how Maximus avoided the single view of Eastern theology and its tendency toward pantheism. This is so important because Maximus's Christological formula can be viewed as a global formula.

Balthasar unravels not only the Christological form of Maximus's synthesis but also the elements within it. He does this by listing the various activities—Maximus as biblical theologian, as Aristotelian, as Logologian in the school of Origen, as monk in the Evagrian tradition, as orthodox fighter for the doctrines of Chalcedon. Elsewhere Balthasar discusses Maximus's Christological solution to the problem of freedom.[27] Balthasar claims that Maximus in particular has great impor-

26. *Kosmische Liturgie*, p. 245.
27. *Theodramatik*, vol. 2, pt. 1, p. 201.

tance for the history of theology. Maximus could develop his world-view only in his given circumstances, and he used those circumstances to the utmost. Against the monophysitism and Origenism of his time Maximus succeeded in restoring the tradition. Against political and religious integralism of Byzantium he upheld the freedom of the gospel for Rome.

Balthasar calls attention to two problems, which Maximus made great contributions toward solving. The first is a response to Hegelian pantheism; the second is whether and how one can unite Eastern and Asian with Western thought and tradition.

Maximus asked Hegel's question: How can multiplicity and unity be brought together? Maximus differed with Hegel's answer in that the multiple syntheses are so conceived that the *asynchytos* does not disappear. Balthasar sees his own study of Maximus as a realization of what Johann Staudenmaier had proposed in the nineteenth century—a way out of Hegel's system. The multiple references to Hegel in *Kosmische Liturgie* thus have a clear purpose.

How does Maximus answer the problem of Eastern religion and Christian faith? Biblical religion does not destroy natural religion. Rather, natural religion is presupposed; and to the extent that Asian religions are synthesized *asynchytos* with biblical faith, they complement one another.

Again Sherwood is a typical critic of this approach to Maximus. Sherwood faults Balthasar for seeing the task of the theologian as "audaciously creative." Sherwood says that Balthasar

> sees the task of the theologian . . . as that of one who would bring into a coherent overall view the objective values of our post-Cartesian world that bears so deep an imprint both from German idealism and from modern science. For this he sees a magnificent exemplar in Origen, in Gregory of Nyssa and particularly in Maximus, who made the Chalcedonian formula the keystone of a theology embrac-

ing all in its unifying grasp. Thus are explained his frequent references to Hegel and to other German idealists, as he leaps directly from the historical context of Maximus to a contemporary situation of the mid-twentieth century.[28]

Balthasar acknowledges a twofold religious consciousness in Maximus. The first is a "relation" which must use the mediation of concepts and thoughts and arouses a longing for unmediated possession. The other is beyond conceptual thought and involves a total perception that transcends all concepts.[29]

## Patrology Reconsidered

The brief excursus through patristic authors from Origen to Maximus in the work of Hans Urs von Balthasar should make clear that his guiding question involves the analogy of being. To take the next step, we must look more thoroughly at Origen and the Greek tradition.

Balthasar holds that Origen laid the foundations for Greek patristic thought. Origen and the other Fathers were closer in time to the writers of the New Testament. More important, they shared the same culture, language, and concerns. Origen knew that the work of the theologian was more than intellectual research—it also involved a mystery.

In *Herrlichkeit*, volume 3, part 1, Balthasar approached Greek antiquity from the perspective of the relation of the divine to the world. So again the issue of the analogy of being determined his analysis. He divided his study into epochs. The first, whose genius was Homer, he called the time of myth.

28. Sherwood, "Survey," p. 433. See also Werner Löser, *Im Geiste des Origenes* (Frankfurt: Knecht, 1976), p. 211.

29. Cf. Maximus the Confessor, *Questiones ad Thalassium* (Migne), 60; *PG* 90, 621C–623B.

This epoch ended with the great tragedians Aeschylos, Sophocles, and Euripides. Writers of this epoch viewed the divine and human relation in terms of the analogy of being.

Balthasar sees in Homer a figure who explained the divine-human question. Homer stressed the unsurpassable gulf between God and man as well as the transcendence of man. The mythical explanation of being is continued in the tragedies of Aeschylos and Sophocles. In them the "Homeric double dogma remains valid: original opposition and unsurpassable distance between God and man—and total dedication of man to God." The first proposition opposes the philosophical tendency to make of being identity, and the second opposes the inclusion of men in the divine. In this paradox is enacted tragedy in all its fateful dimensions.

## Balthasar's Theory of Tragedy

According to Hans Urs von Balthasar, existence itself is tragic. Goods are offered man which are to be affirmed and loved and yet which are denied. There is love of man and woman, but Admetus is summoned to die. His wife Alcestis consents to die in his place. Though Admetus lives, he has lost. Hecuba, queen of Troy, together with her royal daughters, becomes spoil for the conquering Achaeans. There is faithfulness, but Sophocles shows us a Deianeira who sends her husband Heracles the tunic soaked in the poisonous blood of Nessus, who had told Deianeira this would guarantee perpetual marital faithfulness.

Not only is existence a matter of facing the loss of what is desired, but the very stuff of existence is filled with contradiction. Orestes obeys the god Apollo and slays his mother, Clytemnestra, because she had killed her husband. But as a consequence, Orestes is pursued by the Furies. Antigone obeys the unwritten law of God and buries her brother. For this act she is herself buried alive by Creon, the protector of the written law. Hippolytos obeys the goddess Artemis, whom he loves, and so will not marry. He thereby offends another goddess, Aphrodite, whose nature and law Hippolytos violates. It is the same with the Danaids. In befriending man, Prometheus offends Zeus. In such contradictions existence becomes absolute pain. Many tragedies present only this inevitable condition of pain. It is the paradigm situation of the "Suppliants"—man standing alone, without a home, hunted, is the starting point of tragic drama, the extreme representation of existence.

Balthasar carries this explanation of tragedy one step further. Underneath the conflict and contradiction, the suffering and pain resulting from the struggle, is unseen guilt.[30] It is basic and so can be uncovered but not removed; it is present but cannot be fixed. Is the individual guilty? Is Oedipus, for example, guilty? Balthasar finds Oedipus very guilty—from the moment he killed his father. Original guilt can sometimes be traced to the beginning, as in the case of the sons of Atreus. Man is blamed to the extent that he acts responsibly. But he acts in a connection with the gods, whose thoughts and plans he cannot know. Thus the guilty act places him in a greater guilt network, from which there is no escape except by uprooting his entire existence. To the extent that the gods from the time of Homer are only partial aspects of the entire providence, they themselves view only a part of the future events. They too can become involved, as did Apollo, who ordered the matricide and in the end had to fall back on Athena for a solution. A similar situation binding men and gods is visible in Teutonic myth—the twilight of the gods.

30. "Die Tragödie und die christliche Glaube," p. 350.

The second epoch is that of philosophy, whose chief representative is Plato. The third epoch Balthasar calls that of Greek intellectual history, which was characterized by repeated attempts to build a synthesis of myth and philosophy. Virgil and Plotinus stand out in the later period of this epoch.

Balthasar explains the relationship of patristics to these three epochs through two propositions. First, the Church Fathers entered upon a long and intensive conversation with Greek philosophy and were greatly influenced by the result. Second, the early Christians did not enter into a similar dialogue with myth, especially with Greek tragedy. Balthasar feels it is regrettable that they did not do so. Early Christians applauded Plato's theater criticism and as a consequence created a vacuum.

Balthasar's *Theodramatik* is essentially an attempt to make up for this loss. The concept of "glory" means that the Fathers used the ancient meaning to give expression to the "biblical-Christian glorious event." The cost came in doctrine. The teaching on the Trinity was influenced by Platonic schemes of descent; Christology leaned in the direction of monophysitism; in piety the movement of the ascetical life is that of ascending from matter to spirit; and in ecclesiology, the Greek church viewed the hierarchical structure as transitory.[31] The Platonic spirit in the theology of the Greek Fathers was always tempered by symbolism, albeit Platonic symbolism.

Balthasar often compared the theology of the Greek Fathers with that of the Western Fathers. Among the most explicit texts are *Sehen, Hören und Lesen im Raum der Kirche* (1961), the introduction to *Kosmische Liturgie* (the new material in the second edition on pages 19–47), and *Anspruch auf Katholizität* (1974), pages 108–13. The church stands between extreme

31. "Patristik, Scholastik und wir," p. 87.

East and extreme West, between Athos and Wittenberg, between pure seeing and pure listening.

Patristic theology expressed itself in the categories of the time, and these were those of Greek philosophy. Consequently, the relation between God and world was expressed as "participation." This was accomplished through a rhythmical egressus and regressus. In its simplest and most logical form this schema has a pantheistic shadow. Created being is conceived as a less powerful divine being.

Whereas patristic theology expressed the God-world situation as an "exemplar" relationship, medieval scholastic theology saw it as a causal relationship. The trend was away from Plato and toward Aristotle. *Metoche* was replaced by *energeia*. Distance between God and creation as well as the value of the limited were elements that belonged to the analogy between God and world. Despite replacing the danger of pantheism with the danger of rationalism, Balthasar says the real danger in Scholastic theology was what remained of Platonism.[32] Scholasticism did not succeed in ordering natural and supernatural. Aquinas, for example, spoke of a "natural desire" of the creature for the supernatural vision of God. But this is a Platonic notion that threatened to restore pantheism. The teaching on the "desiderium naturale in Deum" resulted in further Platonic elements, including the notion of stressing the ascent from the particular to the universal, from material to spiritual as the basic movement of the human mind.

Balthasar states that what is new in contemporary theology is the attempt to remove "Platonic-Hellenic remnants of Scholasticism." Two directions unite to form a single theme: the progressive discovery of the individual and consequently the

32. Ibid., p. 94.

true worldliness of the world and the progressive emphasis on the personal. This leads to the complete transcendence and complete immanence of the Christian regarding nature—that God appears as the totally other. Balthasar thus sees his own contribution as mastering the task given contemporary theology: to allow the genuinely Christian to appear.

## Balthasar's Patristic Theology

Balthasar's theology can best be understood as a continuation of the patristic tradition.[33] His goal is to allow the genuinely Christian to appear.

An *aporia* in patristic theology is the apparent impossibility of combining Origen's protology and eschatology with Augustine's. The difficulty is that the universal effectiveness of the divine redemptive action and the sanctity of human freedom seem to present a contradiction. Origen and the Greek Fathers represent one horn of the dilemma and Augustine and Western tradition the other. The contest was waged primarily in the teaching on protology and eschatology. It entered Christology only in a secondary manner.

Origen and his followers saw in the eschatological *apokatastasis* the restoration of the original unity of creation in the eternity of God. Inasmuch as this process is inevitable, human freedom appears shortchanged. Augustine stressed the moment of absolute freedom manifested in choice and in this idea founded Western ethical personalism.

Balthasar says man is free and God respects this freedom, even if it is used against God. The world, whose crown jewel is man gifted with responsibility, is affirmative, and God assumes

33. For a similar account see Löser, *Im Geiste des Origenes*, pp. 240ff.

the consequences of this affirmation. The positive value of the world and the freedom of man contain the heart of the analogy of being.

The Greek Fathers ignored the demands of Greek tragedy and instead entered into a dialogue with Greek philosophy. Hence they did not see that the life and work of Christ completed Greek tragedy. The death of Jesus was the "absolute tragedy." The Fathers had interpreted the "descensus Christi ad inferos" triumphantly. Balthasar interprets it as a condition of solidarity with the dead and the God-forsaken and in this sense perfect tragic *pathos*. The decisive point about this "absolute tragedy" is that it is visible only to the eyes of faith, for the tragedy does not end with the "descensus." There is a fifth act: the Resurrection.

Balthasar observes a contemporary obsession with human freedom and a competition as to who can interpret it best. Balthasar himself reviews many theories of freedom in *Theodramatik*, volume 2, part 1. Atheism is preoccupied with this theme: the freeing of reason (the Enlightenment); the freeing of the economically enslaved for humanly worthy work (Marx); the freeing of the individual from the bonds of a past (Freud). "Everywhere at the very doors of freedom the human being appears chained to some past, to a tradition, to a moment in history made absolute, or to some forbidden totem in the realm of nature or culture."[34] Nevertheless, the human being achieves true humanity only in choosing: "So long as Christianity appears to be principally a matter of traditions and institutions, the emancipatory movement of modernity will have an easy time of it."[35]

Another area in Balthasar's theology that demonstrates his

34. *Im Gottes Einsatz Leben*, p. 14.
35. Ibid., p. 15.

extension of patristic theology is the teaching on the relation between action and contemplation. Gregory the Great and Augustine demonstrate the developed patristic teaching on this relation. They assumed the teaching of Evagrius Ponticus, who developed a scheme in which the active life was a means to the contemplative. The roots of the system were both biblical, the Martha and Mary pericope, and philosophical (Stoic, Aristotelian, and Platonic). Balthasar sees the descent of God as having primacy over the ascending motion of man. Man's ascent finds the goal, God, to the extent that man allows himself to be of service in the descent. This descent is action out of love. This interpretation corrects the ascent-oriented Greek patristic understanding of the actio-contemplatio *aporia*.

The theologian has the continual task of understanding the Fathers. This means reformulating their thought in the concepts of contemporary philosophy. The Greek Fathers were tempted to contrast the world of the senses with that of the spiritual, to oppose history to eternity. Origen for the most part avoided the temptation. He divided history into "three ages." The Latin Fathers, led by their appreciation for the Roman understanding of history, valued it as the crystallization of progress. The Fathers were not engaged in developing a philosophy of history. Rather, they saw history as a theological datum.

Balthasar begins by positing that the historical presence of the Logos reveals the folly of "pure" philosophy, that is, thought in universals (*abstractio universalis*). The Logos is not a kingdom of ideas—values and laws ruling history. Current existential emphases have inverted the earlier Neoplatonic view so that the world of the Logos can be opened up as the foundation for the existence of things in time and history. A theologian should recognize that the preoccupations of existentialism are similar to his own.

Balthasar's method for ordering the question is convex and

concave: (1) history in general as a condition for the possibility of the historical Christ; (2) this historical Christ as condition for the possibility of history in general.[36] Elucidation of this method and its integration into theological aesthetics are the subjects of the next chapter.

36. A *Theology of History*, pp. 79ff.

## Chapter 8

# History and Theological Aesthetics

THE GREEK Fathers always suffered from a Platonic theory that contrasted the world of the senses with the purely spiritual, eternal world. Origen divides all history and reality into three ages. The Latin Fathers, on the other hand, were drawn by their appreciation for Roman history to value it as the crystallization of progress. All the Fathers, however, in spite of apparent exceptions, rejected cyclical views of history. Augustine in his own way not only reproduced Paul's quadruple division of history but devised his own complex sevenfold division, mainly, it seems, to justify his refusal to take the account of creation portrayed in Genesis literally. The Fathers did not write a philosophy of history. As theologians they looked at history as a datum, which forced them to consider history not merely as the field of operation for man's free will but also for God's providence.

Balthasar's extension of the work of the Fathers on the theology of history is the subject of this chapter. Balthasar assumes that man cannot build a "theology of history" because the synthesis, the full unity of the subject, is in Christ. Balthasar means by *history* the complex of temporal events that can never be completely public because their undercurrent springs from the person whose strongest impulses involve some form of philosophical or religious commitment. History may attempt to be "scientific," but it cannot avoid the hard fact that its subject acts according to a particular interpretation of ultimate meaning.

Balthasar begins by positing that the historical presence of the Logos on the plane of history reveals the folly of "pure" philosophy. The Logos is not a kingdom of ideas—values and laws ruling history. The Logos is history, and no "ideal" can be abstracted from the events of the life of Jesus. These events constitute of themselves the norm and are not, like the view of the Alexandrians, an allegory within which meaning may be decoded.

Origen, for example, followed a strain of Hellenistic rhetoric and thought that the Old Testament, like the *Iliad*, had woven into its narrative certain myths and allegories. "The incidents, which are historically true," he insists, are more numerous than the "spiritual interpretations" that have been inserted by the Holy Ghost for pedagogical purposes.[1] Origen's allegorization does provide an extension of traditional typology. For example, Origen interprets the theme of the fall of Jericho as symbolic of the fall of the world by changing the spiritual meaning of the episode into a series of hierarchical levels. Allegorically, the fall of Jericho and the sound of the trumpets represent the fall of the world and the joy of the people of God at the coming of Christ and the preaching of his Word. Tropologically, the trumpets represent the joy of the individual Christian whenever he receives Jesus-Joshua within the city of his soul after the fall of the worldly vices that had previously dwelt there. Anagogically the episode is a type of the Second Coming, of the trumpets of the Last Judgment,

1. See Origen, *De Principiis*, 4.3.4.329ff.

and of the final overcoming of the satanic forces of this world (*Hom. Jos.* 7–11, 327–66).

Balthasar's method presupposes that any consideration of the relation between Word and history starts with the question of how the absolute principle that the Logos is Lord of history can be applied. This theory implies not only that the Logos is both judge and redeemer of history but also that in the human sphere the Logos forms history in detail. The answer presupposes a scheme that is both convex and concave: first, history in general as a condition for the possibility of the historical existence of the Logos; second, the historical existence of the Logos as a condition for the possibility of history in general. The two are related as promise and fulfillment. It is impossible to distinguish in this theory any nontemporal content and a temporal container. So it is precisely the temporal and historical existence of Christ which is the visible explanation for the form of existence of the triune God. Time as such is the *form* chosen by Christ and so is an adequate explanation of eternity. The Platonic tension between time and eternity and the conception of eternity as negation of the temporal are put in question. According to Balthasar, Boethius's definition of time (*tota simul possessio vitae*) is insufficient as a starting point. This means that we penetrate eternity not by denying the temporal and the historical but by intensifying it—for example, by taking a good hard look at Bergson's *durée réelle*.

Every philosophy that considers time simply appearance or a "form of intuition" (Kant), as a shadow that will disappear in the sunshine of eternity, must confront the problem of the Logos. Thus it would be wrong to think of Christ before the Passion as living in time by means of some kind of apparition that veiled his glory and that only by way of exception (on Tabor, for example) did he let the veil drop.[2]

2. *Word and Redemption*, p. 26.

The theology of time is a necessary condition for seeing eternity in the mirror of faith. This "seeing" is the core of Balthasar's theological aesthetics. Thus history, as the history of salvation, enters the phase of horizontal accomplishment and receives its meaning and justification. This history encompasses the chaotic course of Israel from Abraham to John the Baptist and all events subsequent to the birth of Christ. The Christ-event is to the course of history what faith is to the man confronted by God's offer of salvation.

The time of the church as the era of the Holy Spirit (in contrast to the Old Testament and the era of Christ) is not a time in which revelation occurs. Rather, it is the expression of the fullness of revelation. Hence one cannot write either a phenomenal or a noumenal theology of history of the time of the church. The order of the Spirit is to such a degree the order of freedom that it cannot be contained in the categories of world and human history.[3]

The Logos contains the fullness of revelation. So it would be foolish to expect that the theology of today or tomorrow with its development of doctrine, all the riches of tradition, could possess a deeper insight into the essence of the Logos than did the early Fathers.

What this means practically is that the church as church cannot develop internally. What is possible is a development of the ecclesiastical presence of Christ in world history. This development must not be understood geographically or quantitatively.[4] Myths vanish and reappear; ideologies order themselves consciously or unconsciously in accordance with or opposed to the program of Christ. The world becomes full of Christian ideas gone mad (in Gilbert K. Chesterton's sense).

3. See *Das Ganze im Fragment*, p. 144.
4. Ibid., p. 197.

## Issues in Ecclesiology

Balthasar argues that a more contemporary conceptualization of the church can be reached from the viewpoint of theological aesthetics than by many supposedly more "relevant" approaches. This means that issues raised in the study of art and *belles-lettres* can shed new light on musty liturgical and ecclesiological questions. Balthasar has been called a great ecclesiologist of the Mystical Body tradition. This tradition is said to be old-fashioned, but fashions have been known to change.

That the church is a mystery of faith has been present in the consciousness of every age. The patristic period lived naively in this consciousness without feeling any need to develop a self-contained ecclesiology. In the Middle Ages the situation was no different. "Even the embittered controversy between the protagonists of pope and emperor remained on the threshold regarding the theology of the Church. The struggle was limited to legal rights; it did not touch at all on the essence of the real matter; for thought was still in the pre-reflexive age."[5] The most one could say was that the content of the church was the kingdom of God, which had arrived, and that its form was Christendom—not the organized Church of post-Reformation times. Between the logical mystery of the relation of Christ and church and the aesthetic mystery of, say, a cathedral, there was only analogy, not identity. No one was tempted to identify cathedral and church (which happens so often today). The analogy was enough, however, up to the period of the Enlightenment to prevent further development in ecclesiology.

The Reformation compelled men to rethink the church. Reflection tended to focus on what remained of Christianity,

5. *Church and World*, p. 17.

on the undivided *visible* church. Within Catholicism the result was a break in church teaching. From this moment the central problem became the *form* of the church in the narrow sense—that of the three functions of the hierarchy. Yet if the church is the Body of Christ, then individual Christians, considered as parts, are members of Christ, not members of the church, which viewed by itself would be a headless body. It is the "head" as resurrected who determines and distributes offices and charismata (Eph. 4:11–16) and consequently the Trinity that is the organizing principle. It is through the Spirit of Christ, the Spirit of the church, that the individual is inserted. Otherwise the New Testament would not be a covenant of freedom.[6]

Balthasar says that we must guard against facile solutions and keep on asking about the real nature of the church. If we cannot express this, then we must further ask what is the form of its manifestation of appearance. Should we simply demythologize what eludes comprehension and revert with Karl Barth to a simple meeting among persons or to the concept of the people of God of the Old Testament, Qumran scrolls, and some forms of Protestantism? Balthasar argues that there is no definite form for the church. Her nature is more than any structural system. He observes that neither the right nor the left can bear the fact that existence in time is fragmentary. Those of the left take the social programs of the prophets and the Sermon on the Mount to be mandates to change society overnight. Those of the right insist that the hieratic-hierarchical form of the church is definitive and timeless. Balthasar seems all along to have carried out the ideal expressed by Michael Novak: "My ideal for the teaching authority of the church would be that persons of intellect would follow conscience and

6. Ibid., p. 18.

reason to the utmost, yet all the while taking responsibility both for bringing the community of faith together and for relating their findings to the great tradition."[7]

An institutional organization is necessary because the community in responding to the historical Christ must have a historical, spatiotemporal form, must take precedence over the individual in order to grow and flourish, and must visibly participate in the apostolic experience. To overcome objections to these "institutional" features, Balthasar argues, one must see the intimate connection between personal discipleship and authority. This implies not only that the personal use of authority is guaranteed by an impersonal authority—which may be the case but certainly provides little satisfaction—but also that the very notion of discipleship entails authority. The apostles had to abandon everything in order to place their lives in Christ. Into the emptiness that resulted poured the grace of office. The apostles followed as individuals. So does every member of the church—each is a unique individual who follows Christ.

One form of modern "personalism" derives from the idea of the actualization of the Old Covenent in the Jews (Jakob Stern, Max Scheler, Martin Buber, Gabriel Marcel). Balthasar says that Christianity goes beyond personalism in the same way it goes beyond the Old Covenant to a situation in which it appears a paradox to followers of both natural religion and biblical personalism.

The Word of the one God cannot be given to all men at the same time and place without overturning existing conditions in the world. The Word can come only in such a way that it is heard by human beings—and that is in the form of a human be-

7. Michael Novak, *Confessions of a Catholic* (San Francisco: Harper & Row, 1983), p. 115.

ing who announces the totally other that is God. This is the theological proposition that distinguishes revelation from "open" philosophical reason and constitutes a scandal to reason.[8]

The gifts each individual receives are that person's "form" in the church. No member qua member lacks a "member-form." Balthasar notes that Protestant theology, especially that of Karl Barth, recalled Catholics to this biblical functionalism and the foundation for official ministry. The assumption of "member-form" should be understood by analogy to the *kenosis* of Christ, even though there can be no structural comparison with the hypostatic union. What Christ is by nature, the Christian becomes by grace. For Balthasar a most important insight is that of the functional and representative character of the Christian *form* of existence. The cleric may display this *form* more clearly. No one would say that the form-giving element (*esse sequitur formam*) in itself is the church. The church requires the material element: the faithful. Believers can belong only insofar as they are included in the form. It is by the grace of this form that members belong to the church, the prolongation of the Incarnate Word in the world. Worship became no longer just giving back the Word of God as praise (*beraka, eulogia, eucharistia*). Rather, it became an annunciation of the passion of the Incarnate Word in an act that is both absolute obedience and absolute love, which unites man and Christ. Christ's absolute obedience to the Father was the condition for making possible a transparency to the Father under the guidance of the Spirit (archetypal faith and hope). Baptism is giving the self the form of Christ's death and resurrection as well as letting the self be given the form of love and membership in the community.

Balthasar relates theological reasoning to personal belief. This manner of doing theology may appear odd or repugnant

8. *Das Ganze im Fragment*, p. 205.

if the principal dimension is ignored—namely, the religious imagination, which relies on a category against which reflection proceeds. This dimension for Hans Urs von Balthasar is the aesthetic. I have already indicated the role of form in the foundation of Balthasar's ecclesiology. The purpose was to provide a setting for the major task ahead—elucidation of Balthasar's theological aesthetics.

## Theological Aesthetics: Vision

Aesthetics focuses all of Balthasar's writing. His theological aesthetics are spelled out in the multivolume *Herrlichkeit*. This work embodies the reduction of the major themes which Balthasar explicates around the idea of the "glory of God." *Herrlichkeit* treats revelation, which can be seen shining gloriously through all its veiled forms. God does not encounter the human creature as a teacher of truth or a merciful redeemer but as the irradiation of personal trinitarian love.

The first part of the work portrays man's meeting with radiance, *doxa*, the initial moment that leads man to recognize the ineffable foundation of the *khabod Jahwe*. The second part illustrates this encounter of the individual and *doxa* in studies of twelve important figures in church history who manifest twelve different theological styles. The third part interprets this meeting of individual and *doxa* in immense frescoes detailing the itinerary of thought from the Greek myths to Heidegger. The final section presents a biblical theology of glory.

Balthasar begins by admitting that his concern is not to retain or transmit the old imagery of the gods and art as something holy but rather to recover that power which enabled citizens of the past to embody the revelation of reality in a variety of myths. Thus the concern is to show how the human mind comes to *see* God. The key concept, as noted earlier, is *theoria*, vision, not the everyday vision whereby the individual observer becomes united with the object, but that in which the mind dwells intently upon the object in an act of "contemplation." Objects that draw man to contemplation are those in which man can take delight. The adjective "beautiful" need not be limited to what is perceptible. Aesthetic attraction also exists in the realm of the relationship of ideas, in a well-constructed mathematical proof or in a methodical argument. Platonic tradition never doubted that there had to be intelligible as well as sensible beauty.

Balthasar argues that God's formlessness is not like that of created things, a defect. God is not something that fails to attain its form. He is that to which all form fails to attain. The mind in contemplating God knows this and knows that in beholding God one sees total fullness. This is a paradox. The mind can *see* beyond itself and understand that there may be something beyond its understanding. The mind can find greater satisfaction in this thought than in anything it actually understands. For God, besides being absolute Being and Oneness, truth and goodness is also absolutely beautiful.

This God has manifested himself in the Incarnation. The Word is not only heard but is seen. So he is the God not only of the Torah or Qur'an but of the cradle and the cross. He is not just the Lord of Hosts but the Beloved of the Song of Songs. He is the Rose of Sharon and the beauty of the heaven of heavens. Such images, Balthasar argues, are aesthetic expressions.

By *aesthetics*, Balthasar first means the Kantian account of the part played by the senses together with the power of memory and imagination in our awareness of God. This idea is fundamental because God does manifest himself. *Theological aesthetics is a study of the perceptible forms in which God is manifested and of the subjective conditions that must be fulfilled if the individual is to apprehend the forms for what they are*. This aesthetics is completed by a theological dramatics, the study of the sustained action or drama of God's Word in the world. This in turn is completed by a theological logic that demonstrates how the reality of the appearance of God is actually understood by the intellect and how it is processed by the analytical operations of reason. All three—theological aesthetics, dramatics, and logic—are meant to constitute a total systematic theology.

Second, Balthasar's work is also an aesthetics in the strict sense of the study of beauty, specifically the divine beauty. It depends on the ontological depths of the beautiful. The sensible appearance of the form of an object expresses under particular conditions its metaphysical form. In the special case of theological aesthetics in which the *appearing* object is divine, the sensible manifestation becomes charged with all the inexhaustible meaning and authority of the divine, so that this beauty is truly called *glory*. Balthasar regrets that modern fashion in aesthetics pursues a different approach, preferring art to beauty and the workings of the mind to the attributes of being. Another way of saying this is that the works of art are explorations of the possible, explorations of formal structures conceived and depicted in space or time. They are explorations of the potentialities of being rather than of what really is. Every sensible form carries its own feeling-value, so that a work of art, a symphony of sensible forms, is a symphony of feeling-tones. Art, then, inasmuch as it explores feeling-values, enlarges one's experience. One might well ask why Balthasar would so obviously choose such a backward-looking, apparently long outmoded method.

One purpose of this book has been to answer this question by examining theological aesthetics in detail. A brief answer would be that for Balthasar there are two wrong answers to the question about Christian faith: one is that it rests on argument and the other that it rests on feelings. The theory that it rests on feelings is usually held by nonbelievers. Having found no cogency in arguments themselves, and wondering what convinces others if not argument, they can think of no alternative but feelings. Christian language plays into their hands. Those who do see that feeling cannot be a legitimate basis for belief usually conclude that for themselves it must be argument or nothing. Then they make the mistake of thinking that Christianity is a jumble of creeds, each of which must be considered and judged separately. Balthasar says both groups fail to see the possibility of a global vision and a global acceptance that involves an intuitive grasp of the faith which is both vivid and convincing and which compels assent while leaving details to be explicated by subsequent reflection and inquiry. This subsequent inquiry is the task of theological logic, a task Balthasar is now completing, with one volume left to be published.

## Eclipse of Transcendental Beauty

Balthasar begins with a category with which most philosophers would rather end, that of the beautiful: "Beauty is the word that shall be our first. Beauty is the last thing the thinking intellect dares to approach, since only it dances as an uncontained splendor around the double constellation of the true and the good in their inseparable relation to one another."[9] It is the final point toward which reason directs itself because it is the reflected glance of the double countenance of the "true" and the "good." Balthasar charges that thinking in every discipline today proceeds computer fashion. It collects immense banks of data and makes very fine specializations but has no overall understanding or appreciation. It is no wonder, he

9. *Glory of the Lord*, 1:18.

says, that the fate of *being* suffers eclipse when the fate of the transcendentals is oblivion. If Aquinas could call being a "kind of light" for the existent thing, must not this "light" be extinguished where the language of light has been forgotten? And where the language of the mystery of reality is no longer spoken, what can be the fate of the subject of mystery other than rejection? All that remains is a "portion" or "fragment" of existence. The witness of being for itself becomes incredible for the man who can no longer *see* the beautiful.

Balthasar says that any discussion of beauty must include the ideas of *mystery of form* and the *radiance from within*. Plato understood this phenomenon inasmuch as he thought of a soul that fell for a second time into matter. This interpretation is understandable because he thought that the unity of what is dissolved in death could not be saved. He had placed this unity in a separate, spiritual world. Greek tragedy was the cry of transient existence standing on the frontier of immortality.

## Eclipse of the Christian Form

Balthasar asks what man is who has no "form" for life? In this sense, "form" is something like role-playing. When a man plays the role of father or husband, he puts on the "form" of husband or father. In this context, one can think of the way marriage "formalizes" life. It involves not just mutual trust in the beloved, not just a response to biological laws and drives, but abandonment to a "form" which the partners can realize equally. It involves an internal mystery of realization.

Being a Christian is itself a form. This form is built into the wonder of the redemption and justification of man. Balthasar argues the need to look to the summit, the form of divine revelation. There is need to see that the cosmos is both expression and exegesis of the divine. As man, Christ uses the whole expression-apparatus of historical existence. He wills that all ages and conditions of life witness the Christian form in the way that Christ who is what he expresses gives witness to the Father.

Without the perception of form, man is neither moved nor enraptured. The process of being torn away in ecstasy is the very origin of Christianity. The apostles were enraptured by what they saw, heard, and tasted. John in particular describes how in meeting Jesus and in conversation with him the outlines of his unique form became clear. Then suddenly, ineffably, the radiance of the unconditioned would break through and compel belief.

## Aesthetic Measure

The category of the "beautiful" appears to transcend the frontier between philosophy and theology. Balthasar argues that if the innerworldly beautiful (as *appearing* spirit) can compress and unify the entire dimension, must not the religious be included and with it the ultimate answer to the question "why something rather than nothing." Such art is visible in Christian forms of life.

Prophetic existence, for example, is living the life of the believer who lets himself be formed as a divine effect. Abraham, Isaac, Jacob, Joseph, and Moses display this art in their lives. Although hidden and unspectacular, it appears in such a way that its profile and archetypal power influenced the entire history of belief.

The beautiful carries its own evidence, which immediately illuminates. The application to revelation of what we think to be beautiful seems impossible or at best betrays a naive piety. Balthasar admits that a theological application of aesthetics may turn into aestheticism. This would betray the content of theology and turn it into a theory of beauty.

Despite the danger, it should not be dismissed a priori. A dangerous road is still a road. It may require special knowledge and equipment, but it is not necessarily impassable. Balthasar argues that the Fathers used the category of the "beautiful" as a core of their methodology.

Given the condition that we may approach transcendental beauty, theology is the only science that can have this beauty for its object. Philosophy can approach the absolute only as principle and end of the world, a border concept of ontology. But such a distinction is a late development. Augustine certainly made no such dichotomy. Descartes was the first to let philosophy slip from its mooring in theology.

The middle of the last century saw the last of the great theological systems that clung to a vision of the unity of philosophy and theology. Hegel's synthesis broke apart into a materialist left and a spiritualist right. Theology as a discipline splintered. Fundamental theology became the demonstration of the historicity of God's revelation. Other studies, especially Scripture studies, attempted to become exact sciences. Dogma became more and more history of dogma. Ethics turned into the feeling of being addressed by God's Word in each changing historical situation. Aesthetics could find no place in the series of changes.

Revival of the aesthetic dimension in theology means a return to the existential method in theology. The danger in overconcentration on the exactness of theological sciences consists in leading the theologian to think he may someday discover the object of his science. The simplest insight into aesthetics, however, illustrates that what is expressed by the reality is a pointing to a concealed greater spirit which is capable of appearing. Nothing we see in this world as beautiful is ever complete or absolute.

In making precise the concern of theological aesthetics, Balthasar distinguishes it from "aesthetical theology." For him this latter term has a pejorative meaning and is exemplified by the work of Johann Gottfried Herder. Matthias Joseph Scheeben exemplifies a possible purification of an excessively aesthetic theology (such as that developed by Herder and the romantics).

Balthasar argues that given the essential correctness of the concept of the appearance of the beautiful, it is possible to develop a genuine theological aesthetics along two main lines: (1) the teaching on vision (*Erblickungslehre*) or fundamental theology, aesthetics in the Kantian sense as the teaching on the perception of God who reveals himself; and (2) the teaching on ecstasy (withdrawal, enrapture, *Entrückungslehre*) or dogmatic theology, the teaching of the aesthetics of the incarnation of the glory of God and man's elevation to participation in it. Balthasar says it may seem odd to use *aesthetics* in this dual sense. Yet in theology there are no simple data that could be determined without objective and subjective participation in the way we know worldly facts. But in this case the object is precisely man's participation in divinity, realized on the part of God as revelation and on man's part as faith. This double "ecstasy"—God to man and man to God"—is the content of dogmatic theology.

It is difficult in the current climate of opinion to express such ideas. As attempts to elaborate a theory of the sign have given way to more radical critiques of such attempts, a principle of textuality entirely closed upon itself and for which no extratextual referent and origin can be reached has become itself an absolute.

If Balthasar's argument is correct, methodically sweeping consequences result—especially the inseparability of fundamental and dogmatic theology. Fundamental theology cannot be thought of as a diving board from which one springs into the waters of pure fiducial faith. Rather, it is a development of evidence first obtained in the light of faith, which itself already was ecstasy. Paul, who normally distinguishes "faith" and "vision," speaks in the locus classicus of his theological aesthetics of a "vision of the reflection of the Lord with revealed countenance" by means of which "we are changed into the image" (2 Cor. 3:18). Thus Paul unites the two, although he treats them separately. Only in the second part of the third volume of *Herrlichkeit* (which consists of two thick volumes) does Balthasar reach what he says the entire work strives after—a theology of glory. These volumes go hand in glove with the first volume, which pursues theological aesthetics as *aisthesis*, as perception and experience of the self-revealing glory of God. The first book of the second part of volume 3 is concerned with the Old Testament and the second book with the New Testament.

The glory of God is not only the chief content of Scripture but also the basic theme. It is important that at decisive places in Scripture God's glory (*khabod*, *doxa*) be revealed before the Word goes forth.[10] The appearance of the absolute is never abstract and without relation to the one approached.

Theological aesthetics treats of every theme of revelation. If other themes apart from glory seem to be independent, especially in the Old Testament (themes of creation, man, worldliness, and the like), these cannot be removed from the horizon of the glory of God. A second concern of theological aesthetics would be that of the creature created in God's "image and likeness." Hence the theme of *image* is in a sense contrapuntal to the theme of *glory*. The relation is obvious from the start: first, because the creature is wholly dependent and

10. *Herrlichkeit*, vol. 3, pt. 2, p. 14.

unable to create himself; second, because he is a replica in which is mirrored the archetype and hence must assume certain aspects of glory; and finally, because the movement of revelation is such as to allow *image* and *glory* to become identified (in Christ).

The third range of themes relates to what God erects between himself and his image—the field that seeks to identify itself in concepts like grace, covenant, and justice. This mystery of biblical revelation is also the ultimate question of theological aesthetics. It can be illuminated only by the New Testament in which the image of God becomes united with the Logos of God and so becomes subsistent grace—the real justice and covenant of God.

The themes of glory, image, and grace do not of themselves bring into focus what is truly decisive. Only when the holiness of God appears in glory and when the sinful creature sinks to the floor beneath the overpowering weight of this glory does it become a true opposition of light and darkness, of sanctity and sin, and the drama begins which transcends the mythical parallels of the struggles with the gods. To understand Balthasar's contribution to this tradition, we had to follow, in Chapters 3 and 4, his explication of the movement from myth to religion in the classical world. Balthasar's use of the Fathers was considered in the previous two chapters.

Balthasar studied the theme of *doxa* in both Old and New Testaments. He draws the relationship of glory (in biblical revelation) to the glory revealed by metaphysics and notes that this is an appearance perceived in the mystical religions. He applies the concept of form as developed in the first volume of *Herrlichkeit* throughout his study of biblical aesthetics. He concludes that the concept of *doxa* in the Old Testament became ever more emptied of content until it meant almost anything one wanted it to mean. The New Testament portrays

Christ recalling for man the presence of the divinity whose glory draws all men to adoration.

## Light of Faith: *Pistis* and *Gnosis*

Balthasar's method demands that he examine the relation between *pistis* (faith) and *gnosis* (knowledge) in both Old and New Testaments. He does not intend to provide a complete explanation or to explain and determine the nature of the scriptural use of the terms. Rather, his intention is to highlight the importance of these two concepts. He selects texts that demonstrate the thesis that biblical *gnosis* is not something lying on the threshold of faith (as *praeambula fidei*) but rather a cornerstone of the theology of the Alexandrian Fathers.[11]

Clement of Alexandria, for example, speaks of knowledge: "Our knowledge and spiritual garden is the saviour himself, into whom we are now planted, after being transferred and transplanted from the old life into good soil. The change of soil leads to fruitfulness. The Lord then, into whom we have been transplanted, is the light and true knowledge" (*Strom.* 6.1.2). Such an account of *gnosis* is possible only through the concept of the Logos, in which the rational object of knowledge is at the same time a person. The move from dialectic to contemplation was easier for the Alexandrians than for the plain Platonists.

Both Clement and Origen viewed the Christian as a gnostic who "understands" his faith. The Christian strives for the appropriation of belief, so that he *sees* unfolded before his vision (*theoria*) the essential content of faith. Augustine claimed that human existence made sense only if reality granted what it commanded, that is, if there are resources beyond human ca-

11. See *Glory of the Lord*, 1:130ff.

pabilities to help fulfill the claims human life makes. The attitude in question is faith, a faith that is not just belief but an existential attitude embracing acceptance and commitment. What makes the attitude "religious faith" is a reference to the divine in the context of which man possesses himself.

Gnostic penetration of the veil of revelation by *theoria* means this vision of faith. Balthasar argues that in theological aesthetics *vision* and *faith* are identical. He tries to avoid both the error of Kierkegaard (the *credo quia absurdum*) and that of Hegel (a scientific *analysis fidei*). He argues that if one brackets the historical aspect of the divorce between philosophy and theology, one has no reason for missing the unity of *mythos* and *logos* in Plato, Hölderlin, Schelling, and Heidegger. Christians have either assumed that biblical revelation is the only true appearance of God and that this appearance marks the end of myth or have followed a path of strict rationalism. Philosophy takes the latter path insofar as it dissolves myth into allegorical symbolism without granting reality its true "revealing" character.[12] Christian thinkers found it easy to follow this path leading to the convenient distinction between philosophy and theology.

In other words, Balthasar claims that the formal object of theology (and consequently of the act of faith) lies at the core of the formal object of philosophy. This object erupts from the depths of mystery as the self-revelation of being. Once this is understood—and such thinkers as Origen, Augustine, Anselm, and Aquinas did not understand *intellectus fidei* differently—the limits of what man using his own resources can achieve may be determined by examining what revelation clarifies. The theological vision of reality (*theoria*) always involves myth. Balthasar finds the biblical teaching on this point

12. *Theologik*, 2:230ff.

in the books of Wisdom and in Paul and John in the New Testament.

Once the relation between the formal objects of theology and philosophy has been recognized, the question about the proper outlines of religious faith can be situated. Under the "light-form" of the *beautiful* reality becomes truly visible. An aesthetic moment needs to be added to all knowledge.

## Elements of the Form of Faith

The Christian may call "faith" an ecstatic opening of spirit into the light of reality. Philo, Plotinus, Proklus, Dionysus, and Maximus called knowledge of the real *pistis*. Producing *gnosis* out of *pistis* has occupied Christian thinkers. Pascal carried on the tradition of Augustine and Bernard. Newman did not consider his "realization" of faith anti-intellectually. Rather, he saw it as a deepening of the conceptual element into a total, personal apperception.

Balthasar also says that the teaching on the *lumen fidei*, which has been stored in the warehouse of liberal theology and the philosophy of religion, need not be rejected. The Christian should realize that the internal religious light anyone sees who seeks God in extrabiblical religions is the same light. Many "rites of natural religion" may be just that as far as external ritual is involved, but in the depths of the religious formation they were the result of the same light of faith that illumines all.

In summary, Balthasar argues that the basic question of fundamental theology is one of the vision of the form and so is an aesthetic question. Opposing a "Christ of Faith" to a historical Jesus results in a "tragic dialectic" which is just as crippling as the rigid rationalism of Catholic apologetics. Restoring the aesthetic dimension will put both tendencies back on course, for both are rooted in a Kantian formalism in which there can be nothing more than a sensible "matter" ordered and worked by categorial forms or by ideas and postulates.

Balthasar credits Pierre Rousselot with restoring a patristic tradition on the "eye of faith," the tradition that faith is the ability to see.[13] All theoretical and practical difficulties of faith as an intellectual act can be resolved when the deeper plateau of love is reached. For it is not just human love, which if made absolute becomes demonic (since a finite being abandons himself infinitely to another finite being), but also philosophical love. Every form of the beautiful perceived in space and time is a fragile expression of what is more than spatiotemporal beauty. But spatiotemporal beauty includes the moment of the death of the beautiful because death belongs to the appearing form of immortal beauty.

The light of faith is determined by the object. Hence the light of faith cannot be thought or experienced simply as spiritual reality. Instead it must be considered the irradiation of the presence of a *lumen increatum*. The sensibly beautiful is not surpassable. It is of itself already spiritualized—but only in the measure in which spirit is embodied within the beautiful. Balthasar studies this tradition in Western thought. His careful analysis, though not always original, always provokes and stimulates. This study of the aesthetic tradition in Western thought as it has influenced Balthasar's *Theodramatik* and *Theologik* is the subject of the next chapter.

13. Pierre Rousselot, "Les yeux de la foi," *Recherches de sciences religieuses* 1 (1910): 244–59, 444–75.

## Chapter 9

# *Theodramatik* and *Theologik*

At the start of the second volume of *Theodramatik* Balthasar asks how to divide a study that embraces the entire field of theology. He says it would be tiring to grasp the method of theological aesthetics anew and after an introduction (1) to explore the history of Christian thought according to various theodramatic outlines; (2) to discuss the relation between "natural" and "supernatural" drama; and (3) to present the scriptural teaching from the Old and New Testaments. The disadvantage of such a sequence would be that the third step might be presupposed for the first before the second could be made understandable.

Balthasar consequently chose a division that consciously and thematically keeps the entire question in view but leads from implicit to explicit in a "theodramatic" series of steps. The same basic themes—God and creature, structure and situation of world and mankind, the course of history—are presented in three stages in the *Theodramatik*. The first stage, the *starting point*, is "*ludi personae*"; the second, the *course of action;* and the third, a *conclusion*, which appropriately is an eschatology. In this chapter I will review the role and the sources of the "theodramatics" in Balthasar's theological aesthetics and at the end will indicate the role of the "theologic."

## Theodramatics

The drama of human existence, which appears full only upon its completion, begins to be perceived in the theater. Not only is the uniqueness of human existence re-presented, but the divine action becomes stuff for drama. The dramatic movement prevents theological aesthetics from petrifying in the simple act of perception.

Balthasar states: "What interests us is the entire complex of theater, the very existence of something like performance and play. This totality is to become transparent to revelation, all of its elements used as forms for theology."[1] He argues that great currents of culture culminate in what can be called the universal stage of drama—event, dialogue, role, politics, action, freedom. Focusing on classical theory, Balthasar traces theories of the theater as they illumine the mystery of existence. Then he reviews attitudes toward the stage. The second section of Volume 1 reviews "the dramatic ensemble" of theater: world, author, actors and actresses, director, audience, performance.

In the first part of the second volume Balthasar focuses on the "persons of the drama," the subjective center of the action, to provide an exposition of limited freedom, without which the mysteries of the Trinity and ecclesiastical soteriology cannot be understood. Man, the player, is revealed acting on a stage poised between heaven and earth.

The third part (Volume 4) considers the "action of the play." The cosmos is a stage upon which actors play their roles. The

1. *Theodramatik*, 1:9. In *Theodramatik*, vol. 3, Balthasar stresses the importance of allowing in a theodramatics the true pathos of the real world together with all its *aporiai* to be made visible, before the free answer of the divine is even heard: "If one does not grant to this self-revelation of the world its proper place and time, because one melds into it the 'always beautiful' of the divine answer, then one is in danger of robbing the God-world relation of its drama" (*Theodramatik*, 3:71).

Apocalypse is a starting point, for this New Testament book examines the conflicts of history over God's presence in Christ, the Lamb. The presentation is in multiple images of epic drama which prophesy a future resolution of the theodrama. The two central actions of this part unfold an anthropology of action and then a kind of Christology. First and second Adam are protagonists; "action" describes the being and narrative of the individual and collective Adam under headings such as finitude, time, and death, freedom and evil. The Lamb is ordered toward sacrifice. Crucifixion and resurrection are located within the Trinity, the ultimate protagonist, and in the church, whose liturgy is sacramental drama. The paschal mystery and the community of saints lead back to the Apocalypse.

Balthasar reminds his readers that the main issue in a theodramatic is not seeing and judging but playing and being able to play. The saints are the authentic interpreters of the divine play. Their understanding must constitute the measure not only for the life drama of the individual but also for the "history of freedom" of all mankind.[2]

Aesthetics considers the appearance of the divine—marked as the rising of *Khabod*, "glory"—among the numberless other appearances in nature and history. Theological aesthetics must also consider the conditions for the possibility of perceiving this appearance. As long as only the motif of glory is considered, the formal standpoint remains theocentric. Human freedom "in this responding reflection of glory appeared thematically only as the gift of grace."[3]

Aesthetic form and its implicit "word" involve arousal, awakening of freedom to react to the call that proceeds from the form. A negative reaction to a work of art or drama does not

2. *Theodramatik*, vol. 2, pt. 1, p. 13.
3. Ibid., p. 20.

have serious consequences. But a negative answer to divine revelation in the world theater has very serious consequences. The transition from aesthetics to dramatics can be viewed in a similar way. Viewing "art for art's sake" is a depraved form of encountering what is beautiful.

The ancient hero, when he stood on the stage, possessed a universal, catholic claim, which he inherited from the catholicity of the mythical rite which presented man to God and God to man. As long as this claim remained alive, drama resisted the defamiliarization of narrative epic. All postmythical drama strives for this catholicity. One asks what re-presentation means—whether one drama replaces another or simply takes its position along with others. The drama of Christ is the inclusive culmination of Greek tragedy just as it is the inclusive end of the individual tragic figures of the Old Testament. Christianity fulfills what is positive in myth and at the same time destroys what is vacuous. The divine is not so interwoven in the drama of history that the conclusion of the struggle is uncertain; but the divine is also not elevated beyond the world so that whoever will assume the standpoint of God must elevate himself beyond the dramatic into epic distance.[4]

It is not enough that God is involved with the world and man. If the drama is to come to a question of playing together, man must also enter into the play of God. Man is invited to audition, but he must freely accept this invitation to act in the play. This is the situation for a theodramatic hermeneutics. Balthasar explains that the process involves discussing (1) the basic law of the self-illumination of the phenomenon; (2) the relation of the apparently uninvolved word of the witness to the dramatic, self-explanatory word; and (3) the structure of that which one calls theologically "proof." This three-stage process reflects the three "systems" in Balthasar's trilogy.

4. Ibid., p. 55.

We enter the theater to experience an action that explains itself through its presentation. In a similar fashion, to comprehend a symphony, we must listen to it in its temporal succession. In letting the music or the play affect us, we are forced to pay attention. It is a very different experience from simply reading the play or the musical score. The ancient Greek playwrights thought they were producing a play for a single performance; they certainly did not think they would be reperformed, let alone read and reread.

Dionysus was the god of the dramatic festivals, the patron of both comedy and tragedy. The play, as a ritual act, questioned the act of worship by reviving, in a context offering a moral problem, both emotionally and intellectually, the ritual of which it transcends. In the *Bacchae*, for example, between the ritual death of Pentheus, which we observe, and the blessing of Cadmus, in which we believe, there is no point that unites these signified actions other than the cause of both: the action of the god, who as actor moves the drama forward. The "proof" is presented through the very rite of the drama.

The question about the structure of theological proof—which really belongs to "theologik"—Balthasar only adumbrates in the *Theodramatik*. All theological proof is based on the factual and historical. The paradox, however, is that the Logos exists precisely in this contingent particularity. The historically unique must also be the divinely unique—otherwise the historically unique dissolves into myth or pure symbol.

Balthasar argues that the period of dramaturgy running from Shaftesbury to Herder and on the way from Lessing to Goethe was ruled by the Prometheus principle.[5] Ancient Greece, de-

5. Balthasar was immersed in this issue from the time of his doctoral dissertation, *Apokalypse der deutschen Seele*, published in three volumes totaling 1,612 pages. The first volume was republished as *Prometheus* and accounts for almost one-half of those pages. Its thesis underlies the argument of the *Theodramatik*.

spite Aeschylos, had no such principle—not even a Faustian one. All such forms of "titanism" tend to destroy the person. This is the Titanic, Promethean tendency that Plato envisioned when philosophy tried to overwhelm the world of myth. It is the reasoning that will not accept the incomprehensible decision of the gods. Prometheus's struggle against Zeus symbolizes this reaction.

We must situate this principle in its historical context. Europe was the successor of Christendom, just as Christendom inherited Greco-Roman civilization. In a cultural sense, Europe came into being only with the demise of Christendom, generally with the onset of the Reformation. Before 1650 most works of importance were written in Latin. Many believed the Catholic Counter-Reformation would prevail. Before 1650 the power of the reforming movements, Lutheran, Reformed, and the like, was in flux. By midcentury it appeared that Catholicism would be limited to only part of Europe.

The near success of the Reformation caused a move to conservatism in the Counter-Reformation. The openness and freedom characteristic of the medieval church came to an end. From the point of view of Roman Catholic intellectual life, Kant was Martin Luther in philosopher's clothes; both promoted the triumph of subjectivism. What Luther began, Kant finished.

In reaction, Rome convinced the world that it had no modern history. Had not both Origen and Aquinas said that the water of Greek philosophy could be transformed through revelation into the wine of theology? The waters of Leibniz and Descartes lacked sparkle and capacity for such transubstantiation. Rome rejected not only modern institutions but also modern cultural forms. This is the background for projecting the theology of the future. As T. F. O'Meara wrote, "We need to take seriously this real and seminal encounter of Catholic intellectual life with Romantic idealism precisely because, between Trent and Vatican II, it was a rare event. In its goals and style it begins and molds Catholic theology in the modern world."[6] Balthasar's work might be called a prime demonstration of that thesis.

Eventually, Catholic thought and life tried to accommodate to the new situation. In Germany they did so through the mediation of post-Kantian idealism in the same way they had previously done with the thought of Plotinus and Aristotle. In one sense Schelling helped fashion this epoch. He offered an alternative to Hegel. Schelling affirmed the world of nature and history. He became the gateway from the Romantic view of art to the Catholic tradition of mysticism and symbol. Balthasar noted: "He is really an apocalyptic figure from whom all is arranged around revelation, around the disclosure of mystery, around breakthrough into the mysteries of God. From this magical and mystic style, different from Fichte's asceticism and Hegel's logic, emerges the fact that he is a prophet and a poet."[7]

Hans Urs von Balthasar's first major book was an examination of the German soul in apocalyptic times. His dissertation surveyed terror and eschatology, secular and Christian morality and aesthetics in German thought from Fichte and Goethe through Novalis and Schelling to Hegel. This enterprise of the young Swiss synthesizer offers an original reading of Schelling, who, Balthasar argues, wrote an eschatology of the fall and the divine abyss. Freedom, necessity, and indifference float above the primal ground of the All. This is a system of mysticism and physics for an age moving from Luther and Böhme to Nietz-

6. T. F. O'Meara, O.P., *Romantic Idealism and Roman Catholicism: Schelling and the Theologians* (Notre Dame: Notre Dame University Press, 1982), p. 4.

7. *Prometheus*, p. 206.

sche. Schelling labored on a never-finished bridge from subject to object, from myth to Christianity. In the last analysis he did not know where to lay the foundation stone.[8]

## Sources of Balthasar's Theological Dramatics and Logic

It is not accidental that the term "ideology" and its referent first surfaced following the French Revolution, which, among other removals, tore traditional religion from the center of European political and social life. "Ideology" has been defined in different ways, although a few common elements belong to all variants. First, it refers to a global system of ideas or symbols that shapes history and so social reality and consequently allows one to position the community holding that ideology. It becomes a Weltanschauung with a social base and a communal function. Second, as used by both Napoleon and Marx, ideology has a pejorative connotation, indicating an unwarranted claim on the truth. Because religion originally made no claim to be science, it was not considered an ideology. For Marx, however, such a claim conceals a form of self-interest. When the term "ideology" is used, it often signals a disdain for the group holding the beliefs in question. Third, as a symbolic structure focusing the life of a society, an ideology must be shared by the members of the group for the group to be effective. This sharing implies intellectual assent to the symbolic structure and commitment to group goals.

As ideologies replaced religion after the French Revolution, personal religion in evangelical or cultic form arose to give structure and meaning to personal life in the new industrial world. As this world moved into a postindustrial period, the religious element did not disappear but assumed its place along-

8. See *Theologik*, 2:235ff.

side other ideologies. Nineteenth-century attention to aesthetics was an attempt to revise the meaning of transcendence precisely when the traditional apparatus of sublimation—spiritual, ontological, and psychological—appeared to be expiring. Balthasar picked up the hermeneutical side of the movement, a remarkably successful way to read, which preserved the authority of the past.

Balthasar sees very clearly that today's struggle is for a theology that can mesh with the problematic of the technological rather than the medieval world. Such a movement has been made possible by the careful work of the tradition, the historical recovery of biblical, patristic, and medieval sources founded on the classical tradition. Balthasar's own work in rediscovering and reformulating this corpus must be assigned a prominent place. His interpretation of the tradition rests on a Teutonic base built by a series of thinkers from Kant to Heidegger. The most succinct formulation of this later metaphysical tradition is found in *Herrlichkeit*, vol. 3, part 1, section 2.

Kant's first great critique was aimed directly at the ideal of pure reason represented at that time in the work of Christian Wolff and a dry scholasticism. Kant's critique, whatever its other difficulties, demolished the philosophical naieveté of pure rationalism. Kant struck the core presupposition of that school: the mistaken analogy between mathematics and philosophy. In mathematics in Kant's pre-Riemannian period pure reason could yield universal and necessary results because the mathematician can construct mathematical concepts and categories by representing those space-time concepts in a pure a priori intuition. The philosopher, however, does not possess a similar a priori intuition of being, the object of his study. A philosopher must pursue a more modest because more critical path: the construction of a transcendental method based on a critical analysis of human consciousness. Kant called for a

"Copernican revolution" in philosophy by insisting that anyone who did metaphysics first had to defend critically the "conditions for the possibility" of any such knowledge. Although the negative conclusions of Kant's enterprise have received the principal attention of most "realist" commentators, Kant's conclusions were challenged by subsequent German philosophy. Nevertheless, the philosophic ideal of pure reason was upset and the possibility of all and every precritical approach to philosophy, including scholasticism, was called into serious question. No matter where the accent is placed, Kant's "critical idealism" left "no more room for an experience of the being of the world as an appearance of the glory of God."[9]

Kant's criticism, however, opened the door of the vast corridors of German Idealism to art. The "dynamic" sublime, which concerns power and sets man and nature in desperate opposition, became an obsessive structure for the thinkers who followed. When Nietzsche finally proposed "heights of the soul from which even tragedy ceases to look tragic," he carried the sublime to the ultimate extreme. Without some sense of the beyond, some credible discourse of the supernatural, the sublime founders or becomes merely a philosophical problem. This, incidentally, was just as true in antiquity. A purely humanistic sublime would constitute an oxymoron.

Hegel compounded the difficulty by introducing a more general theorem—the dialectic—which demanded that every philosophic ideal be made explicit. For Hegel any attempt at scientific explanation or explication of an implicit ideal involves an ever-increasing abstraction of that ideal. But that involvement serves only to increase the problematic, for no abstraction can express the whole of man's desire and capacity for that mimetic ideal. Any explication, however abstract, for ex-

9. *Herrlichkeit*, vol. 3, pt. 1, sec. 2, p. 818.

ample, a Scholastic theory of grace, cannot express the actual living situation because in every abstraction there remains an opposition between the explication of the ideal and the desires of the subject in whom that ideal is implicit. That opposition is the Hegelian alienation, that is, the alienation of the subject from an abstract ideal that cannot represent the real situation. The Hegelian critique expresses the existence of the critical problem of the philosopher's scientific ideal. Not only is the ideal of pure reason criticized as in the case of Kant, but the Hegelian argument pushes that criticism still further: any scientific or philosophical ideal will be an abstraction; it will ultimately prove inadequate; that inadequacy will expose the reality of alienation, which may give rise to another explication and still another. Hegel's own solution (mediation-resolution via the dialectic) has been interpreted very differently.

In appealing to Socrates, Johann Georg Hamann cast his vote for an alliance with the classical tradition. In radically reinterpreting Socrates, however, he served notice that he did not understand that tradition in the same way as the rationalists. He agreed with the Enlightenment in looking back to Greece for wisdom but disagreed over what was seen. This difference comes into focus in his *Memorabilia*, in which Socrates is presented as a precursor of Christ, not as the only rational alternative. This was part of a patristic inheritance that included Justin Martyr, Lactantius, and Minucius Felix. Hamann sought the literary form that could not only be truer to the spiritual reality of Socrates but could also conform to the paradox of the "Knechtsgestalt Christi"—that is, the appearance in "the form of a servant" (Phil. 2:7). Hamann was convinced that the frequent metamorphoses of Greek gods into lower forms was an anticipation of the Incarnation in the "form of a servant." Balthasar does not share this view, but his approach is very similar. Balthasar claims, however, that Teilhard's thought displays an even greater similarity, for Teilhard maintained that the myths contain genuine anticipations of the Incarnation.[10] Hamann's was an extreme form of appeal to the classical tradition. The mainstream, ultimately, represented no less radical a turn.

As for Kant "philosophy" meant rational criticism of traditional concerns, so for the Idealists, it meant a search for the Logos in nature, art, and institutions. The leaders in this research were Fichte, Schelling, and Hegel, along with Schopenhauer, whose thought is based on Kant and Schleiermacher, who focused on religion. All, however, were schooled by Kant; all wanted to present a single world-view through a deification of reason extended to embrace intuition and feeling, conscious and unconscious. Common to these thinkers and the literary figures such as the Schlegels, Tieck, and Novalis, was a revived interest in the world of mythos—art, literature, and mysticism. Balthasar grew up encased in this intellectual greenhouse.

For Kant, both the beautiful and the sublime are pleasing on their own account, but the pleasure or delight induced by the two are wholly distinct. That which is beautiful by nature is so by virtue of its form, and this consists in limitation. But the sublime evokes the sense of limitlessness, which is somehow totally present to the viewer.[11] For Kant the sense of the sublime makes possible apprehension of the infinite or the transcendent as immediately present.

Johann Gottlieb Fichte wanted to view the world as a unit based on the absolute primacy of moral consciousness, a picture as powerful as the tautologies from which he claimed to derive it: "My world is the object and sphere of my duties and nothing else at all." His argument in *nuce* was that the ego

10. *Theodramatik*, 4:137; see also *Theologik*, 2:232ff.
11. *Herrlichkeit*, vol. 3, pt. 1, sec. 2, pp. 859ff.

posits itself as existing; the ego posits the nonego as not itself; the nonego is posited within the ego. The motive is that "the Ego is obliged to posit itself as perceptive." Fichte called this the dialectic of thesis, antithesis, and synthesis.[12]

In the same way that Fichte began with Kant's *Critique of Practical Reason*, Schelling began with the *Critique of Judgment*, which exhibits reason as operative in art, culture, and the science of organic life. For Schelling it is the objective world, not the individual psychology, which man must study to find traces of the absolute. This notion appealed to Balthasar as a theoretical ground for his aesthetics.

Since the absolute is found in perception, contemplation, and artistic creativity rather than in logic or abstract reasoning, Fichte's pure ego, Schelling claimed, is a useful postulate for explaining the mimetic aspect of self in nature, art, mythology, and religion. In his *First Draft of a System of Natural Philosophy,* Schelling argued that we must see that intelligence continually and unconsciously unfolds the world of our perception just as it consciously procures the creation of the ideal world. There is a relation between nature and art in the sense that art calls attention to aspects of nature we would otherwise fail to realize. Art, Schelling says, is more productive than science as a source of self-revelation: "The idea of the gods is essential for art."[13]

In the *Philosophy of Art* Schelling argues that it is the function of art and not of philosophy to manifest the "identity of the conscious and the unconscious in the Absolute." Symbolic and mythological art enjoys special status because it provides both the subject matter of significant works of art and material of philosophy. Given the absolute unknowability of the abso-

12. Ibid., pp. 882ff.
13. *Theologik*, 2:234.

lute, he raises the question adopted by Balthasar: Why is there anything at all? Why not nothing? Schelling's answer was a theory of history as displaying "the evolution of the divine principle in history." The beginning is the moment when "God alienates himself from himself." This is the genesis of infralapsarian man, the man of the silver, bronze, and iron ages of Hesiod. This process, as the entire content of the myths demonstrates, is essentially tragic.[14]

Comparative mythology led Schelling to think we can find necessary, a priori conditions about the interrelationships of myth. A genuine myth can never be just the invention of one man. But myths cannot be simply the product of certain people because the people as a tribe or cultural group is the creation of its myths.[15] For Western man this is the amalgam of the Greek and the Judaeo-Christian traditions. The former involves an idealization of nature; the latter, of human social life and history.

The Judaeo-Christian tradition includes myths of fall and redemption, apocalyptic glory and happiness, whereas the Greek tradition is one of revelation. The use of images from Babylonian myth in the Old Testament opened the way for Christian use of the mythology of the Greeks by the Fathers and the later Christian humanists.[16] The connection among Old and New Testaments and the classical tradition can be seen at many places, whether in mythical images or ethical statements such as those in the Wisdom Books.

14. Ibid., p. 235.

15. See ibid., p. 233.

16. See *Herrlichkeit*, vol. 3, pt. 2. Balthasar later noted, "No matter how different the expressions are, one sees so little how they could be stopped. Every thought must, in order to be understood, be included in the form of 'I think—I am', which is formally unsurpassable and consequently absolute (divine)" (*Theodramatik* vol. 3, pt. 1, sec. 2, p. 79.

Georg Wilhelm Friedrich Hegel studied at Tübingen, and it was there he met Hölderlin, who became his closest friend (until Hölderlin began to go "mad" in his thirties). He met Schiller at Jena, where he was appointed to a chair of philosophy. Schiller's *Letters on Aesthetic Education* had already influenced Hegel. In the *Letters* Schiller makes art, and in particular poetry, the result of the combination or synthesis of two drives—an urge toward play and an urge toward order. Both Schiller and Hegel used the concept of *Geist*, spirit, as a creative force manifesting itself in individual consciousness.

Balthasar observes that drama for Hegel constitutes the high point of all artistic creation.[17] Hegel provides an analysis of Greek tragedy and says the greatest achievement is the *Antigone*. Because drama was the summation of art, the proposition can be advanced that comedy leads to this peak as well as to the breakup of art as such. Balthasar notes that Hegel means this proposition to be taken seriously and says it is repeated frequently.

Poetry and art are for Hegel one of the two moments united in philosophy. He undertakes to resolve the yearning for identification, but his resolution is the same as in the tradition: man finds both nature and spirit within himself, insofar as he comes to know them in reality, as absolute idea. To know is to become like them. Like know like; the human spirit becomes what it knows (Aristotle), and it knows only that which comes as a result of its self-realization in self-consciousness (Hegel). Goethe's *Faust* (part 1, 11, 500, 512–13) expresses this idea poetically:

17. *Theodramatik*, 1:50: "Drama must, because according to content as well as form develop to its fullest totality, and must be viewed as the supreme stage of poetry and art." Balthasar quotes Hegel's *Ästhetik*, vol. 2, and uses it to bolster his argument.

*Ich bin's, bin Faust, bin deines gleichen!*
(It is I, Faust, I'm just like you!)

The apparition retorts:

*Du gleichst dem Geist den du begreifts.*
*Nicht mir!*
(You are like the spirit that you grasp, not me!)

To the question with what subsequent art is concerned, Hegel gives a number of answers. The first is that it is assumed by Rome as simply an expression of imperial power. The second says that the Greek gods should not be viewed as human in the way the Christian Jesus Christ is human. The third answer, however, is both more interesting and more problematic. Hegel contrasts the multiple forms of art of every genre with the classical by calling them "romantic." He cannot ignore Dante, Shakespeare, Calderon, Cervantes, Goethe, and Schiller. He says that the romantic is in itself the principle of the breakup of the classical ideal.[18]

In Balthasar's view, the issue becomes finding an analogy between innerworldly drama, which obtains its visible form in the theater, and the drama between God and man (Theodramatik). He says Hegel is of interest only as a possible contributor to this analogy. Balthasar admits that no thinker before Hegel had expressed Christian revelation so powerfully in dramatic categories and that we can follow him in this, because Hegel saw between the Old and New Testaments a synthesis of the basic dialectic rhythm of the world process.[19] Ultimately for Hegel, tragedy as play and Christian passion as seriousness disappear and the analogy required to build a Theodramatik disappears in an identity.

18. Balthasar takes this idea from Hegel's *Ästhetik*, vol. 1.
19. *Theodramatik*, 1:61.

Despite his critique, Balthasar observes that one is tempted to think Hegel right because personal Christology is no longer practiced. He lists several issues that must be addressed:

1. Mission in the ecclesiastical sense, which is rooted in the teaching on Christology and the Trinity, is neither "worship" nor "character" but a reality which the Christian must by "worship" realize as character. This subjective mission is both a stewardship of the world and truly universal.

2. The difference between the "substantial" task of the church as a whole and that of the individual must be reaffirmed. The former is similar to the role of the ancient chorus in a Greek tragedy, the latter, the hero, now re-presented on a new level.

3. Because Christian mission always has a universal content, its realization both within and outside of the ecclesiastical sphere contains an inevitable fullness of dramatic tension, conflict, and opposition.

4. Each mission participates in the total mission of Christ. So each Christian existence is a drama mirroring the mission of Christ. Hegel failed to see this aspect in romantic drama. From such a viewpoint, many of the chief works of Calderon can be understood, as well as those of Shakespeare.

5. Behind all this stands the basic problem of theodramatics, at which Hegel ultimately took aim: In what sense is the theological drama a drama of God? Does God participate in the acting? What is the relation between the immanent and economic Trinity (which in Hegel become identified)? Hegel's philosophy brings such theological questions to light.[20]

Ultimately, dramatic action can be represented only against the backdrop of the gift (*Vorgabe*) of absolute meaning, and

20. See *Herrlichkeit*, vol. 3, pt. 1, sec. 2, pp. 911ff.

after Hegel this gift can no longer be rationally described. Such an absolute for the Christian can be understood only in the gamble that is belief. Other views can be put forward, such as those of Nietzsche or Marx. There is no purely "private" play. In Athens the drama was a civic event, sponsored by and for the *polis*; Shakespeare played before a kingdom, a court, a republic—for or against! For Corneille, long before Hegel, the purpose of the state is the most palpable form for the stage. In Lope de Vega the prince can be a villain, yet his principality is unaffected. Racine dreams of the lost power of Rome. Society as such cannot replace the horizon of meaning of the tragic. It must be nourished, justified, by blood and suffering, as in Ibsen.

That which is meaningless, however, if that is the last word, destroys the action and ends up in the dust bin (Beckett). Alleged absolute freedom, which God and devil can play (Sartre) ends in boredom. Revolt as absolute attitude (Camus) is absurd because it must continually presuppose the very condition it denies.

The hero of classic tragedy was a king, the son of a god, or a Titan, an immediate appearance of the divine world, larger than life. Shakespeare's kings and great men share a reflection of this mythic grandeur when they mingle in the world of the little man and the fool. Like the heroes of French tragedy and those of Calderon and Schiller, they are "characters" in the Hegelian sense. They relate one to another.[21]

In order to preserve itself, drama must again borrow the splendor of ancient myth; again an Antigone, Medea, Electra, an Orpheus, Oedipus, Amphitryon, an Orestes (even if so discretely disguised as in Eliot's *Family Reunion*), an Achilles (Kleist), a voyage of the Argonauts (Grillparzer), etc. Giraudoux, Hoffmansthal, Shaw, Cocteau,

21. See *Theologik*, 2:43ff.

> Gide, O'Neill, Anouilh change the material . . . from genuine tragedy through parody to social criticism.[22]

Freud is a modern mediator, a replacement for the ancient notion of the demonic, the dimension of the irrational. Even when one knows the laws of inheritance as does Ibsen, one still does not know what role they play in human action. The existential question becomes more difficult the more science can say about it.

Behind Marxian radicalism stands as starting point a biblical spirit of prophecy, whose Christian form, according to Marx, has failed historically but in an atheistic revolution can be realized. But from this viewpoint Marxism simply cannot be undramatic and nontragic. If the tragic today assumes such dimensions that humanity "experiences more anxiety and pain than can be shown on the stage" (Herbert Marcuse), if mankind is not to flee into Nirvana, it must again look to the Christian for a way into the future.[23] Examples of how the theater must be humanized, made into the stage for real people, may be found in such playwrights as Thornton Wilder and Bertholt Brecht. Balthasar claims that no modern poet has conducted a finer dialogue with Christianity than Brecht, though "none harsher" either.[24]

Hegel's *Phenomenology* ends with what came to be called "Absolute Spirit": natural religion, religion of art, revealed religion, absolute knowledge (philosophy). Art is a form of religion that exists in statues and pictures and gives rise to a tension between love of the beautiful around consciousness of absolute demands, among them a demand for the revelation of a divine individual. Those who are aware of the absolute

22. *Theodramatik*, 1:70.
23. Ibid., pp. 75–76.
24. *Spiritus Creator*, p. 406.

present in this divine individual in the form of love may obtain an absolute knowledge. The *Phenomenology* represents Hegel's movement toward accepting life, including its problems, because life produces rational social order, aesthetic religion, and philosophy. This became a central notion for Schopenhauer and Nietzsche.

For Hegel art is finding ideal forms in the material and in works that have an individuality of their own. The beauty of nature is a manifestation of spirit, but it is surpassed by the human imagination in a successful work of art. There are three main types of art: symbolical, classical, and romantic. Symbolic art is hieratic, a means of representing the religious or magical; classical art is the purest expression of static form; romantic art "delivers itself to the inward life," displays the tension between spirit and its body. Romantic art becomes the equivalent of Christian art, whose highest expressions are music and poetry, just as the highest expressions of classical art are sculpture and painting.

If Schelling's writings at Jena first were dedicated to the philosophy of nature, his lectures were on a general system of transcendental philosophy. The time at Dresden and the companionship of such literary figures as the Schlegels led Schelling to incorporate art as well as nature into a transcendental framework. Fichte also traveled to and from Jena, where he lectured alongside Schelling. When Shelling was twenty-five years old, he published the *System of Transcendental Idealism* at the Easter book fair of 1800. This system embraced natural sciences as well as painting and plastic arts. The system announced parallel worlds: self and nature. Idealism was objective; the world of nature was not a mental projection. The ideal is just as dependent on the real as spirit is dependent on nature for ultimate synthesis. A preestablished harmony unites the parallel histories. The climax of the system was art, the place where spirit became embodied. In the artistic imagination, realized in paint or stone, the idea assumed matter. The spirit of the knowing self was free and creative, possessing intuition into absolute spirit. In art the creation of the artistic mind, the synthesis of matter and form, reflected the universe in which the real and ideal joined in history and play.[25]

Schelling wrote that the Homeric epic was the poetic paradigm of the real world. In the journey of the individual and collective self we view Odysseus leaving home to become objectified, to find his true identity, on his travels back to Ithaca: "History is an epoch whose poet is God. Its two main parts are found in the process of humanity; the first is humanity's emergence up to the highest point away from God; the second is the return. The first part is the *Iliad*; the second is the *Odyssey*."[26]

Schelling and his Jena circle believed that the numinous has three loci: nature, art, and the depth of the free self. Before long they included history. Balthasar notes the impossibility of pursuing the wandering thoughtways of Schelling's philosophy of art, but he is greatly indebted to such passages as "the realistic mythology reached its bloom in Greek myth, the idealistic poured itself out in the course of time wholly into Christendom."[27]

Shortly after he arrived in Munich, Schelling came to know Baader. Baader was a truly extraordinary character. By profession he was a miner, but he was obsessed with mysticism and philosophy. His writings adumbrated ecumenism, nihilism, and socialism. Balthasar describes Baader as the "Titan" of

25. *Herrlichkeit*, vol. 3, pt. 1, sec. 2, pp. 897ff.

26. Friedrich Wilhelm Schelling, *Werke*, 15 vols. (Stuttgart, 1856–61), 6:57.

27. *Theologik*, 2:234.

German Idealism.[28] Aesthetic terms always ultimately apply because of, and aesthetic qualities always ultimately depend upon, the presence of features that, like curving or angular lines, color contrasts, placing of masses, or speed of movement, are visible, audible, or otherwise perceptible without any exercise of taste or sensibility.

Throughout this discussion we have been grappling with a central notion, that of form. In this section I intend to focus upon what this notion means and its central role in Balthasar's dramatics. The investigation and elucidation of this notion seems to me to hold the answer to many of the problems and paradoxes of theology. The issue involves the way pleasure in aesthetic contemplation is derived from the perception of the harmony of the imagination and the understanding in the apprehension of the form of an object.

According to Kant, an aesthetic judgment is either empirical or pure. An empirical aesthetic judgment asserts that a certain object is either pleasant or unpleasant, that is, it asserts that an object is or is not a source of empirical satisfaction. A pure aesthetic judgment asserts that a certain object is beautiful or sublime. The latter, whether empirical or pure, consists of a subject, copula, and predicate. The predicate in either case is a feeling of pleasure or displeasure in the presentation of an object. The crucial difference is that in a pure aesthetic judgment the feeling of pleasure or its opposite in the presentation of the object is a determination that goes to the form of the object of sense, whereas in the case of the empirical aesthetic judgment, the feeling of pleasure or dis-

28. *Prometheus*, p. 240. Balthasar holds that everything that came after German Idealism implies a new edition of older models of hope. Thus Marx and "the ideal of the total cybernetics, with which the ancient attitude of Prometheus seems to be revived" would be interpreted. See also *Die Wahrheit ist symphonische*, p. 154; *Theologik*, 2:331.

pleasure is a determination that does not go to the form but to the matter of the object. Balthasar relates the Kantian theory to Kant's experience of wonderment in gazing at the star-filled heaven. This was an experience of wonder or of the sublime.

In determining that an object is sublime we estimate the form of the object. If a color or tone is capable of being beautiful in itself, then it is more than sensation; it is a play of sensations. If we say that this play of sensations is beautiful, that is, if our judgment is a pure aesthetic judgment on the beautiful, then we must be concerned with the form of these sensations. If particular colors and tones are beautiful plays of sensations, rather than merely agreeable sensations, then the investigation of what, exactly, is involved in saying that they are beautiful will aid in solving the question of meaning of form, since if they can be said to be beautiful, there is a reflection on their form.

In speaking of the form of objects of sense as play, Kant divides play into play of figures in space and play of sensations in time. The apprehension of the form of an object of sense is the apprehension of the temporal or spatial relationships among a given manifold of sensations. Imagination unites sensations. Sensations so united display a form—that is, they exhibit spatial and temporal relationships, play or figure. If the form exhibited by the one manifold of sensations agrees with the faculty of concepts, pleasure results and the object of sense is judged beautiful. Only the form and not the matter of sensation can accord with understanding. Balthasar situates this as the horizon of world theater.

In the *Critique of Aesthetic Judgment* Kant's analysis is not of the cognitive relation but of a somewhat different kind, wherein the human mind knows the object, not as something to be known but as something to be estimated aesthetically. The artist originates new possible relations among sensations, new forms, which are concomitants or analogues of indefinite thought or concepts. The artist must also determine the proper expression for those aesthetic ideas—he must find the expression that permits the harmony of imagination and understanding to be perceived in his art; he must communicate his intuition. The artist as creator makes a work of art in accordance with the free exercise of his intellectual gifts. He re-presents aesthetic ideas. To present an aesthetic idea is to give form a specific, perceptible embodiment. The artist freely and spontaneously creates those forms which have the appearance of being natural, for they are final forms. The artist re-presents the same forms which nature presents, forms that lead to a subjective, pleasurable harmony of imagination and understanding, which is the mimetic process.

Because the aesthetic experience carries within itself its evidence, Balthasar believes he avoids a Kantian categorial origin for this experience in the subject. The paradigm for this experience is divine revelation in the form of Christ. The form and the act are inseparable.

Balthasar says that a great work of art appears like an original creation, a miracle on the stage of history. Every such work has presuppositions, but these conditions do not explain it completely. Mozart's *Magic Flute* was preceded by many Viennese and Italian models, but how can one account for the uniqueness of Mozart's work?

A great work of art is never obvious and immediately intelligible in the prior, immediately understandable language that lies ready to hand, for the new, unique language that is born with it is its interpreter. It is "self-explanatory." For a moment the contemporary world is taken aback, then they understand, and begin to speak in the newly minted language (e.g., "the age of Goethe") as though they had invented it themselves. The unique word makes itself understandable by itself. The greater a work of art, the more extensive, generally, will be the cultural sphere it dominates.[29]

Balthasar observes that philosophies of art, those of Schelling and Hegel, for example, try to project the arbitrarily erupting imagery and the Weltanschauung reflected therein against a horizon of universal understanding. "And is there any reason why they should not succeed? Yet the 'miracle' that is the achievement of a great work of art remains inexplicable."[30]

In the vertical drama in which the players (God above, man below) fix the dimensions of the stage, the stage itself is an important part of the play.[31] The movement from both poles centers on the Incarnation. Inasmuch as the church is the elongation of this movement, "she lives out of heaven to earth and from earth to heaven."[32] The action in time becomes more tragic, both for man who is capable of gambling away his salvation and for God who must judge where he wished to bring love.[33]

Balthasar called Hegel's language about the "death of God" an attempt philosophically to represent God as a necessary process and theologically as "free self-revelation."[34] The death of Jesus from such a viewpoint is a pure expression of Trinitarian life. The mystery of Good Friday and Holy Saturday represents the loneliness of the love between Father and Son in the Spirit in such a way that the melding of these events, the

29. "Warum ich noch ein Christ bin," p. 22.

30. Ibid., Balthasar situates Hegel in the tradition of the Stoa, Plotinus, Dionysus, Scotus Erigena, Cusanus, Ficino, Spinoza, Herder, and Goethe, all of whom in some fashion interpreted the cosmos as an explication of the divine. See *Herrlichkeit*, vol. 3, pt. 1, sec. 2, p. 906.

31. *Theodramatik*, 4:96.

32. Ibid., p. 114.

33. Ibid., p. 173.

34. Ibid., p. 203.

reunion, the resurrection, can follow only as a "secret of eternal life" in total "loneliness."

The elevation of the tragic element now appears to be the same as the situation of the *apokatastasis*, the total reconciliation. The question becomes one of eternal damnation versus universal salvation. Balthasar argues that insofar as the judgment occurs only in the suffering love between Father and Son in the Spirit, all Old Testament satisfaction about the punishment of the evil must be muffled radically.

Balthasar cites Hofmannsthal's play *Der Turm* in this context and notes that a beggar appears on stage who can only speak and repeat a single word, "unworthy."[35] The king says to the beggar, "Wholly soft has hell grown into you and it is there called abandoned by god." The "radical evil" Kant found in man, which Goethe seconded, had found no echo in Idealist philosophy and theology.

Balthasar establishes the possibility of a return of creature to God in the sense of a completion and without loss of the quality of being a creature through three propositions. First is the description of divine life which in a superessential manner contains all elements. Second, this possibility is achieved by a theology of the world in its pilgrim condition, which reaches its goal by a transforming death. Finally, this is accomplished by the thought that in spite of and because of its true, free createdness the world cannot be "outside" of God. So it is not a question of a movement of the world from outside to inside the divine, but rather a transformation of the condition of the world within, a nearness and immanence to the divine.[36] The opposition of heaven and earth ultimately reflects the mystery of Christ—man and God. Balthasar holds that in the face of

35. Ibid., p. 267.
36. Ibid., p. 361.

death it is impossible to encourage belief unless man is sustained by the vision of the splendor of the form of Christ.

Balthasar confesses that he has had to describe the completion of the world by means of images and symbols. "But when we look back over the long, meandering way in the volumes of the *Theodramatik*, does not what has been presented seem too simple, given the labyrinthian character of the world and the abyss in, around, and surrounding of the incomprehensibility of God?"[37] Was what was described as a drama in which God had the role of protagonist presented too simplistically? To set the central scene of the play in act, the essential mystery of the divine basis of the world had to be shown under three aspects. God, who gave man commandments, was injured by the disobedience of his creatures; he sends his eternal Son from Heaven to Earth, but he is rejected; his death reconciled God and world. On the basis of the passion of the Son and his followers, God wins the *agon*, the theatrical contest. Balthasar asks whether after all statements of such a simple scheme one must place a question mark.

Balthasar quotes from Büchner and again from Hoffmannsthal's *Der Turm*. Büchner reportedly said on his deathbed: "We do not have too much pain; rather we have too little; for it is through pain that we go to God." And Sigismund in *Der Turm* states: "Man is a unique glory (*Herrlichkeit*), and he does not have too much suffering and pain, but rather too little of them. That I say to you."

The splendor of the form of Christ can be perceived only by one who is willing to suffer, to take up the cross and lose himself, to forget his selfish needs. This is the role of the protagonist in a tragedy.

37. Ibid., p. 447.

Balthasar's *Theodramatik* ends in a Trinitarian-Christological eschatology. The splendor of the form of Christ derives first from the self-sufficient freedom and love between the persons of the Trinity and secondarily from their love for creation. The problem of eternal damnation is reversed in Hegelian fashion. Instead of asking what man has lost when he has lost God, the question becomes what does God lose when he loses Man?

The gratuity of creation is based on the more fundamental gratuity of divine internal life. From the "gloria Dei" in creation every suspicion of a divine solipsism is removed. Inner participation of creation on Trinitarian life is a gift of each divine person in the other whereby every appearance of a mere eternal "glorification" is overcome.[38]

The *Theologik*, the third part of the trilogy, has the task which Balthasar himself ultimately says is impossible, the attempt to develop the third transcendental, divine truth, which overcomes the opposition of heaven and hell.[39]

I have tried in this chapter to outline how Balthasar relates the *Theodramatik* to theological aesthetics. The concept or motive of world theater is the key. Liturgy and sacrifice are shown to be one, or in other words the unity of Balthasar's aesthetics and dramatics has been re-presented.[40] "World theater" is a category of universal dimension whose transcendental horizon is captured in the concept of theater.[41] The discussion of how Shakespeare and Calderon become important for theology in Balthasar's approach must be the subject of another volume.

38. Ibid., p. 464.

39. *Theologik*, 2:330.

40. *Theodramatik*, 3:51. Concrete examples from drama are given on p. 461.

41. Manfred Lochbrunner, *Analogia Caritatis* (Freiburg in Breisgau: Herder, 1981), p. 212.

I conclude this discussion with a repetition of the signal importance of Greek tragedy in Balthasar's work. He draws a parallel between the sacraments and Greek tragedy in its cult dimension. This leads to a new definition of the tragic which becomes a demonstration that "a totally different existence, another world must exist, the knowledge of which . . . can be given only in an indirect manner."[42] The importance in Greek tragedy of suffering, re-presentation, sacrifice, and reconciliation are important moments for theological speculation. Had the Fathers concerned themselves as much with Greek dramatic literature as with Greek philosophical thought, the history of Christian dogma may very well have been different.

42. *Theodramatik,* 1:47.

# Epilogue

We have seen that Balthasar developed his theological aesthetics in two parts, first as an epistemological investigation of the "sight" of faith (*Erblickungslehre*) and second as a doctrine of ecstasy (*Entrückungslehre*), a presentation of the divine ecstasy, the procession out of the Godhead into the world as manifestation of glory and as narrative of the way the human is seized "dramatically" by this glory and taken up into the Godhead. The divine appears in the form of Christ, the perceptible form of the divine, the "aisthesis tou theou." The process of manifestation is revelation, and the divine epiphany becomes the object of theology.

The theological aesthetics also constitutes an aesthetic in the normal sense of the word, a study of beauty. For Balthasar this sense follows from the first denotation of the word. Beauty is transcendental in the same way that truth and goodness are. Everything that exists is true because it can be grasped by the intellect; everything that exists is good because it can become an object of love; everything is beautiful because it can provide pleasure in the act of apprehension. Balthasar holds that without beauty the true would be just what is logically correct and the good would be the same as what is useful. What asserts itself beyond the correct and useful is a delight in the apprehension of the object of beauty.

As *splendor formae* beauty has an ontological depth. Perceptible form of an object is self-expression of its metaphysical form. Works of art are explorations of the possible, explorations of formal structures that can be imagined and projected in space or time. So art is an exploration of the formal possibilities of being and of the possibilities of human emotion-reaction in the face of the forms of being. Platonism always held that sensible beauty was but a reflection of absolute beauty and a means whereby the soul may begin its ascent.

Beauty is concerned with form (*formosus, speciosus*) and with the splendor that radiates forth. It is the form, the *Gestalt*, which is the expression of the artistic vision, and yet the glory that shines forth is nowhere present except in the form. The beauty of a work of art is not an aspect, not something over and above the actual work itself; rather, the beauty is in the work, which itself is somehow miraculous. Part of Balthasar's originality may be seen in the way he chooses the transcendental "beauty" as the intersection between Western thought and Christian revelation. He builds on a foundation of German Idealism as elaborated in Chapter 9.

The term "aesthetics" is from the Greek *aisthesis*, "perception," and from the time of Baumgarten and Kant has also designated a branch of philosophy. Hegel expanded the concept to include a philosophy of the fine arts. Balthasar begins with the simple experience of the beautiful as interpreted by this tradition.

Aesthetics, therefore, is concerned with form, shape, composition, expression, and seeing such forms *as they are*. Just as the artist is "inspired" and filled with enthusiasm, so too those who *see* are seized with the divine spirit (*enthousiasmos*). What is seen is the *doxa* of the form, but this glory is the glory of being. Balthasar argues that the mystery in such beauty is the irruption of the eternal into the material in such a way that one can speak of the event of beauty, the entrance of the numinous into this world. To see beauty is to be overcome by the glory that breaks out of this person, this poem, this picture, this flower. Once the beauty is seen, its possessor can no longer simply have utilitarian value, something to be used or classified or even discarded. We are confronted by the sense of its otherness. The explanation for this interpretation depends on Balthasar's exposition of the classical tradition, discussed in Chapters 3 and 4. A study of this tradition can alert the theologian to aspects of theology which otherwise have been neglected. The experience of the sublime for Balthasar, as for Kant, draws us up into a higher realm. Balthasar has as goal not to rob the beauty of the world to save theology but to alert men to the radiance of the divine *kenosis*, which is the source and completion of all beauty.

Aesthetic contemplation of Christ's form is the basic act of faith as a mode of understanding. This form acquires the greatest possible evidence in the splendor of the greatest possible necessity.

The images and concepts with which Balthasar works derive from an original mythopoeic activity which created a particular world-view. Its origin was in the Old Covenant. This original vision was developed and shaped under the impact of centuries of prophetic criticism and insight in Israel. When men holding this world-view encountered Greek culture, religious reflection became philosophically self-conscious, attending more to problems of analysis and systematic conceptual construction. It continued to be expressed, however, in the images, concepts, and metaphors derived from its mythic origins.

Others have studied the work of Balthasar from a different perspective. Achiel Pielman, for example, chose to focus on his theology of history. Roberto Vignolo accented the aesthetics as a new fundamental theology. Jeffrey Kay approached Balthasar's thought as a theology of crisis. Wolfgang Müller stressed the impossibility of a genuine theological aesthetics. Michael Hartman took the opposite view and studied aesthetics as a basic concept for fundamental theology; Georges de Schrijver examined the "marvelous" in the human-divine aspect of the analogy of being; Johann Schmid focused on the analogy itself in *Herrlichkeit;* and John Sachs studied pneumatology and spirituality in Balthasar's works.[1]

I have tried to show how Balthasar has read the literature and art of the classical and patristic traditions to produce his theological aesthetics. Literature and the arts share with theology that they are essentially products of an imaginative constructive activity. In addition to aesthetics, Balthasar's attention to the mode of apprehending and articulating the real which is the focus of aesthetics constitutes a major contribution to theological method.

Balthasar's aesthetics embraces the whole of dogma. It calls for the category of "necessity," which builds an analogical bridge to the reality of art. Great art is self-revealing and in the process displays its necessity. "The great work of art is not spelled out nor made understandable in language that is already at hand or understood. Rather the new, unique speech which is born with it gives the explanation in self-explication."[2]

Balthasar's system is not simply one of aesthetics or drama, not a history of Christian motifs in art and literature, even though a structure of culture informs them. The aesthetics involve a reconsideration of Christian culture. As T. F. O'Meara said with reference to the *Theodramatik*, "Two admirable quali-

1. See the list of studies on Balthasar at the end of the list of Balthasar's works in the Bibliography.
2. "Warum ich noch ein Christ bin," pp. 19, 20.

ties stand out in particular: the wealth of insights brought from so many areas of the humanities to illumine Christian belief, and the original concept of the systems themselves."[3] O'Meara goes on to say that the reader may feel annoyed at times at the haste in composition or the repetition of large sections. He says their sources are almost exclusively European. The pathos of British and American theater as exemplified in George Bernard Shaw, Eugene O'Neill, and Harold Pinter is not prominent. "Whether Anglo-Saxon and American ethicians would see life as a drama between cosmic forces of good and evil, a drama capable of resolution in heroic but clear choices is questionable."[4]

It is true that the majority of authors Balthasar has studied are not English or American. Yet he has included Gerard Manley Hopkins as a major example of a theological style. He began volume 2 of the *Theologik* with a poem by T. S. Eliot, the last sentence of which captures the spirit of Balthasar's theological aesthetics: "O Light Invisible, we give Thee thanks for Thy great glory!"

Being is not inert matter waiting for man's activity. Rather, as philosophers from Plato to Heidegger have claimed, it is illumination. The ancients spoke of being as *physis*, related to the root of the verb *phainesthai*, "to appear" or "to cause to appear." The philosophers of the Middle Ages called this *manifestabilitas*. This active, appearing, nonhidden quality "can be called the *word* of Being if one understands it as an annunciation beyond all that has been or can be formulated in speech. It witnesses to the source of all annunciation and therefore to the source of the ability to speak as well."[5] The Greek *kalon*

3. T. F. O'Meara, "Art and Theology," *Theological Studies* 42 (1950): 275.
4. Ibid.
5. *Herrlichkeit*, vol. 3, pt. 1, p. 962.

(beautiful) displays this quality, for its root is *kalein*, "to call." Augustine, Leibniz, and Malebranche interpreted the light of being as "word." Gadamer also displays the affinity of light and word by relating the Neoplatonic metaphysics of light to his own and to Heidegger's theories of language. For Heidegger beings are words in the language of being, so that the word of being is an evocation, a "ringing silence" that resounds out of the polarity of essence and existence, making all human speech possible. Schelling and Fichte had emphasized this summoning character of being. Being's raison d'être is its revelation of itself in beings.

The power immanent in beauty reveals the immanence of the absolute. This immanence pervades history. It appears in the sacramental light streaming from the anthropomorphic gods and goddesses of ancient Greece. For Plato the analogy between material and spiritual numbers reveals the immanence of divine beauty.[6] The very world is a "magnificent symbol of the divine essence that expresses and reveals itself in parables."[7] One can begin with the hypothesis that the encounter with literary beauty, the rhetorical sublime, is structurally cognate with the transcendence excited in the encounter with the "natural" sublime.

The history of literary studies teaches that the history of ideas is a history of metaphors fashioned and refashioned. Kant found a problem in the affective correlative of a semiotic discontinuity in the inexplicable passage between one order of discourse and another. A general semiotic of the sublime would find the same discontinuity between sensation and idea as between idea and world. Balthasar attempts to bridge the discontinuity between what can be grasped and what is felt to be

6. Ibid., pp. 109ff.
7. *Theologik*, 1:221.

meaningful. The data of experience cannot be verified except by implicit acts of metaphor. Behind each act of intellectual metaphor is an imitation, an identification or mimesis.

Contemporary criticism would instruct us in how little of our work belongs to individual vision and choice. Yet Balthasar's aesthetics as an aesthetic of the beautiful is a humanizing method because it emphasizes spirit over sense. Balthasar answers a preoccupation of the more advanced academic criticism. This is the dilemma of modernism, with its incurable ambivalence regarding authority. What is new is the opposition between authority and authenticity, between traditional mimesis and originality.

The heroic pessimism of the twentieth century revolts at this interpretation of beauty because the nature of transcendence is misunderstood. Modern man plays Sisyphus. Nietzsche's superman, Zarathustra, unites ecstasy and sickness. The glory of being as witness to the absolute is lost and God is said to have died.

Divine revelation is the supreme work of art in history and the form of Christ is the "Urbild des Schönen."[8] Insofar as art is prophetic, it anticipates the future; it is out of season or ahead of time. When the right time, the *kairos*, arrives, the meaning of the work of art unfolds of itself. Art as mystery, however, cannot be reduced to prophecy; for as mystery, art is timeless; it overrides contingent history by illuminating all the ecstasies of time; past, present, future. The problem of the work of art is thus the problem of utopia; as mystery it refuses restriction to place and time.

Balthasar serves admirably the work of the theologian in examining the various images of religious language. Yet critics have overlooked this contribution, perhaps because such use

8. *Herrlichkeit*, vol. 1, pt. 1, p. 459.

of the imagination is normally associated with literary figures and not with theologians. For example, one of Balthasar's examples of a "style" of seeing God is represented by the poet Gerard Manley Hopkins. Hopkins replaced the modern axiom of the autonomy of the artistic imagination with the older notion of poetry as rhetoric. It can be argued that most of Hopkins's poetic techniques were developed to serve this purpose. Along with his use of "sprung" rhythm, the highly mnemonic sound structure of the poems and their commonplace themes, his poetry suggests deep roots in the ancient mimetic tradition that defined poetry as a kind of rhetoric. This tradition embraces "poems-for-pictures" theory because it prized *energeia* (pictorial vividness that is "seen") and *ekphrasis* (providing the object with a voice). Hopkins termed this "inscape."

In Hopkins's Dorothea poem, for instance, we see a Dantean emphasis on light per se, in which, as in many other poems, it becomes clear that Hopkins is committed to the tradition that is "deeper than a mere return to middle age forms," as he put it, a true "medievalism in *feeling* through medieval subjects."[9]

Earlier I characterized Balthasar's theology as emphasizing the divine descent. In this descent God comes the whole way, not just to meet human understanding and be heard but to be seen and touched. He is not the God merely of the Torah or the Qu'ran but of the cradle and the cross, the bread and the cup; not merely the Lord of Hosts, but the Beloved of the Canticle of Canticles. His is the true Rose of Sharon and the beauty of the heaven of heavens. As a doxological act Balthasar composed his theological aesthetics. Manfred Lochbrunner

9. Gerard Manley Hopkins, *Journals* (London: Oxford University Press, 1959), pp. 26, 33.

summed up Balthasar's approach: *Herrlichkeit als Liebe Gottes,* "Glory as God's love."[10]

We have seen that Balthasar intends first of all an aesthetic in the Kantian sense—an account of the part played by the senses together with the powers of memory and especially imagination in awareness of the divine. This is fundamental because the divine reveals itself in the sensible world. Christ, the perceptible form of God, has to be mediated by the historical record and the ritual of the church. In particular, this mediation is continued through the various ways the imagination has been seized and kindled by the form. Theological aesthetics studies these perceptible forms and the conditions that must be present to apprehend them for what they are.

Modern aesthetics prefers to talk about art rather than beauty and the functioning of the mind rather than the transcendentals of being. Modern aesthetics claims the source of form is in the constructive powers of the mind. We receive shapeless and manifold impressions. By selection and synthesis we make for ourselves a world-view that has order and form. We find the world or a Picasso painting beautiful to the extent that we are successful in constructing our selective synthesis. The forms are value-laden so that in synthesizing them we express basic emotions and attitudes. Further, we project symbolic meanings into things and processes and people, and in terms of these symbols we construct mythologies that reflect our deepest loves, hates, and fears.

Balthasar's aesthetics focuses on the beautiful, whose twin constituents are "form" and "light." This is most easily recog-

10. Manfred Lochbrunner, *Analogia Caritatis* (Freiburg in Breisgau: Herder, 1981), p. 190. See also p. 113 for a bibliography of the controversy between Rahner and Balthasar.

nized in great art. Great art explains itself and in that manifests its necessity. Balthasar believes all great art grows from a religious and mythical power of inspiration, as exemplified by the Greek theater. During the fifth century at Athens a mystery was created that we only now are beginning to understand theologically.

Balthasar says aesthetic theology is the judgment of the manifestation of the divine by existing standards of beauty. This happens when, for example, we try to make the Bible interesting by presenting it as a great work of literature or treat its voice as an instance of what we know to be poetic or mythological composition. Thus aesthetic theology differs from theological aesthetics.

"Seeing" Christ in the light of faith is the foundation of all Christian belief. It is what makes theological propositions carry semantic content. The *lumen fidei* opens for the soul a new world of experience. Neither mystic nor common layman can have an authentic experience alone. The experience must be understood within the framework of tradition. Varied appearances to a variety of perceivers who can share their experiences are the only means for communicating a sense of the fullness of the object. The knowledge of God in Christ is mediated by accounts from many sources, each of which represents a different manner of apprehending and perceiving. The archetypal experience is that which Christ himself in his human nature had of the Father and of himself.

Every witness is a person, living at a particular time and place, witnessing to something manifested there and then in perceptible form. The testimony cannot be reduced to spiritual truths. Understanding it means we must engage the imagination as well as the intellect. The senses are re-formed by the Spirit to become vehicles of the invisible. This is the horizon of Origen's talk about "spiritual senses." They are one means of the divine revealing itself. The Scriptures, Old and New Testaments, are one form in which Christ and the Father are revealed. Balthasar encapsulates the tradition on material historicity, the unity of humanity and trinity in the luminous form of Christ.

In this book the emphasis has been on how in the course of tradition the beauty and glory of the divine have again and again been seen and expressed. Balthasar examines this tradition and highlights not just writers with a beautiful style but those who have a distinctive vision. Wherever the vision is genuinely seen, it carries conviction. Balthasar develops the reasons for this in the theological dramatics. He provides the ontological foundation in the logic.

How Balthasar's work diverges from some of the main currents in contemporary theology may be seen by observing his differences with the late Karl Rahner. Lochbrunner rightly observed that these differences between the colleagues and "old masters" of German-language theologians is a living question of contemporary Christendom.[11] Balthasar's criticism of Rahner's *Geist in Welt* and *Hörer des Wortes* was a consequence of a distinction between a philosophical and a theological concept of "potentia oboedientialis." Balthasar's position on this was influenced by Karl Barth.

Both Rahner and Balthasar appealed to the Council of Chalcedon to demonstrate their "orthodoxy." Rahner contended that Chalcedon cannot be considered as definitive. Because the definition of two natures and one person in Christ was intended to counter the heresy of the monophysites, it cannot be taken as valid for later conditions. Paradoxically, Rahner held

11. Ibid., p. 114.

that the tradition tended to emphasize Christ's divinity over his humanity. Rahner argued that if Jesus was fully human, he must have had a genuine human existence. Yet Rahner had difficulty accepting Balthasar's account of the pain of Christ.

Rahner and Balthasar agree ultimately in their metaphysics. For Rahner, being becomes present to itself and attains its perfection by being symbolized. The symbolic nature of being means that it reveals itself to the "other," and in this finds itself in knowledge and love. Every symbol is the self-perfection of one being in another. Balthasar has seized on this moment of self-revelation of being as the basis for aesthetic experience.

A major criticism Balthasar voiced of Rahner was the lack of a clear theology of the Cross.[12] Balthasar argued that Rahner's Kantian orientation left open the question of the theological suitability of the categorial and the transcendental. How can the incomparability of the historical revelation of Christ be preserved in Rahner's transcendental approach? Balthasar said that either one must then be satisfied with a relative picture of the historicity of the Christ event or introduce a new method, different from that of Kant.

Balthasar called Rahner the most powerful theologian of his time. But he added, "Rahner chose Kant, or if you wish, Fichte, the transcendental approach. I have chosen Goethe—as a student of literature." Balthasar was particularly influenced by Goethe's understanding of form and how it is perceived. Both theologians thought within a Kantian framework,

12. *Cordula*, p. 91. Balthasar attacked Rahner's gradual adoption of an anthropological norm, which he believed to be evolutionary Christology which Solowjew, building on Schelling, Hegel and Darwin, had presented in the last century as the most modern form of Christianity. For Rahner's position in detail, see "Chalkedon—Ende oder Anfang," in Alois Grillmeier and Heinrich Bacht, eds., *Das Konzil von Chalkedon*, (Würzburg: Grünemann, 1954), 3:3–49.

however, and their differences are more like those between Thomas Aquinas and Bonaventure than between Thomas and Luther.

There is one issue, however, on which it is important to take Rahner's criticism of Balthasar seriously. Rahner asked whether the theological aesthetics was not just another form of gnostic monophysitism. Does not man become a necessary partner of God in such a way that divine truth dissolves into human truth? Balthasar answered that the Incarnation becomes the alphabet for historical human nature so it can serve as the expression of a divine speaker. "When God becomes man, man becomes such an expression, a valid and authentic translation of the divine mystery."[13] Man becomes in every dimension the supreme language of God in revelation. Revelation is the perfect divine work of art in history. In this interpretation the danger consists in possibly seeing divine glory as the glory of being. Balthasar repeatedly denies that he makes this mistake and frequently cites the "maior dissimilitudo in tanta similitudine" doctrine of the Fourth Lateran Council.

In the Preface to the final volume of *Theodramatik* Balthasar wrote that Karl Rahner had called his theology "gnostic" and added that if Rahner could have seen his chapter on the pain of God, he would have found his judgment confirmed even more.[14] Yet Balthasar appeals to the Council of Chalcedon to demonstrate the orthodoxy of his position. He states that the *Theodramatik* concludes with a development of what Rahner rightly and emphatically called the mystery of God.

13. *Verbum Caro*, p. 74.

14. In *Theodramatik*, vol. 3, Balthasar devoted ten pages (pp. 252–62) to showing the lack of a "dramatic moment" in Rahner's soteriology. He bases his argument on the question of how the "pathos of Christ" is part of the redemption.

He intends what Heidegger called the "wonder of wonders," what Wittgenstein had in mind with his utterance: "Not *how* the world is, is the mystical, but *that* it is."[15]

If the elucidation of Balthasar's thought in these pages has shown him to be somewhat old-fashioned (in the sense of adherence to the classical tradition), the excuse must be that the Western tradition has looked at its art and literature with a conventional eye. Modern criticism would not admit that such a perspective could produce new results. The true greatness of this tradition of art and literature must be measured in part by the questions and approaches it provokes in the minds of those who love it.

To criticize the massive work of Balthasar as a whole is not an easy task. Despite its concentration on disparate authors (Homer to Heidegger) and on both spiritual and literary topics, the work is so dense and interwoven that it cannot be broken into parts. Every page reflects the astounding knowledge and keen analysis of the author. It is refreshing to read theology written in the manner of literary criticism.

In the *Theologik* Balthasar has tried to mend the split between love and science, between philology and theology. He admitted that his work could be criticized on the basis of his method. At one level his reply was that where a method is the same as the way and the way is the truth ("I am the way and the truth"), a study of the transcendental truth must be methodologically problematic. "Because the Logos named himself also Truth, there is no seamless truth other than the exposition of God and indeed of God the Father in the Holy Ghost, which is at the same time the most pronounced and immediately available justice as well as the deepest mystery."[16]

15. Ludwig Wittgenstein, *Tractatus Logico-Philosophicus* (London: Kegan Paul, 1922), p. 187.

16. *Theologik*, 2:330.

As a final word in this book I would like to return to one fact that epitomizes Balthasar's theological aesthetics. Tragic death reveals the inadequacy of philosophy, religion, and the theological a priori for the maintenance of wonder. When confronted by death, man comes to know himself and to realize with Euripides that the only true lover is the one who loves eternally. Greek tragedy found a different solution to the problem of death than that of Promethean monism. In *Theodramatik* a key concept comes from classical Greek tragedy. The origin of this tragedy is rooted in the possibility of reconciliation. It is important to recall that tragedy, in the complex modes of its expression, was an act of worship to Dionysus; its artistic features do not make it the kind of artistic literature which postindustrialization aesthetics would have it be. In discussing tragedy, comedy, and tragicomedy, Balthasar asks a series of questions. How can the good appear on stage, while the criterion for that good threatens to disappear in the struggle of relativity? How can the stage become a place of judgment, where human action is set beneath an ultimate, judging light? How this mystery, which, when applied to Christianity, surpasses all literary description, can be developed, Balthasar hints he will indicate in a later context.[17] He has not yet done so. On that note of promise I end this book.

17. "Geist und Feuer," *Herder Korrespondenz* 30 (1976):75.

# Bibliography

**Major works of Hans Urs von Balthasar cited in the text or notes in shortened form.**

"Analogie und Dialektik." *Divus Thomas* 22 (1944): 171–216.

*Der antirömische Affekt. Wie lässt sich das Papsttum in der Gesamtkirche integrieren?* Freiburg: Herder, 1974.

*Das Antlitz der Kirche.* Einsiedlen: Benzinger, 1942.

*Apokalypse der deutschen Seele: Studien zu einer Lehre von letzten Haltungen.* Vol. 1, *Der deutsche Idealismus.* Salzburg: A. Pustet, 1937. 2d ed. with new preface: *Prometheus, Studien zur Geschichte des deutschen Idealismus.* Heidelberg: Kerle, 1947.

*Apokalypse der deutschen Seele.* Vol. 2, *Im Zeichen Nietzsches.* Salzburg: A. Pustet, 1939.

*Apokalypse der deutschen Seele.* Vol. 3, *Die Vergöttlichung des Todes.* Salzburg: A. Pustet, 1939.

*The von Balthasar Reader.* Ed. Michael Kehl and Werner Löser, trans. Robert J. Daly and Fred Lawrence. Edinburgh: T. T. Clark, 1982.

*Bernanos.* Cologne: Hegner, 1954.

*Das Betrachtende Gebet.* Einsiedeln: Johannesverlag, 1955. Trans. A. V. Littledale, *Prayer.* London: Geoffrey Chapman, 1961; reissued, London: SPCK, 1975.

*Der Christ und die Angst.* Einsiedeln: Johannesverlag, 1951.

*Cordula oder der Ernstfall.* Einsiedeln: Johannesverlag, 1966. Trans. Alexander Dru, *The Moment of Christian Witness.* Glen Rock, N.J.: Newman Press, 1969.

*Der dreifache Kranz.* Einsiedeln: Johannesverlag, 1977.

*Einfaltungen.* Munich: Kösel, 1969.

*Einsame Zwiesprache, Martin Buber und das Christentum.* Cologne: Hegner, 1958.

*Elisabeth von Dijon und ihre geistliche Sendung.* Cologne: Hegner, 1952.

"Erich Przywara." In *Tendenzen der Theologie im 20. Jahrhundert,* pp. 354–59. Ed. Heinrich Schultz. Stuttgart: Olten, 1966.

"Die Entwicklung der musikalischen Idee." *Sammlung Bartels* 2 (1925): 3–38.

*Das Ganze im Fragment.* Einsiedeln: Benziger, 1963. Trans. William Glen-Doepel, *A Theological Anthropology.* New York: Sheed and Ward, 1967.

*Glaubhaft ist nur Liebe*. Einsiedeln: Johannesverlag, 1963. Trans. Arthur V. Littledale and Alexander Dru, *Love Alone*. New York: Herder and Herder, 1969.

"Die Gnostischen Centurien des Maximus Confessor." *Herders Theologische. Studien* 61 (1941): 1–156.

*Die Gottesfrage des heutigen Menschen*. Vienna: Herold, 1956. Trans. Hilda Graef, *Science, Religion and Christianity*. London: Burns and Oates, 1958.

*Göttliches und Menschliches im Räteleben*. Einsiedeln: Johannesverlag, 1974.

"Die Grossen Regeln des Heiligen Basilius unter Beiziehung ausgewählten Kleinen Regeln." *Menschen der Kirche*. Einsiedeln: Johannesverlag, 1974.

*Henri de Lubac. Sein organisches Lebenswerk*. Einsiedeln: Johannesverlag, 1976.

*Herrlichkeit. Eine theologische Ästhetik*. Vol. 1, *Schau der Gestalt*. Einsiedeln: Johannesverlag, 1961. Translated by Erasmo Leiva-Merikakis, *The Glory of the Lord: A Theological Aesthetics*. Volume 1, *Seeing the Form*. Edinburgh, T. T. Clark, 1979.

*Herrlichkeit. Eine theologische Ästhetik*. Vol. 2, *Fächer der Stile*. Einsiedeln: Johannesverlag, 1962. Translated by Erasmo Leiva-Merikakis, *The Glory of the Lord*. Vol. 2, *Studies in Clerical Styles*. Edinburgh and San Francisco: T. T. Clark, 1982.

*Herrlichkeit. Eine theologische Ästhetik*. Vol. 3, pt. 1, sec. 1, *Im Raum der Metaphysik: Altertum*. Einsiedeln: Johannesverlag, 1963. Trans. Robert Girard and Henri Englemann, *La Gloire et la Croix*, Vol. 4. Paris: Aubier, 1981.

*Herrlichkeit. Eine theologische Ästhetik*, Vol. 3, pt. 1, *Im Raum der Metaphysik*, pt. 2, *Neuzeit*. Einsiedeln: Johannesverlag, 1965.

*Herrlichkeit. Eine theologische Ästhetik*. Vol. 3, pt. 2, sec. 1. *Alter Bund*. Einsiedeln: Johannesverlag 1966.

*Herrlichkeit. Eine theologische Ästhetik*. Vol. 3, pt. 2, sec. 2. *Neuer Bund*. Einsiedeln: Johannesverlag, 1969.

*Das Herz der Welt*. Zurich: Arche, 1945. Trans. Hilda Graef, *Heart of the World*. San Francisco: Ignatius Press, 1980.

"Die Hiera des Evagrius." *Zeitschrift fur Katholische Theologie* 63 (1934): 181–206.

*Im Gottes Einsatz Leben*. Einsiedeln: Johannesverlag, 1973. Trans. *Engagement with God*. London: SPCK, 1975.

*Karl Barth. Darstellung und Deutung seiner Theologie*. Cologne: Hegner, 1951. Trans. John Drury, *The Theology of Karl Barth*. New York: Holt, Rinehart and Winston, 1971.

"Katholisch: Anmerkung zur Situation." *Communio* 4 (1975): 383–89.

*Katholisch. Kriterien* 36. Einsiedeln: Johannesverlag, 1976.

"Katholische Religion und Kunst." *Schweizer Rundschau* 27 (1927): 44–54.

*Kennt uns Jesus -kennen wir ihn?* Freiburg: Herder, 1980.

*Klarstellungen. Zur Prüfung der Geister*. Freiburg: Herder, 1971.

"Kleiner Lageplan zu meinen Büchern." *Schweizer Rundschau* 55 (1953): 212–25.
*König David: Text zu den Bildern von Hans Fronius*. Einsiedeln: Johannesverlag, 1955.
*Kosmische Liturgie. Höhe und Krise des griechischen Weltbildes bei Maximus Confessor*. Freiburg: Herder, 1943. 2d ed. *Kosmische Liturgie. Das Weltbild Maximus des Bekenners*. Einsiedeln: Johannesverlag, 1961.
"Kunst und Religion." *Volkswohl* 18 (1927): 354–65.
*Der Laie und der Ordenstand*. Einsiedeln: Johannesverlag, 1948.
"Metaphysik und Mystik des Evagrius Ponticus." *Zeitschrift fur Aszese und Mystik* 14 (1939): 31–47.
*Mysterium Christi*. Leipzig: St. Benno Verlag, 1970.
*Neue Klarstellungen*. Einsiedeln: Johannesverlag, 1979.
*Nouveaux points de repère*. Paris: Fayard, 1980.
*Origenes Geist und Feuer: Ein Aufbau aus seinen Schriften*. Salzburg: Müller, 1938. Trans. R. J. Daly, S.J., *Origen: Spirit and Fire, A Thematic Anthology of His Writings*. Washington, D.C.: Catholic University of America Press, 1984.
*Parole et mystère chez Origène*. Paris: Cerf, 1957.
"Patristik, Scholastik und wir." *Theologie der Zeit* 3 (1939): 65–104.
*Pneuma und Institution. Skizzen zur Theologie*, Vol. 4. Einsiedeln: Johannesverlag, 1974.
*Présence et pensée: Essai sur la philosophie religieuse de Grégoire de Nysse*. Paris: Beauchesne, 1932.
*Rechenschaft* 1965. Einsiedeln: Johannesverlag, 1965. Trans. Berthe Widmer, "In Retrospect." *Communio* 5 (1975): 197–220.
*Reinhold Schneider*. Sein Weg und sein Werk. Cologne: Hegner, 1953.
*Romano Guardini. Reform aus dem Ursprung*. Munich: Kösel, 1970.
*Schleifung der Bastionen*. Einsiedeln: Johannesverlag, 1952.
*Spiritus Creator, Skizzen zur Theologie*. Vol. 3. Einsiedeln: Johannesverlag, 1967.
*Sponsa Verbi. Skizzen zur Theologie*. Vol. 2. Einsiedeln: Johannesverlag, 1960. Trans. Arthur V. Littledale and Alexander Dru, *Church and World*. New York: Herder and Herder, 1967.
*Theodramatik*. Vol. 1, *Prolegomena*. Einsiedeln: Johannesverlag, 1973.
*Theodramatik*. Vol. 2, *Die Personen des Spiels*. Pt. 1, *Der Mensch in Gott*. Einsiedeln: Johannesverlag, 1976.
*Theodramatik*. Vol. 2, *Die Personen des Speils*. Pt. 2, *Die Personen in Christus*. Einsiedeln: Johannesverlag, 1978.
*Theodramatik*. Vol. 3, *Die Handlung*. Einsiedeln: Johannesverlag, 1980.
*Theodramatik*. Vol. 4, *Das Endspiel*. Einsiedeln: Johannesverlag, 1983.
"Les thèmes johanniques dans la règle de S. Benôit et leur actualité." *Collectanea Cisterciana* 1 (1975): 3–14.
*Theologie der drei Tage*. Einsiedeln: Benziger, 1969.
*Theologie der Geschichte*. Einsiedeln: Johannesverlag, 1950. Trans. anon., *A Theology of History*. New York: Sheed and Ward, 1963.

*Theologik*. Vol. 1, *Wahrheit der Welt*. Einsiedeln: Johannesverlag 1985.
*Theologik*. Vol. 2, *Die Wahrheit Gottes*. Einsiedeln: Johannesverlag, 1985.
*Therese von Lisieux. Geschichte einer Sendung*. Cologne: Hegner, 1950.
*Thomas von Aquin. Besondere Gnadengaben und die zwei Wege menschlichen Lebens. Kommentar zur Summa Theologica*. Vol. 2, pt. 2, pp. 171–82, *Deutsche Thomas Ausgabe*, Vol. 23. Heidelberg, Graz, and Vienna: Kerle/Pustet, 1954.
"Die Tragödie und der Christliche Glaube." In *Spiritus Creator*, pp. 347–65.
*Verbum Caro. Skizzen zur Theologie*. Vol. 1. Einsiedeln: Johannesverlag, 1960. Part 1. Trans. Arthur V. Littledale and Alexander Dru, *Word and Revelation*. New York: Herder and Herder, 1964. Part 2. Trans. Arthur V. Littledale and Alexander Dru, *Word and Redemption*. New York: Herder and Herder, 1965.
*Der verziegelte Quelle*. Salzburg: Otto Muller, 1939.
*Wahrheit*. Vol. 1, *Wahrheit der Welt*. Einsiedeln: Benzinger, 1947. Reprinted with new introduction as *Theologik*. Vol. 1. Einsiedeln: Johannesverlag, 1985.
*Die Wahrheit ist symphonisch*. Einsiedeln: Johannesverlag, 1972.
"Warum ich noch ein Christ bin." In H. V. Balthasar and J. Ratzinger, *Zwei Plädoyers*, pp. 11–52. Munich: Kösel: 1971. Trans. John Griffiths, *Two Say Why: Why I Am Still a Christian by Hans Urs von Balthasar and Why I Am Still in the Church by Joseph Ratzinger*. London: Search Press; Chicago: Franciscan Herald Press, 1971.
*Das Weizenkorn. Aphorismen*. Luzern: Räber, 1944.
"Wendung nach Osten." *Stimmen der Zeit* 136 (1938): 32–46.
*Wer ist ein Christ?* Einsiedeln: Benziger, 1965. Trans. John Reedy, *Who Is a Christian?* New York: Newman Press, 1968.
A complete bibliography of Balthasar's writings for the period from 1925 to 1975 is provided in *Hans Urs von Balthasar, Bibliographie, 1925–1975*, compiled (up to 1965) by Berthe Widmer, revised and enlarged by Cornelia Capol (Einsiedeln: Johannesverlag, 1975), and revised again in 1980 and 1985. A bibliography is also found in *Hans Urs von Balthasar, Istituto Paolo VI, Bibliographie* (Roma, 1984).

**Selected Secondary Literature**

Albus, Michael. *Die Wahrheit ist Liebe. Zur Unterscheidung des Christlichen bei Hans Urs von Balthasar*. Freiburg: Herder, 1976.
Babini, Eugenio. "Il rapporto tra filosofia e teologia nel pensiero di Hans Urs von Balthasar." Dissertation, University of Bologna, 1976–77.
Beaudin, Marcel. "L'obéissance de Jésus Christ comme lieu d'apparition de la vérité de Dieu et de la vérité de l'homme chez Hans Urs von Balthasar." Dissertation, University of Montréal, 1978.
Escobar, Pedro. "Zeit und Sein Jesu Christi bei Hans Urs von Balthasar." Dissertation, Institut Catholique, Paris, 1973.

Fessio, John. "The Origin of the Church in Christ's Kenosis: The Ontological Structure of the Church in the Ecclesiology of Hans Urs von Balthasar." Dissertation, University of Regensburg, 1974.

Hartman, Michael. *Asthetik als ein Grundbegriff fundamentaler Theologie. Eine Untersuchung zu Hans Urs von Balthasar.* Freiburg: Herder, 1985.

Heinz, Hans. *Der Gott des Je-mehr. Der christologische Ansatz Hans Urs von Balthasars.* Bern and Frankfurt: Lang, 1975.

Johri, Michael. "Descensus Dei. Teologia della croce nell'opera di Hans Urs von Balthasar." Dissertation, University of Lucerne, 1980.

Lochbrunner, Manfred. *Analogia Caritatis. Darstellung und Deutung der Theologie Hans Urs von Balthasars.* Freiburg: Herder, 1981.

Löser, Werner. *Im Geiste des Origines. Hans Urs von Balthasar als Interpret der Theologie der Kirchenväter.* Frankfurt: Knecht, 1976.

Marchesi, Giorgio. "La Christologia di Hans Urs von Balthasar." *Analecta Gregoriana* 207. Rome, 1977.

Moda, A. *Hans Urs von Balthasar. Un' esposizione critica del suo pensiero.* Bari, 1976.

Pielman, Achiel. *Hans Urs von Balthasar et la Théologie de l'histoire.* Bern and Frankfurt: Lang, 1978.

Schrijver, Georges de. *Le merveilleux accord de l'homme et de dieu: Etude de l'analogie de l'être chez Hans Urs von Balthasar.* Paris: Mame, 1983.

**Selected Articles**

Cobb, James B. "A Question for Hans Urs von Balthasar." *Communio* 5 (1978): 53–59.

Dru, Alexander. "The Achievement of Hans Urs von Balthasar." *Continuum* 6 (1968): 418–24.

Foley, George. "The Catholic Critics of Karl Barth." *Scottish Journal of Theology* 14 (1961): 136–55.

Kay, Jeffrey A. "Aesthetics and a Posteriori Evidence in Balthasar's Theological Method." *Communio* 2 (1975): 289–99.

Keefe, Dennis J. "A Methodological Critique of von Balthasar's Theological Aesthetics." *Communio* 5 (1978): 23–43.

Lubac, Henri de. "Un témoin de Christ: Hans Urs von Balthasar." *Civitas* 20 (1965): 587–600.

Mackinnon, Donald. "Masters in Israel III: Hans Urs von Balthasar." *Clergy Review* 54 (1969): 859–69.

O'Donovan, Leo. "Evolution under the Sign of the Cross." *Theological Studies* 32 (1971): 601–26.

O'Meara, Thomas. "Of Art and Theology: Hans Urs von Balthasar's Systems." *Theological Studies* 42 (1981): 272–76.

Pannenberg, Wolfhart. "Zur Bedeutung des Analogiegedankens bei Karl Barth. Eine Auseinandersetzung mit Hans Urs von Balthasar." *Theologische Literaturzeitung* 78 (1953): 18–23.

Proterra, M. "Hans Urs von Balthasar: Theologian." *Communio* 2 (1975): 270–88.
Rahner, Karl. "Hans Urs von Balthasar." *Civitas* 20 (1965):601–4.
Reedy, Gerard. "The Christology of Hans Urs von Balthasar." *Thought* 45 (1970):407–20.
Riches, J. K. "The Theology of Hans Urs von Balthasar." *Theology* 75 (1972):562–70, 647–55.
Roberts, Louis. "The Collision of Rahner and Balthsar." *Continuum* 5 (1968):753–57.
———. "A Critique of the Aesthetic Theology of Hans urs von Balthasar." *American Benedictine Review* 16 (1965):486–504.
Sachs, Johann. "Die Theologie der Zukunft: Hans Urs von Balthasar." *Zeitschrift für deutsche Theologie* 34 (1977):234–56.
Schmid, Johann. "Neue Versuche der Theologie unserer Zeit." Dissertation, Munich University, 1982.
Schmitz, Karl L. "Divine Initiative and Christian Praxis." *Communio* 5 (1978):44–52.
Schrijver, Georges de. "Die Analogia Entis in der Theologie Hans Urs von Balthasars. Eine genetisch-historische Studie." *Bijdragen* 38 (1977): 241–81.
Sherwood, Polycarp. "Survey of Recent Work on St. Maximus the Confessor." *Traditio* 20 (1964):428–537.
Valentin, Paul. "Kénose, amour et gloire: La mort du Christ dans l'esthétique théologique de Hans Urs von Balthasar." In B. Sesboue, ed., *Annoncer la mort du Seigneur*, pp. 40–50. Lyons and Fourviére: Cerf, 1971.
Vignolo, Roberto. "Teologia e preghiera. In margine all'opera di Hans Urs von Balthasar." *La rivista del clero italiano* 55 (1974):403–8.
Vorgrimler, Herbert. "Hans Urs von Balthasar." In *Bilanz der Theologie im 20 Jahrhundert*, 4:122–42. Freiburg: Herder, 1971.
Wiedmann, Franz. "H. U. v Balthasar, Herrlichkeit I und II." *Philosophisches Jahrbuch der Görresgesellschaft* 74 (1966–67:210–16.

# Index